RENEWALS 458-4574

DATE DUE

MAR 6			
JAN 08			
GAYLORD			PRINTED IN U.S.A.

Managerial Decision Making

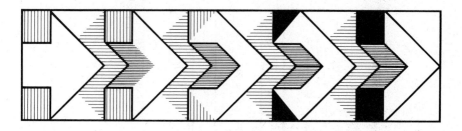

Management Applications Series

Alan C. Filley, University of Wisconsin, Madison
Series Editor

Performances in Organizations: Determinants and Appraisal
L. L. Cummings, University of Wisconsin, Madison
Donald P. Schwab, University of Wisconsin, Madison

Leadership and Effective Management
Fred E. Fiedler, University of Washington
Martin M. Chemers, University of Utah

Managing by Objectives
Anthony P. Raia, University of California, Los Angeles

Organizational Change: Techniques and Applications
Newton Margulies, University of California, Irvine
John C. Wallace, University of California, Irvine

Interpersonal Conflict Resolution
Alan C. Filley, University of Wisconsin, Madison

*Group Techniques for Program Planning: A Guide to Nominal
 Group and Delphi Processes*
Andre L. Delbecq, University of Wisconsin, Madison
Andrew H. Van de Ven, Kent State University
David H. Gustafson, University of Wisconsin, Madison

Organizational Behavior Modification
Fred Luthans, University of Nebraska, Lincoln
Robert Kreitner, Western Illinois University

Task Design and Employee Motivation
Ramon J. Aldag, University of Wisconsin, Madison
Arthur P. Brief, University of Iowa

*Organizational Surveys: An Internal Assessment of
 Organizational Health*
Randall B. Dunham, University of Wisconsin, Madison
Frank J. Smith, Sears, Roebuck and Company

Managerial Decision Making
George P. Huber, University of Wisconsin, Madison

Managerial Decision Making

George P. Huber

University of Wisconsin, Madison

Scott, Foresman and Company   Glenview, Illinois
Dallas, Tex.   Oakland, N.J.   Palo Alto, Cal.
Tucker, Ga.   London, England

Library of Congress Cataloging in Publication Data
Huber, George P.
  Managerial decision making.
  (Management applications series)
  Includes bibliographies and index.
  1. Management—Decision making.   2. Decision-
making.   I. Title.
HD30.23.H78   658.4′03   79-24590
ISBN 0-673-15141-7

12345678910-VHJ-85848382818079

Foreword

The Management Applications Series is concerned with the application of contemporary research, theory, and techniques. There are many excellent books at advanced levels of knowledge, but there are few which address themselves to the application of such knowledge. The authors in this series are uniquely qualified for this purpose, since they are all scholars who have experience in implementing change in real organizations through the methods they write about.

Each book treats a single topic in depth. Where the choice is between presenting many approaches briefly or a single approach thoroughly, we have opted for the latter. Thus, after reading the book, the student or practitioner should know how to apply the methodology described.

Selection of topics for the series was guided by contemporary relevance to management practice, and by the availability of an author qualified as an expert, yet able to write at a basic level of understanding. No attempt is made to cover all management methods, nor is any sequence implied in the series, although the books do complement one another. For example, change methods might fit well with managing by objectives.

The books in this series may be used in several ways. They may be used to supplement textbooks in basic courses on management, organizational behavior, personnel, or industrial psychology/sociology. Students appreciate the fact that the material is immediately applicable. Practicing managers will want to use individual books to increase their skills, either through self study or in connection with management development programs, inside or outside the organization.

Alan C. Filley

Preface

How important is decision making in management? Peter Drucker stated in one of his most prominent books that decision making is "the first managerial skill." Charles Kepner and Benjamin Tregoe, cofounders of a prominent management consulting firm, have noted that "No good manager needs to be convinced that problem analysis and decision making are the most important things that he does. . . . His success virtually depends on doing these things well." David Miller and Martin Starr, professors of management at Columbia University and well-known writers in the field of management, have referred to decision making as "the main responsibility and function of the manager," and have observed that managers are "regarded and evaluated in terms of success in making decisions."[1]

I'm convinced, as a result of my experience as an industrial manager, educational administrator, and management consultant, that these strong statements accurately portray the importance of decision making to the professional manager. But even if one endorses a more modest position, there can be absolutely no doubt that the careers and lives of good decision makers are more professionally rewarding and more personally satisfying than the careers and lives of poor decision makers. Managers who are good decision makers tend to spend their time capitalizing on the results of their wise choices. Managers who are poor decision makers expend their energy dashing around remedying mistakes and figthing fires; they seem always to have had "a frustrating day."

This is a book about how to make decisions. I wrote it for managers and managers-to-be. Its purpose is to help managers and future managers improve their decisions and the decisions of their subordinates and associates as well. It describes techniques that anyone can use

[1]See page 10 for references.

to increase his or her already existing decision-making skills. It also explains how to decide when or whether a particular technique should be used, and how it should be used if it should be used. Because several of the techniques will be new to most managers, it seems important to point out that each of the techniques presented in this book has been closely examined and has been found to be useful by *both* researchers and practitioners. These techniques are not speculative or esoteric; they are proven and practical. To help make this clear, many of the example applications are taken from published and referenced accounts of situations in which the techniques were actually used.

Some of the techniques described require no arithmetic skills at all. Some of those described in Chapters 4–7 require high-school algebra for full implementation. Most fall in between. For those readers who are averse to math, I have preceded every equation with a sentence that says exactly the same thing the equation says, but in plain English.

As I mentioned earlier, I wrote this book for two kinds of people. One is the manager who wants to upgrade his or her managerial skills. I know what it is to be a manager—I've been one for years—and I've learned through experience how important it is to make sound decisions. I also know how to teach this material to practicing managers, having done so in numerous managerial short courses.

The other person for whom this book is written is the manager-to-be, typically a student in a college or university. I believe the book fits the needs of this person well. My colleagues and I have taught this material in both graduate and undergraduate courses for eight semesters now. We hope we have it finely tuned. The feedback from students indicates that we do.

The book itself is divided into three parts. Chapters 1 and 2 comprise the first part and, as they are in the nature of an overview of decision making, form a foundation for the remainder of the book. The second part is concerned with improving the decisions of individual managers. It contains five chapters. Chapter 3 examines the difficulties inherent in correctly evaluating the information surrounding a decision situation, while Chapters 4–7 describe easy-to-use analytic techniques for improving decisions by overcoming these difficulties. The third part of the book is concerned with the use of committees, study teams, and other decision-making or decision-aiding groups. It contains four chapters. Chapter 8 analyzes the difficulties that managers encounter when they attempt to use groups to aid them in their decision-making efforts, while Chapters 9–11 describe easy-to-use techniques for improving group effectiveness by overcoming these difficulties. Chapter 12 is concerned with predicting and influencing organizational decisions.

During the past months of work on this project, my wife and children have been very gracious and understanding about the inconveniences caused by my absences. For this I am most grateful.

In closing I must say that I enjoyed writing this book. I hope the reader enjoys using it.

George P. Huber

Contents

Part One
Overview of
Decision Making and
Problem Solving

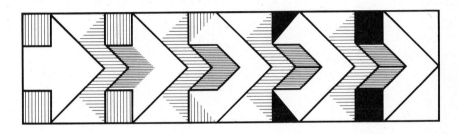

1
Introduction

This book is concerned with decision making. Its purpose is to help managers improve their decisions and the decisions of their subordinates and associates as well.

In order to help achieve this overall purpose, this first chapter has three functions: (1) to highlight the importance of decision making to the manager, (2) to describe a major source of knowledge that managers can draw upon to improve their decisions, and (3) to outline the nature and scope of the remainder of the book.

WHY STUDY DECISION MAKING?

Given the challenging nature of their jobs, it is not surprising that most managers are active in seeking ways to enhance the abilities and skills that lead to effective performance. Many of these self-improvement efforts are directed toward improving decisions and decision-making capabilities. Evidence of this abounds—in the existence of hundreds of management consulting firms in any large city, in the enrollment of practicing managers in university courses in decision making, and in the conversations of the managers themselves at professional meetings or social gatherings.

2

Why is there so much interest in the improvement of managerial decision making? There seem to be at least three reasons. First, the quality and acceptability of a manager's decisions can have a considerable impact on his or her professional career and personal satisfaction. Authoritative recognition of the impact on careers is plentiful. For example, David W. Miller and Martin K. Starr, professors of management at Columbia University and well-known writers in the field of management, refer to decision making as "the main responsibility and function of the manager," and then point out that managers are "regarded and evaluated in terms of success in making decisions" (Miller and Starr, 1967, p. 13). Similarly, Charles H. Kepner and Benjamin B. Tregoe, cofounders of a prominent management consulting firm, note that "No good manager needs to be convinced that problem analysis and decision making are the most important things that he does," and then observe that "His success virtually depends on doing these things well" (Kepner and Tregoe, 1965, p. 24).

The impact on satisfaction follows from the fact that if a manager's decisions tend to be of low quality, or if they tend to be resisted by those who are affected by them, then the manager expends his or her energy in the often frustrating task of remedying mistakes rather than in the more satisfying activities associated with capitalizing on successes. Thus one reason that decision making is important to managers is that the results of their decisions so directly affect their careers, their rewards, and their satisfactions.

The second reason that individual managers seek to improve their decision-making capabilities is that the quality and acceptability of their decisions affect the performance of the organization on whose behalf they make the decisions. There is no doubt that a manager's decisions have an impact on the goal achievement of the parent organization, the unit he or she supervises, and his or her coworkers. For this reason too, then, most managers feel responsible for developing their decision-making capabilities.

The third reason that managers seek to enhance their decision-making abilities and skills follows from the fact that a great deal of a manager's time is expended in getting decisions either made or implemented. A desire to decrease the amount of time and effort that managers spend in making and guiding decisions is a strong motivator for seeking improvement in decision-making capabilities. However, we find that even when managers are primarily involved in implementing a decision, they are still quite involved with making decisions. This is easy to see by recalling that the effectiveness of any implementation depends greatly on a series of managerial decisions on how to plan, organize, staff, and control the implementation effort. Thus, although implementation-related activities may absorb a good deal of a manager's time, he or she will be intimately and continuously involved in decision-making activities as well. Because decision-making activities absorb so much time and effort, most managers attempt to increase their capability for carrying out these activities.

What is perhaps most interesting is that this high level of interest in improving decision making is prompted by only the perceived problem. The actual problem is much greater. The fact is that many of our decisions are of much poorer quality than we realize.[1] One reason we do not recognize their lack of quality is that our defenses—such as our ability to selectively forget about our "bad" decisions and remember our "good" ones—or our ability to rationalize—seeing poor results as the consequence of uncontrollable events while seeing good results as the consequence of our actions—make us feel as if we are doing much better than we are. And while some of our coworkers will point out our mistakes, many more will reinforce our gracious misperceptions, either because they were part of the decision-making effort themselves or because they do not want us to retaliate by pointing out their own shortcomings.

Another reason we do not know that the difference between our actual performance and our potential performance is so large is that we are, for the most part, unaware of the methods that can be used to achieve a greater proportion of high-quality decisions. Our lack of awareness stems from many sources, including lack of formal managerial training, lack of coaching by a manager experienced in decision methods, and involvement in work activities to an extent precluding involvement in self-development activities. In any case, all of us have a problem of less than satisfactory decision-making performance to some degree, and some of us have it to a considerable degree.

The situation is portrayed in Figure 1-1, where we can see that the actual difference between the quality of most decisions and their potential quality is much larger than the perceived difference.

Although it is difficult for most people to be fully aware of the degree to which their decision making needs improvement, it is a compliment to their judgment that so many managers are seeking ways to more

[1]*In this book, when we refer to the quality of decisions, we will be using the word "quality" in its broadest sense and will intend for it to encompass all reasonable criteria including, for example, timeliness and acceptability to those affected by the decision.*

Figure 1-1.   Difference Between Actual and Potential Quality of Decisions

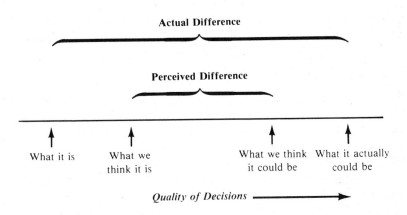

fully develop their decision-making capabilities. Clearly these managers are not content to rely on experience *alone*. They are wise not to do so. Alvar Elbing, in discussing the problem of approaching decision making as a systematic discipline, explains why:

> Decision making is a process in which everyone has already ac-quired a good deal of experience. . . . Much of that experience has been reasonably successful, at least successful enough to have kept us alive and brought us to our present situations.
>
> However, past experience in decision making is no guarantee that our experiences have taught us the best possible methods of . . . decision making and problem solving. Learn-ing from experience is usually random. Furthermore, although we all *learn experiences,* there is no guarantee that we *learn from experiences.* In fact, it is possible to learn downright errors and second-rate methods from experience, as in playing golf without taking lessons from a professional. As with the golfer, so with the manager: it is only training in systematic method which enables us to correctly analyze situations so that we can truly learn from experience in those situations. (Elbing, 1970, pp. 13–14)

Given the importance of decision making, it is not surprising to find that a great deal of effort is being directed toward its systematic study and improvement. Much of this work is being carried out by scientists in universities, large corporations, and consulting firms. The results of their work form a valuable and important knowledge base for us to draw upon, particularly when these results are first screened for their managerial relevance and practicality.

DECISION-MAKING RESEARCH: AN IMPORTANT SOURCE OF KNOWLEDGE

In order to identify their focus on decision making and their common interests with others in the area, many scientists who study decision making—whether their training has been in psychology, political science, statistics, or whatever—refer to themselves as "decision scientists." For the sake of convenience, we will apply this term to all those scientists who, at least during the period when they produced the results that are of interest to us, were studying decision making.

For a variety of reasons, decision scientists have tended to specialize, to work in different sections of the overall field. One important sectioning is referred to as the "descriptive-prescriptive" dichotomy. Those scientists in the "descriptive" camp focus on understanding how decisions are made. For example, they develop models or theories for predicting how a decision maker *would* change his or her opinion as new information became available. In contrast, scientists in the "prescriptive" camp focus on improving decisions. They attempt to prescribe decision-making behavior. For example, they might use statistical theory to determine how a decision maker *should* revise his or her opinion in light of new information.

As a result of this sectioning of the overall field, two separate bodies of knowledge have developed. One deals with how decisions are made, and the other deals with how decisions can be improved. Material from both bodies of knowledge is clearly relevant to the goal of improving decision making.

Using the ideas and insights from descriptively oriented research to predict decision processes and decision outcomes will enable the manager both to plan more effectively around the decisions of others and to intervene more effectively when these decisions seem wrongheaded. Using the methods and techniques from prescriptively oriented research as a basis for guiding the decision processes of himself or herself and of others will enable the manager to cause a greater proportion of these decisions to be of high quality.

This book draws on both bodies of knowledge and describes the best of the decision-aiding techniques that have been developed. It also shows how and when the techniques should be used. Because several of the techniques will be new to most managers, it seems important to point out that *each of the techniques presented in this book has been closely examined and has been found to be useful by both researchers and practitioners.* These techniques are not speculative or esoteric; they are proven and practical. To help make this clear, many of the example applications are taken from published and referenced accounts of situations in which the technique was actually used.

NATURE AND SCOPE OF THE BOOK

This book is divided into three parts. Part I is an overview of decision making. It contains two chapters, of which this is one, that together form a foundation for the remainder of the book. Part II is concerned with improving the decision making of individual managers. It contains five chapters. Chapter 3 examines the difficulties inherent in correctly evaluating the information surrounding a decision situation. Chapters 4–7 describe easy-to-use analytic techniques for improving decision making by overcoming these difficulties. Part III of the book is concerned with the use of committees, study teams, and other decision-making or decision-aiding groups. It contains four chapters. Chapter 8 analyzes the difficulties managers encounter when they attempt to use groups to aid them in their decision-making efforts. Chapters 9–11 describe easy-to-use techniques for improving group effectiveness by overcoming these difficulties. Chapter 12 discusses techniques for predicting and influencing organizational decisions and also contains an overview of the book.

Chapters 3 and 8, which describe the difficulties encountered by decision-making managers, draw heavily on the findings of those decision scientists who are primarily interested in describing and understanding decision making as it actually happens. Undoubtedly, experienced managers will recognize much in these chapters that they have learned by direct observation of their own decision-making behavior or that of their associates. The seven chapters describing techniques for improving decision making draw heavily on the work of those decision scientists who design and test approaches and procedures for helping managers overcome the difficulties they encounter in their decision-making efforts.

While discussing the scope of the book, we should perhaps explain what we mean by *decision making*. This term is sometimes used to describe the narrow set of activities that are involved in choosing one alternative from a set of available alternatives. On other occasions it is used to describe the broad set of activities involved in finding and implementing a course of action. In the first case, *decision making* is used in place of the narrower but less familiar term *choice making*. In the second case, it is used in place of the more encompassing but less specific term *problem solving.*

The scope or definition of *decision making* has not been an issue with decision scientists, probably because the setting or context in which it is used always seems to make the meaning clear. In this book we will use the terms *choice making* and *problem solving* to describe, respectively, the narrow and broad sets of activities that are sometimes referred to as decision making. We will use the term *decision making* to refer to an

Figure 1-2.   Scopes of Choice Making, Decision Making, and Problem Solving

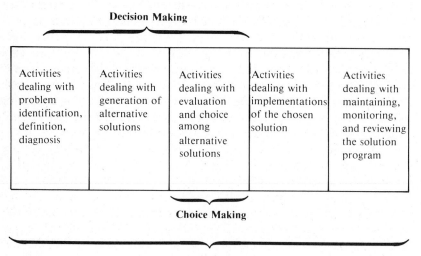

intermediate-sized set of activities. Figure 1–2 clarifies these distinctions. Here we see that solving a problem may involve a great many activities, some of which take place after a decision has been made. On the other hand, making a choice from a given set of alternatives involves relatively fewer activities.

The process of decision making begins when a problem is being explored and ends when an alternative has been chosen. It is important to note that the full scope of decision making, as we use the term in this book, includes developing a full understanding of the problem. It is for this reason that Figure 1–2 shows the decision-making process as encompassing some of the activities dealing with problem identification, definition, and diagnosis. With these thoughts in mind, we will define decision making as *the process through which a course of action is chosen.*

As a final thought in this presentation of definitions, we should note that while we do mean to define choice making as a process more limited in scope than the process of decision making, we do not mean to distinguish a "choice" from a "decision." These two words both refer to the immediate outcome of the decision-making process.

SUMMARY AND OVERVIEW

In this introductory section we noted three reasons why decision making is of considerable importance to managers: (1) it affects their career rewards and satisfactions; (2) it affects the lives and fortunes of the people with whom and for whom they work; and (3) it takes up a good deal of their time and effort. We then noted that its importance has led decision making to be studied by many scientists, that these scientists tend to adopt either a descriptive or prescriptive approach in their work, and that in either case their results can be used as a basis for improving our decision-making capabilities. Finally, we discussed the role of decision making as it relates to choice making and problem solving.

The next chapter is designed to add to the foundation on which the remainder of the book will build. One way in which it contributes to this foundation is by examining the process of problem solving as the context in which the process of decision making takes place. Another way is by describing some of the counterproductive or cost-ineffective behaviors that we all tend to exhibit as we go about the activities involved in solving problems, behaviors that the techniques in succeeding chapters will help us overcome.

REFERENCES AND RELATED READINGS

Drucker, P. F. *Management: Tasks, Responsibilities, Practices.* New York: Harper and Row, Publishers, Inc., 1973.

Elbing, A. O. *Behavioral Decisions in Organizations.* Glenview, Ill.: Scott, Foresman and Company, 1970.

Kepner, C. H., and B. B. Tregoe. *The Rational Manager.* New York: McGraw-Hill, Inc., 1965.

Miller, D. W. and M. K. Starr. *The Structure of Human Decisions.* Englewood Cliffs, N.J.: Prentice-Hall, Inc., 1967.

2
Problem Solving: The Context for Decision Making

This chapter is concerned with problem solving. Its purposes are (1) to provide a broad perspective on the subject of decision making, and (2) to add to the foundation on which the succeeding chapters will build.

The chapter has six sections. The first is quite short and describes what we mean by a problem. Each of the remaining five discusses one of the five steps involved in solving problems. Before discussing these steps, it seems reasonable to first define what we mean by a problem.

WHAT IS A PROBLEM?

What is a problem? A practical working definition is "a problem exists when there is a difference between the *actual* situation and the *desired* situation." As an example, a problem exists when the warehouse contains 70 units but the customer order calls for 100 units. As another example, a problem exists when the departmental staff currently numbers 17, but the number of employees required to serve current client demands is 25.

As managers, we are continually faced with problems. At any

given moment we could probably identify many situations where there is a difference between what we have and what we want. When one of these situations becomes serious enough to demand action on our part, we might call it an *active* problem. Fortunately, many problems, like volcanos, are not active. They exist and can be referred to as volcanos or problems whether active or not, but they are not demanding of our attention. All problems in this book will be considered active problems.

From our definition of what a problem is, we can see that to solve a problem a manager must change either the actual situation or the desired situation. In many cases, changing the actual situation means increasing performance, such as producing the extra 30 units that define the inventory problem described above. In other cases, it means persuading someone else to change the actual situation, such as having another of the company's warehouses supply the additional 30 units.

In some circumstances, weighing of the pro's and con's will indicate that the problem can be appropriately "solved" by changing the desired situation rather than the actual situation. For example, we might ask the customer to order 70 units now and the remaining 30 next week (by which time we expect to have developed an acceptable inventory). Although there is a danger in using this approach, as the stated desires of the others involved might change while their real desires might not, it is occasionally a very practical approach for solving a problem.

Given that problems can be solved by changing either the actual or desired situation, we can define problem solving as *the conscious process of reducing the difference between an actual situation and the desired situation.*

With these definitions in mind, let us discuss the five steps involved in solving problems. The steps and the activities included in them are summarized in Table 2–1. As we consider these steps, we will examine some of the effectiveness-reducing tendencies that individuals or groups frequently exhibit at these points in the overall problem-solving effort. Again, our purposes in examining the nature of the problem-solving process are to gain additional perspective on decision making and to continue forming the base on which the following chapters will build. The first step focuses on the nature of the problem.

EXPLORING THE NATURE OF THE PROBLEM

The first step, *exploring the nature of the problem,* involves identifying, defining, and diagnosing the problem and its causes. When properly carried out, it helps us avoid "solving the wrong problem."

TABLE 2-1.　　Steps in Problem Solving

1. Explore the nature of the problem.
   (Includes those activities dealing with problem identification, definition, and diagnosis)

2. Generate alternative solutions.
   (Includes those activities dealing with generation of alternative solutions to the problem)

3. Choose among alternative solutions.
   (Includes those activities dealing with evaluation and choice among alternative solutions)

4. Implement the chosen alternative.
   (Includes those activities dealing with implementation of the chosen solution)

5. Control the solution program.
   (Includes those activities dealing with maintaining, monitoring, and reviewing the implemented solution)

To solve a problem, we must have some idea of both the actual and the desired situation. Managers employ a variety of approaches in their attempts to determine the actual situation. For example, they might read performance reports, have progress review meetings, or maintain "open door" policies. To ascertain the desired situation they might conduct employee and customer attitude surveys, read government regulations, or converse with their superiors. In many cases, the information bearing on the existence of a problem is obtained only by being sensitive to what those around the manager are thinking and feeling but not necessarily saying.

There are three tendencies that frequently interfere with adequate problem exploration:

1. The tendency to define the problem in terms of a proposed solution • For example, "the problem is that the public relations department is understaffed" focuses on one possible solution and reduces the likelihood that other solutions will be considered. The more basic problem may be that the organization needs, but does not have, a favorable public image. Viewed in this way, there are a number of possible solutions besides enlarging the public relations staff. Perhaps the department can use different public relations strategies. Perhaps it should hire a consultant to determine why the quality of public relations activities is not as high as the firm desires. The danger in defining the problem as the lack of implementation of a particular solution is that it reduces or eliminates the search for other solutions which are perhaps more satisfactory.

2.   *The tendency to focus on narrow, lower order goals* • In identifying the desired situation, a manager may focus on narrow, lower order goals. In contrast, the more successful managers, or at least those managers who tend to move upward in their organizations, are those who keep in mind the need to achieve broader, higher order goals. For example, the rise in the number of conglomerates in the past two decades caused many executives to realize that the goal of their organization was not to produce and sell a particular product line, but rather to make a profit through whatever legitimate endeavor it could. In other cases, and especially in face of court actions, it became clear that even this was not the appropriate higher order goal. Rather it was to survive by finding a niche in the nation's economic and industrial makeup where the constraints imposed by government, consumer groups, competitors, and stockholders were either satisfied or effectively played off against each other. Perhaps the most dramatic recognition of higher order goals was by the March of Dimes organization in the 1960s. After having contributed greatly to conquering polio, it chose not to disband but instead to raise funds for research directed toward overcoming birth defects. Clearly, the original goal had been achieved. It then became clear that "the" goal was really a higher order goal: to survive as an organization that served the needs of its members for either employment or the opportunity to provide altruistic service.

Although achieving lower order goals is a means of achieving higher order goals, the more sophisticated manager views achievement of lower order goals as a means to achieve other ends, rather than as an end in itself, and defines problems accordingly.

3.   *The tendency to diagnose the problem in terms of its symptoms* • Sometimes dealing with symptoms is appropriate. Often, however, the manager must dig deeper. For example, taking aspirin for tension headaches (a symptom) may be appropriate problem-solving behavior. But if the headaches are severe, frequent, and debilitating, it becomes appropriate to diagnose the causes so that they, and not the symptoms, can be addressed.

How far we should go in probing through the layers of a problem varies from one situation to another. Each layer may be both the cause of a superficial problem and a symptom of a basic problem. Most managers probably probe too little and hence spend much of their time fighting the repeatedly erupting symptoms of the same problem. We are all guilty, to some extent, of dealing with symptoms rather than causes. We recognize the fact only occasionally, as when we exclaim "Oh, not that again!" Thus, a third tendency that managers and other problem solvers exhibit in the problem-exploration step is that they tend to diagnose the problem only in terms of its symptoms, rather than in terms of its causes.

We should note here that in many cases the problem is identified and defined for us by others, such as our superiors or assistants. This does not mean that problem exploration should not be a part of the problem-solving process. It simply highlights the fact that each step within the overall problem-solving process does not need to be carried out by the same individuals or groups.

Let us turn to the second step in the problem-solving process.

GENERATING ALTERNATIVE SOLUTIONS

The second step in the problem-solving process, *generating alternative solutions,* involves identifying items or actions that could reduce or eliminate the difference between the actual situation and the desired situation. In other words, it involves identifying alternative solutions to the problem.[1]

The effectiveness-reducing behavior frequently exhibited at this point in the problem-solving effort is *the tendency to slight the alternative-generation process in favor of proceeding to the alternative-evaluation process.* In other words, efforts to *generate* alternatives are not separated from efforts to *evaluate* alternatives already identified.

Many readers will recall having observed this tendency in problem-solving meetings where most of the meeting was devoted to arguing the merits of the first solution proposed, rather than to identifying a set of alternative solutions to be considered. Because the tendency diverts the group's members away from the idea-generation process, it reduces the opportunity for high-quality solutions to be identified.

Old-fashioned "brainstorming," with its instructions to participants not to criticize the ideas put forth, was an early attempt to deal with this tendency. Recently developed techniques are even more effective in both overcoming this tendency and generating high-quality solu-

[1]*For the sake of brevity, we will use "alternatives" in place of "alternative solutions."*

tions. We will examine these techniques in detail in Chapter 11. Here we will simply note that people often rush through the alternative-generation process in order to move on to steps that more directly reduce the tension created by the problem. This shortchanging of the alternative-generation process is a shortsighted strategy that in most cases guarantees a solution of lesser quality.

CHOOSING AMONG ALTERNATIVE SOLUTIONS

The third step in the overall problem-solving process is *choosing among the alternatives.* For the sake of brevity, we will refer to this step as *choice making.*

There are a number of difficulties that managers encounter during their choice-making efforts. The summary effect of these difficulties is *the tendency to be unsystematic in the use of decision-relevant information.* Because these difficulties and this tendency deserve detailed examination and because they lead so directly to the use of decision-aiding techniques, we will devote much of the next chapter and parts of subsequent chapters to detailed discussions of them. At this point we will turn to a brief discussion of the different types of decision situations. It is important that we undertake this review since each type of situation leads to an observably different choice-making process.

The first type to be discussed will be referred to as the *conspicuous-alternative situation.* Such situations are characterized by the availability of an acceptable and conspicuous alternative. As we will see in Chapter 3, the typical behavior in these situations is to accept and implement this available alternative. An example of the situation type would be an instance where we were driving on an unfamiliar turnpike and noticed that we were nearly out of gas.

In such a situation, we would probably "choose" the very next gasoline station in preference to the other gas stations that are undoubtedly available further along the freeway. Choice making here is trivial. Our only concern should be the validity of our belief that the benefits to be gained from further search for alternatives are small relative to the costs of the search. In decision situations where both the benefits and the costs of additional search for alternatives are large, it is generally cost-effective to explicitly compare these benefits and costs before choosing whether to accept the immediately available solution or to search further in hope of finding a superior solution. Chapter 7 describes a systematic approach for choosing between these two alternatives.

A second type of decision situation is one where a number of alternative solutions are available and where the quality of the solution is important. An example would be the choice of a site for constructing a new office building. Because of the multiplicity of alternatives, we will refer to such decision situations as *multiple-alternative situations.* In situations of this type, where the benefits gained from choosing the best alternative are large, it seems reasonable to implement a systematic choice-making process. Chapters 4 and 5 describe such a process.

The third type of decision situation occurs when the alternative-generating step identifies no acceptable solution. When we encounter such a situation, we have three options.

1. We can lower our aspirations or the aspirations of those who presented the problem to us. In other words, we can lower the minimum requirements so that a previously rejected alternative becomes acceptable.

2. We can continue to search for alternatives, hoping to find one that is acceptable.

3. We can attempt to design an acceptable alternative.

The third of these options, the design of alternative solutions, is frequently employed when it is unlikely that any ready-made alternative will satisfy the requirements or constraining conditions. For example, in an academic setting, it is unlikely that the curriculum used in one university's MBA program would satisfy all the constraints imposed by the faculty, politics, and resources of some other university. Consequently, a faculty would be much more likely to custom-design an MBA program rather than adopt a ready-made program from another university. The design option is also used when quality is important and when it is felt that a solution can be designed that is superior to the available alternatives.

Two efforts involved in the design process include identifying and choosing among the components for the solution being designed. For example, we must choose which media outlets to include in the design of an advertising campaign and which routes to include in the design of a municipal transportation system. These efforts correspond to the alternative-generation and choice-making steps described earlier.

The need for this looping back, from one step in the problem-solving process to a previous step is clearly seen in the case of a design effort. Actually, it is typical of the overall problem-solving process. Managers frequently learn something that they wish they had known in a previous step and loop back in the problem-solving process to take account of the new knowledge. A common example of looping back occurs when employee resistance to implementation of the choice surfaces new information about either the nature of the original problem or the nature of the criteria that should have been used in choosing among the alternative solutions to the problem.

We will refer to the type of decision situation described in the above paragraphs as a *designed-solution situation.*

In summary, we see that the nature of the choice-making step can vary considerably, depending on the results of the alternative-generation process or the nature of the decision situation. In the *conspicuous-alternative situation,* the choice-making process amounts to choosing between implementing the available alternative and searching for more alternatives. In the *multiple-alternative situation,* the choice-making process consists of comparing the merits of the alternative solutions. In the *designed-solution situation,* choice making changes its nature and becomes a design process in which interdependent component-generation efforts and choice-making efforts are employed to create an acceptable solution to the problem.

For a problem to be solved, not only must a solution be identified and chosen, but it must be implemented. Thus the fourth step in the problem-solving process is *implementing the chosen solution.*

IMPLEMENTING THE CHOSEN SOLUTION

This step involves planning and enacting the activities that must take place in order for the chosen solution to actually solve the problem. For example, if building a new plant is chosen as the solution to the problem of less than maximum profits, then implementation would involve planning and enacting all the activities necessary to design, construct, and prepare for the operation of a new manufacturing plant.

Inadequate managerial attention to the implementation step is one of the main reasons why good solutions frequently do not solve the problems they were intended to solve. Certainly "the assumption that a decision to make a change is tantamount to its success is not viable where human behavior is concerned" (Elbing, 1970, p. 318). Considering this, and recognizing that managers implement their decisions by directing the behavior of others, let us review some of the effectiveness-reducing tendencies that are frequently observed at the beginning of the implementation step.[2]

[2] *A number of the techniques described in Chapters 9–11 are effective in reducing the occurrence of these mistakes.*

   1.   The tendency not to ensure understanding of what needs to be done ● One important way to help achieve understanding of what needs to be done is to involve the implementors in the choice-making step. When this is not possible, a strong and explicit attempt should be made to identify any misunderstanding, perhaps by having the implementor explain what he or she thinks needs to be done and why.

   2.   The tendency not to ensure acceptance or motivation for what needs to be done ● Again, an important approach to ensuring acceptance and motivation is to create involvement of the implementors in the choice-making step. Other efforts are to cite payoffs for effective implementation (e.g., the problem will be solved) and show how completion of various tasks will lead to successful implementation.

   3.   The tendency not to provide appropriate resources for what needs to be done ● Many implementations are less effective than they could be because adequate resources, such as time, staff, or information, were not provided. In particular, the allocations of such resources across units and tasks are often assumed to be appropriate because they were appropriate for implementing the previous plan. These assumptions should be checked.

   We note here, before leaving our discussion of implementation, that because the quality of a decision is a function of its "implementability," experienced managers concern themselves with implementability during their decision-making efforts. Thus, although implementation is not part of the decision-making process, it still affects this process.

   Let us move on now to discussing the last step in problem solving.

CONTROLLING THE SOLUTION PROGRAM

   The fifth and final step in the problem-solving process is *controlling the solution program.* In this step, the manager takes the actions necessary to see that what actually happens is what was intended to happen. For example, if we chose to use an incentive-bonus system to increase the performance of our salespeople, controlling the solution program would mean maintaining records and disbursing bonuses in accord with what we intended when we chose this solution.

   This step is really the program administration step—the monitoring and supervising of a program that has survived implementation and is, we hope, an effective solution to the problem. The word "control," however, indicates that to ensure that this solution is solving the problem, we should compare the actual goal achievement with the desired goal achievement. An effectiveness-reducing behavior often observed at this point is *the tendency not to provide in advance for the information necessary to monitor the solution program.* As a result, a less than satisfactory, patchwork evaluation is the rule rather than the exception.

Even a solution that has been carefully chosen and implemented can encounter unforeseen conditions, conditions that cause it to be a less-effective solution than it was thought to be during the choice-making step. When this comparison indicates a significant difference between the actual and desired situations, we have a "problem," and the problem-solving process begins once again. The costs associated with such "reactive" problem solving would be less if it were not for the second effectiveness-reducing behavior, *the tendency not to develop contingency plans in advance* for anticipatable problems.

SUMMARY AND OVERVIEW

In this chapter we analyzed the nature of management problems and reviewed the steps that must be taken to solve such problems. Evidence indicates that managers who recognize and consciously manage these individual steps are more successful than those who focus too quickly on the choice-making step or who are less analytical about the overall process. As part of our review of these steps, we discussed the effectiveness-reducing tendencies that managers and other decision makers frequently exhibit as they carry out the activities involved.

The next five chapters deal with decision making by individuals. In the first of these, we examine some of the difficulties that managers encounter as they attempt to make decisions. In the subsequent four, we describe techniques that managers can use to overcome these difficulties and thereby improve their decisions.

OPPORTUNITIES FOR FURTHER THOUGHT

1. Describe a situation that you know of where inadequate attention to the problem-exploration step caused, or nearly caused, the "wrong" problem to be solved.

2. Describe a situation that you know of where one of the effectiveness-reducing tendencies described in conjunction with the problem-exploration step actually occurred.
3. Describe a situation that you know of where the tendency to slight the alternative-generation process in favor of the alternative-evaluation process caused, or nearly caused, a good alternative to get sidetracked or set aside.
4. Describe a situation that you know of where one of the effectiveness-reducing tendencies described in conjunction with the implementation step actually occurred.

REFERENCES AND RELATED READINGS

Elbing, A. O. *Behavioral Decisions in Organizations.* Glenview, Ill.: Scott, Foresman and Company, 1970.

Maier, N. F. *Problem Solving and Creativity in Individuals and Groups.* Belmont, Calif.: Brooks/Cole Publishing Company, 1970.

Part Two
Individual Decision Making

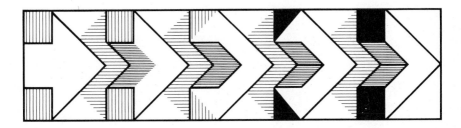

3

Individual Decision Making: The Case of the Boggled Mind

This chapter is concerned with individual decision making, the process through which an individual chooses a course of action. Later in the book we will concern ourselves with group decision making.

The focus of the chapter is on information. It has two sections. The first discusses some of the psychological and situational obstacles that face managers as they attempt to identify and use information in making their choices. The second discusses the types of information used in managerial decisions. Together these discussions serve as an important foundation for the remaining chapters of the book.

THE NATURE OF INDIVIDUAL DECISION MAKING

This section describes some of the factors that interfere with the making of high-quality decisions. In the early parts we will discuss the nature of what are called "limits on rationality." These are the limitations on either our intellectual capabilities or our resources in any given decision situation that cause most decisions to be of lower quality than they might be. In later parts we will point out how these limitations lead to lower quality decisions, and in later chapters we will show what can be done to overcome them.

Limits on rationality

> The capacity of the human mind for formulating and solving complex problems is very small compared with the size of the problems whose solution is required for objectively rational behavior in the real world—or even for a reasonable approximation to such objective rationality. (Simon, 1957, p. 198)

This observation, from the man who won the Nobel prize for his studies of managerial decision making, highlights the central issue of this chapter—the fact that decision quality is limited to a considerable degree by the limiting nature of the human intellect.

Anthony Downs, a decision scientist specializing in the study of bureaucracies, has also studied the issue of a limited human intellect. He has observed that

> 1. Each decision maker can mentally weigh and consider only a limited amount of information at one time. (Downs, 1966, p. 75)

Although Downs would be the first to admit that his observation is not profound, its implications are. Anticipating a discussion that we will undertake shortly, we can predict that our intellectual limitations will, unless we do something to overcome their effects, interfere with our consideration of all the potential alternatives or of all information about any particular alternative. This tendency for people to make decisions without full use of the available information is greatly increased by two other important features of organizational life noted by Downs. They reflect a typical situation faced by managers.

> 2. Each decision maker can devote only a limited amount of time to decision making.
> 3. The functions of most officials (managers) require them to become involved in more activities than they can consider simultaneously; hence they must normally focus their attention on only part of their major concerns, while the rest remain latent. (Downs, 1966, p. 75)

The first of Downs' three observations reflects, using the phrase introduced by March and Simon (1958, p. 136), a "cognitive limit on rationality." The other two are typical characteristics of the manager's workload. Downs groups all three and labels them as simply "limits on rationality." We will as well.

What are the effects of these limits on our rationality? There seem to be two direct effects and two indirect effects.

A direct effect: The use of simplistic decision strategies

One direct effect of limits on our rationality is that decision makers do not really attempt to obtain an optimum or best solution to a problem. Instead they use simplistic decision strategies, relatively simple procedures or rules of thumb that do not require information-processing capabilities beyond those of the unaided human information-processing system. Two of these simplistic strategies have been widely discussed by decision scientists and are briefly described here to clarify the effects of the limits on our rationality.

One of these strategies, labeled "satisficing" by March and Simon (1958, p. 141), is the decision strategy where alternatives are examined as they become available, and the first one that satisfies all of the decision maker's requirements is chosen for implementation. March and Simon argue that satisficing is widely and, in many cases, appropriately used.

> Most human decision-making, whether individual or organizational, is concerned with the discovery and selection of satisfactory alternatives; only in exceptional cases is it concerned with the discovery and selection of optimal alternatives. To optimize requires processes several orders of magnitude more complex than those required to satisfice. An example is the difference between searching a haystack to find the sharpest needle in it and searching the haystack to find a needle sharp enough to sew with. (March and Simon, 1958, p. 141)

Satisficing would be an appropriate strategy when the cost of delaying a decision or searching for more alternatives is high relative to the expected payoff from having found a better alternative. An example would be the case where we were driving on an unfamiliar freeway and noticed that we were nearly out of gas. Unfortunately, decision makers tend to get into the habit of using simplistic decision strategies and then use them when they are not appropriate, such as when the cost of further search for better alternatives is low relative to the likely gain from such search.

Another important but simplistic strategy, labeled "incremental adjustment" by Lindblom (1965), is where a decision maker responds to a problem to the smallest extent possible. When employing this strategy in its pure form, the decision maker makes only the minimum incremental adjustment necessary to move the problem from a status where it demands attention to one where the difference between the actual and desired conditions is at least tolerable. An example would be the case where a legislator, faced with the prospect of having an antipollution bill defeated, would add an exemption that would obtain the few votes necessary to ensure passage and hence solve the problem. Another example would be the case of a homemaker, who, faced with a shortage of electrical outlets in a room, begins using multioutlet adapters. Such a strategy is workable, efficient, and much used. In the short run, it tends to be effective. In the long run, the side effects of many such patchwork solutions cause the pattern of decisions (e.g., the body of laws or network of wires) to be unworkable and ineffective, as when a fuse blows. Gore (1964) describes a large number of case studies of actual organizational decisions where the incremental adjustment strategy was used.

Either of these two strategies allows us to deal with a problem without processing a greal deal of information. They and other simplistic decision strategies are sometimes called *heuristics*. Their use is a direct consequence of the limits on our rationality.

A second direct effect: The use of inadequate models

A second direct effect of the limits on our rationality is that, as decision makers, we are unable to visualize the whole of the decision situation we face. Actual decision situations are more complex than decision situations as we view them. As March and Simon point out, "Choice is always exercised with respect to a limited, approximate, simplified, 'model' of the real situation. We call the chooser's model his 'definition of the situation'" (March and Simon, 1958, p. 139).

When this simplified model of the decision situation does not contain an element of information whose inclusion would increase the chances of our making a higher quality decision, we call it an *inadequate model*. The use of inadequate models is a consequence, in part, of the same limitations on our intellect and time that we discussed above. It is also a consequence of the typical decision situation where the information necessary for a more complete representation of the problem is largely unobtainable. The last three of Downs' six limits on rationality elaborate on the characteristics of such situations.

> 4. The amount of information initially available to every decision maker about each problem is only a small fraction of all the information potentially available on the subject.
> 5. Additional information bearing on any particular problem can usually be procured, but the costs of procurement and utilization may rise rapidly as the amount of data increases.
> 6. Important aspects of many problems involve information that cannot be procured at all, especially concerning future events; hence many decisions must be made in the face of some ineradicable uncertainty. (Downs, 1966, p. 75)

These six limits on our rationality cause us, in general, to exclude from our model of the situation some elements of information that are relevant to making a high-quality decision. In essence, the limits of our intellect, the demands on our time, and inaccessability of information, all acting in concert, cause us to describe many decision situations with inadequate models. Thus the use of inadequate models is a second direct effect of the limits on our rationality.

Two indirect effects: Increased efficiency and decreased quality

Our uses of simplistic strategies and inadequate models are direct consequences of the limits on our rationality. They enable us to make decisions with relatively little information and hence conserve time and other resources. This increased efficiency in the use of resources, being a consequence of the two direct effects, is an indirect effect of the limits on our rationality. We often find the greatest use of simplistic strategies and inadequate models in instances where time and other resources, such as computational aids, are in short supply.

The other consequence of the use of simplistic strategies and inadequate models, and the second indirect effect of the limits on our rationality, is that the chosen solutions will not necessarily have the quality of solutions generated with more elaborate and time-consuming decision processes. We do not get something for nothing. In the long run, a decrement in the effectiveness of the solution is the price that must be paid to incur the desired savings in decision-making resources.

Before closing this discussion, we should note that fatigue, interruptions, and other stress-producing factors decrease our intellectual capabilities and the effectiveness with which we use our time. This in turn tends to increase our use of simplistic decision strategies and inadequate decision models and thus decreases the quality of our decisions.

These last few paragraphs have described some of the psychological and situational difficulties that managers encounter as they attempt to identify and use information for making decisions. The following predictive statements summarize what was said:

1. Limits on rationality lead to the use of simplistic strategies and inadequate models.

2. Use of simplistic strategies and inadequate models leads to (at least short-run) savings in time and other resources.

3. Use of simplistic strategies and inadequate models leads to solutions that tend to be of less than maximum quality.

4. Use of simplistic strategies and inadequate models is increased when time and other resources are decreased and when stress-producing factors are increased.

These ideas and their relationships are portrayed graphically in Figure 3–1.

This first section has highlighted the key role of information in managerial decision making and hints at the fact that improvement in managerial decision making might be achieved by improving the

Figure 3–1.   A Partial Model of Individual Decision Making

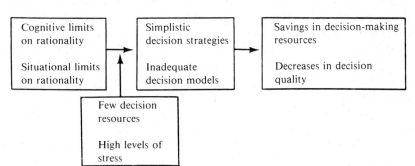

manager's ability to identify and use the information relevant to his or her decision situation. As Kepner and Tregoe put it, "How can the manager improve his performance in analyzing problems (and making decisions)? The key to the answer lies in the fundamental fact that *the raw material of management is information.* That is all that any manager has to work with. . ." (Kepner and Tregoe, 1965, p. 39).

The idea that effective use of information improves decision-making performance is important enough that we will devote the second section of the chapter to a detailed discussion of the types of information used in decision making.

THE INFORMATION USED IN DECISION MAKING

Both our own observations and many research studies show that, in *important and complex* decision situations, decision makers attempt to gather a good deal of information before making their final choice. Let us listen to Richard R. Shinn, President of Metropolitan Life Insurance Company:

> The first step toward making good decisions is getting reliable, timely, well-considered information. Once you have high-quality input, many decisions practically make themselves. Pertinent facts lead inevitably in a certain direction. The question is, how inclusive are the facts at hand? Very often I find that differences of opinions arise among my associates because they are working from different or incomplete sets of facts. (Burger, 1978, p. 36)

Since the remaining chapters of this book describe approaches and techniques for improving the use of information, it seems important to take a close look at the nature of this critical resource. We will organize our discussion around seven types of information.

Not all of these types will be used in every decision situation, but all will be used at some time or other. Most will be used in any complex managerial decision situation. In addition, we should recognize that different managers tend to use information in different ways. For example, the decision-making-style research by McKenny and Keen (1974), in which they categorize managers as being "systematic thinkers" or "intuitive thinkers," clearly indicates that managers in either category make extensive use of information. They just use it differently. For example, when acting as systematic thinkers they may be using the decision-related information in some sort of cause-effect analysis. When acting as intuitive thinkers, they may be using information, perhaps subconsciously, to relate the present decision situation to one they have observed before and for which they have a diagnosis or solution (Simon, 1979). Of course individual managers do not always follow the same style, but vary their styles depending on the time available, their familiarity with the issue, and other aspects of the decision situation.

This typology and listing of information types will serve two purposes. One is to complete the foundation on which the remaining chapters will build. The other, more subtle, purpose is to enhance our vocabulary with a set of terms that will help us sharpen our own thinking. The idea that the availability of appropriate terminology is an important determinant of how well we deal with complex situations and how well we can communicate our thinking to others is suggested by various studies, ranging from research highlighting the fact that multilingual people tend to think in one language at a time to research highlighting the fact that decision-making groups dealing with technical matters are relatively ineffective until they develop a common vocabulary. Morris, focusing on uncertainty as one of the elements of managerial decisions, expresses the idea as follows:

> The suppression of uncertainty is clearly connected with the lack of a readily available language for expressing it. One of the most useful contributions of a decision analyst is to supply such a language. (Morris, 1977, p. 30)

The first three types of information in the categorization can best be described as "basic" in the sense that they form the basic structure of the choice situation. All other information about the situation elaborates upon or deals with these three types.

Basic information

1. One of these basic types concerns the identity of the *alternatives* from which the choice is to be made. For example, "buy stocks" and "buy bonds" are possible alternatives for the person choosing among investment strategies, as are "build plant at site A" and "build

plant at site B" for the corporation choosing among possible new plant locations. In many situations, "take no action" is an alternative that should be considered. So are "search for other alternatives" and "search for more information about the alternatives under consideration." As these examples indicate, alternatives are action statements associated with the allocation of resources. The identity of at least some alternatives is the most basic type of information. Without it, a choice cannot be made.

2. Another basic type of information concerns the identity of the possible after-the-choice *future conditions* in which the chosen alternatives may have to function. Future conditions are possible events or environments that will affect the quality of a decision. For example, a relevant set of possible future conditions for the person investing in the stock market is "no recession," "minor recession," "moderate recession," and "major recession."

The term *states of nature* is often used in referring to such future conditions. It was coined by decision scientists attempting to describe their work in a very casual way. One of these examples concerns the states of nature, "rain" or "shine," for the choice of investing in umbrellas or sunshades to sell at a football game. A more realistic example concerns possible weather conditions as a factor in deciding whether to invest in various agricultural plantings or commodities. In competitive situations, the future conditions are often referred to as "opponent's strategies." This term is appropriate when dealing with choices in marketing, military, or political situations.

The intersection of an alternative and a condition is called an *outcome*. For example, if we choose the alternative "buy stocks" and the after-the-choice condition is "moderate recession," the nature of the outcome would generally be unfavorable relative to buying bonds.

3. The third basic type of information concerns the identity of the *criteria* that are used to evaluate each alternative. For example, if we choose the alternative "plant beans" instead of "plant corn," and the eventual market for beans is poor while that for corn is good, we would score relatively low on the criterion "profit." However, because beans add nitrogen to the soil, we would score relatively high on the criterion "prepare soil for future corn plantings." In almost all managerial decisions, an important criterion is "cost," or more generally, "resources required." As these examples indicate, criteria are goals that are relevant in the choice situation.[1] The identity of the criteria is clearly basic to choice making because without it we have no basis for making a choice.

[1] *The verb is often unstated. For example, our goal is to "reduce cost" in those situations where "cost" is a criterion.*

An example use of basic information

To make the ideas of the previous few paragraphs more specific, let us consider how they could be applied in the following example situation:

> After the last Christmas season, quite a few of the employees and officers of the bank mentioned to Mr. Jones, the operations manager, that during the holidays the bank experienced a number of problems, including a large number of complaints about service, an overcrowded lobby, long lines at the drive-up windows, and an unusually high number of gripes and errors on the part of the employees. After some exploration of these problems, Mr. Jones determined that their common cause was the inadequate size of the workforce relative to the increased work requirements of the holiday season.
>
> Yesterday the bank's president phoned Mr. Jones and said that he would like to hear how Jones planned to deal with the matter during the forthcoming holiday season.
>
> After consulting with a number of people in the bank and the banking community, Mr. Jones decided that there were three *alternatives* worth considering: (1) make no changes, as the problem is common to the industry, (2) do not allow vacation time to be taken, and require overtime, and (3) hire temporary employees.
>
> Although Mr. Jones determined that the increase in work requirements could take any value between 200 transactions per day and 750 transactions per day, he decided that for his preliminary analysis he would examine just two *future conditions,* a moderately low increase of 300 transactions per day and a moderately high increase of 600 transactions per day.
>
> From his own experience and from discussions with the bank's president and other bank employees, Jones determined that the relevant *criteria* for evaluating the alternatives were (1) customer dissatisfaction, (2) employee complaints, and (3) operating costs.

In order to organize his thinking and some of the relevant information, the operations manager might sketch up the matrix of Figure 3–2 as a partial model of the decision situation. In this matrix, if the alternative "temporary employees" were used to deal with the condition of a "workload increase of 600 transactions per day," and if the only

Figure 3-2.   Decision Matrix Showing Operating Costs per Day for the Bank Workload
Problem

Future Conditions

Alternatives	Increase of 300 transactions per day	Increase of 600 transactions per day
Make no changes	*0*	*0*
Draw on regular staff	*– $40*	*– $160*
Use temporary employees	*– $60*	*– $120*

criterion being considered were the operating costs associated with these
employees, then the payoff (in the lower right-hand cell) would
be "– $120."

Conceivably, the operations manager might construct a similar
matrix to better organize his thinking about the effect on customer
dissatisfaction. Such a model might enable him to organize and communicate his thinking even if the entries in the cells could be made no
more specific than "High," "Medium," or "Low." Thus a fuller representation of the manager's situation might be the conceptual model
shown in Figure 3-3. When or if a manager should actually construct
such a model as an aid to organizing his or her thoughts will be discussed
in future chapters.

Although information about alternatives, future conditions, and
criteria is basic to choice making, in certain situations information about
either future conditions or criteria might be less important than information about alternatives. For example, in choices concerning investment in
precious metals versus investment in corporate bonds, it may be that information about only one criterion is relevant—that being the expected

Figure 3-3.   Decision Model Showing Basic Types of Information for the Example
Decision Situation

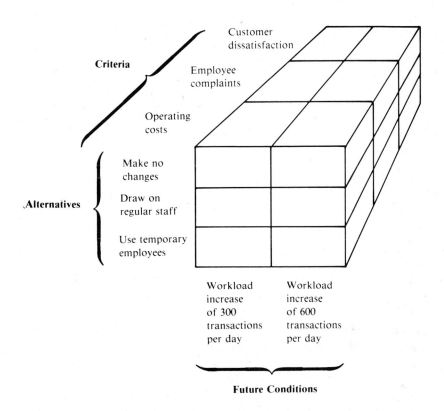

financial return at the end of some specified time period. On the other
hand, information about the whole array of possible economic conditions may be relevant. In another example, information about many
criteria would probably be important in choosing the hours for a town's
only shopping center, but information about possible forthcoming conditions would not be. Thus, the decision maker should make a conscious
determination of whether detailed information about both future conditions and criteria is of practical importance. In some situations, it will
not be.

    With this fact as a rationalization and also for the sake of
simplicity, the decision models in most textbooks show the alternatives as
row headings and the identity of either the future conditions *or* the

criteria as column headings. At later points in this book we, too, will use two-dimensional arrays as useful simplifications. Now let us move to a discussion of other types of information used in decision making.

As a preview of this discussion, the reader might wish to refer to Table 3-1. This listing of types of information reminds us that in any but the most trivial decision situation, our capacity for formulating and solving complex problems is small compared with the information relevant to solving the problems. Fortunately, however, our capacity for formulating and solving complex problems can be greatly extended through the use of the techniques described in succeeding chapters. These techniques focus on the appropriate use of information and draw upon the typology shown in Table 3-1.

Two of the remaining four information types elaborate on the basic types discussed earlier.

Elaborating information

4. One type of elaborating information concerns future conditions. It is the *probability* or likelihood that a particular future condition or outcome will occur.

Sometimes this probability does not depend on the alternative chosen and is the same for all outcomes within the future condition. For example, if the probability of a growing season with less than ten inches of rain is .20, we would not expect this value to change if we planted corn instead of beans. In such cases there would be one probability value for each column heading of the decision model, and it would apply to each

TABLE 3-1.   Types of Information Used in Choice Making

Basic Information
1.   Identity of the alternatives
2.   Identity of the future conditions
3.   Identity of the criteria

Elaborating Information
4.   Probabilities of the future conditions
5.   Importances of the criteria

Performance Information
6.   Payoffs (or costs)
7.   Constraints

cell under that heading. In other cases, the probability does depend on the alternative chosen, as when the likelihood that a competitor will lower prices is partly determined by the price we choose to ask. In these situations, the probabilities would be specific to the outcomes, and there would be one probability for each outcome of the decision model.

5. The other type of elaborating information concerns criteria. It is the relative *importance* or weight attached to each criterion.

Not all of the goals or criteria that are relevant to a given choice situation are equally important. For example, when choosing a location for a corporate headquarters, the goal of having access to a large blue-collar labor force might be relatively less important than locating in a community that would be attractive to professional employees. However, in choosing a location for a labor-intensive manufacturing plant, the opposite might be the case. Certainly the relative importances of these two criteria would vary across the two choice situations. Since in most cases different alternatives do not equally satisfy the various criteria, it is important in choice making to know whether the criteria on which an alternative scores high are among the more important criteria or the less important.

As we will see, there are many situations where detailed information concerning either probabilities or criterion weights is not critical and can be considered informally, if at all. In other situations, detailed information about both is important and should be considered in a very formal and systematic way. Our purpose here is not to make a general judgment about whether or when each type of information is or should be used, but rather to examine the nature of the information itself. By doing this, we will be better prepared to use the decision-improving techniques described in later chapters of the book.

The last two types of information relate to the usefulness or performance of the various alternatives.

Performance information

6. One type of performance information concerns *payoffs*. Reviewing Figure 3–3, we recall that an entry in any one of the cells of the decision model is the payoff associated with that particular outcome considered with regard to the associated criterion. Thus, for the criterion "operating costs," dollar values would be the payoff entries in the respective cells. For the criterion "customer dissatisfaction," the number of customer complaints about speed or quality of service might be used as the payoff entries.

7. The second type of information relating to the performance of alternatives concerns *constraints*. Constraints are maximum or minimum criterion levels that must not be violated by the chosen alternative. For example, if one criterion is "cost," the budget level may be a constraint that disallows any alternative with a price tag above a certain ceiling. Another way of viewing a constraint is as a performance standard that must be satisfied. For example, if we are choosing a secretary, a "minimum typing speed of fifty words per minute" may be a constraint that we would use, at least in the early stages of the choice-making process. In the bank workload situation discussed earlier, a managerially imposed constraint on the maximum expected length of the line at the drive-up window might be six cars.

To review these last few pages, we have discussed the several types of information used in choice making and have listed them in Table 3-1. Not all are used in every situation, or course, but it takes little imagination to see that *all are used in some situations* and that *most would be used in any complex managerial choice situation.*

An example

To see how some of these types of information might be used, let us look at the situation of a large construction company that has the opportunity to bid on building a small apartment complex. A good analysis might lead to much of the relevant information as displayed in Figure 3-4. There are three alternatives:

1. Do not bid.
2. Bid low (e.g., $1 million).
3. Bid high (e.g., $1.2 million).

There are also, in this example, three future conditions that the bid might encounter:

1. Low bidding competitor(s) (e.g., lowest competitor bid is less than $1million)
2. No low bidding competitor and at least one moderate bidding competitor (e.g., lowest competitor bid is about $1.1 million)
3. Only higher bidding competitors (e.g., lowest competitor bid is more than $1.2 million)

Figure 3-4.   Decision Matrix Showing Profits for the Construction Bidding Problem

Future Conditions

	Lowest competitor bid is less than $1 million	Lowest competitor bid is about $1.1 million	Lowest competitor bid is more than $1.2 million
Do not bid	*0*	*0*	*0*
Bid $1 million	*− $5000*	*$95,000*	*$95,000*
Bid $1.2 million	*− $5000*	*− $5000*	*$295,000*

(Alternatives)

If profit (as the dominant criterion) is equal to the accepted bid minus both the construction cost of $900,000 and the bid development cost of $5000, then the essence of the situation can be displayed with the model shown. Each cell entry is the profit associated with respective outcome. The $95,000 entry in the center cell, for example, is equal to the gross profit of $100,000 (a successful $1.0 million bid minus the $900,000 construction cost) less the $5000 cost of preparing the bid.

The model of Figure 3-4 portrays three of the types of information just discussed (i.e., the alternatives, the possible future conditions, and the payoffs). It does not portray information on criteria or their relative importance, presumably because criteria other than profit or constraints on profit are of little concern. It also does not portray the information on constraints or on the probabilities of competitors' actions.

How can the information presently available be used to arrive at a decision? This is another way of asking for information about a decision rule or a guideline for making a choice. What is a reasonable rule to use for transforming this information into a decision? We will address the general issue of decision rules in greater detail in a later chapter. For now we might mention two possible rules:

1. Choose the alternative that allows for the largest possible payoff.

2. Obtain estimates of the probabilities that our bid will encounter each of the three competitive conditions shown, and use this information to help choose the alternative that would give the greatest expected payoff.

For the purposes of this example, assume that we select the latter rule for arriving at a decision. If we determine that there is a fifty–fifty chance for only moderate bidding competitors, and essentially no chance for the high-bids-only condition, then a close examination of the model indicates that we should choose to bid $1 million. This alternative, of bidding $1 million, is the most favorable because it gives us a fifty–fifty chance of receiving a $95,000 payoff. Either of the other two alternatives gives us either zero payoff or a loss.

What does this simple example of choice making teach us? For one thing, it demonstrates that we do not need, or at least may not use, all seven types of information to make a particular decision. In this example, depending on which of the two decision rules we choose, we would need only four or five types of information. Another lesson we can learn from this example is that different decision rules require different information (e.g., the first decision rule does not require estimates of the probability of future conditions; the second one does).

SUMMARY AND OVERVIEW

This chapter has highlighted the fact that actual individual decision making produces decisions that are lower in quality than we would wish. This is in large part a consequence of our limited ability to identify and use relevant information.

What can be done to overcome this unfortunate state of affairs? There are two commonly used approaches. One is for managers to extend their intellectual capabilities and other resources through the use of decision-aiding groups. Chapters 9–11 describe a number of techniques that have proven useful in making groups more effective as aids to managers. The second approach is for managers to sharpen their thinking and use of information by employing one of the several decision-aiding techniques that have been developed for identifying and using decision-related information. Chapters 4–7 describe a number of such techniques that have proven useful in this regard.

Chapter 4 describes a technique that has shown itself to be particularly useful when the complexity of the decision situation is a consequence of the need to consider more than one criterion or attribute of the alternatives from which we are choosing. Decisions arising from such situations, which are frequently encountered in managerial practice, are generally referred to as *multicriterion* or *multiattribute* decisions.

OPPORTUNITIES FOR FURTHER THOUGHT

1. Describe a situation that you know of where a decision maker was, at least temporarily, boggled by what we might call "information overload." How did the decision maker handle the situation?
2. Explain the statement that "most decision-making managers tend to have both too much information and too little information."
3. Take a decision situation you are familiar with, and describe it in terms of the alternatives, the future conditions (if appropriate), the criteria, and the constraints. Describe how you distinguished between the criteria and the constraints.

REFERENCES AND RELATED READINGS

Burger, C. "The Chief Executive." *TWA Ambassador* (September, 1978): 35–40.

Downs, A. *Inside Bureaucracy.* Boston: Little, Brown and Company, 1966.

Ebert, R. J. and T. R. Mitchell. *Organizational Decision Processes,* New York: Crane, Russak and Company, Inc., 1975.

Gore, W. J. *Administrative Decision Making: A Heuristic Model.* New York: John Wiley and Sons, Inc., 1964.

Kepner, C. H. and B. B. Tregoe. *The Rational Manager.* New York: McGraw-Hill, Inc., 1965.

Lindblom, C. E. *The Intelligence of Democracy.* New York: The Free Press, 1965.

March, J. G. and H. A. Simon. *Organizations.* New York: John Wiley and Sons, Inc., 1958.

McKenney, J. L. and P. G. W. Keen. "How Managers' Minds Work." *Harvard Business Review* (May–June 1974): 79–90.

Morris, W. T. *Decision Analysis.* Columbus, Ohio: Grid, Inc., 1977.

Simon, H. A. *Models of Man.* New York: John Wiley and Sons, Inc., 1957.

Simon, H. A. "The Forms of Rationality." Plenary address presented at the Joint National Meeting of the Operations Research Society of America and the Institute of Management Sciences, 16 October 1979, at Milwaukee, Wisc.

Wright, P. "The Harrassed Decision Maker: Time Pressures, Distractions, and the Use of Evidence." *Journal of Applied Psychology* 59 (1974): 555–561.

4

Improving Decisions Involving Multiple Goals: Two Case Studies

This chapter is concerned with how a manager should make decisions in situations where it is important to consider more than one goal or criterion. Such situations are commonplace. Consider, as examples, the following:

1. *Selection of a new director of marketing:* The acceptability of any particular candidate for a top-level marketing position depends on, among other things, the candidate's background knowledge in marketing, background knowledge in the industrial and product setting, ability to work with top-level executives, and achievement orientation.

2. *Location of a new corporate office:* Whether or not location A would be preferable to location B depends on, among other things, the cost of the land and buildings, the expected productivity of the local employees that must be hired, and the attractiveness of the location to professional and managerial employees.

3. *Continued funding of a government program:* Whether or not it is advisable to fund a particular program depends on,

among other things, the performance of the program to date, the anticipated need for the program in the future, the funds available, and the organizational and political consequences of discontinuing the program.

Decisions involving the use of more than one goal or criterion are called *multicriterion* decisions.

Although groups may be involved in making multicriterion decisions, our focus in this chapter is not on how a manager should manage group efforts, but rather on how he or she should identify and use the information relevant to decisions such as those described above. In the later chapters of the book, we will be concerned with overcoming the difficulties encountered by groups engaged in multicriterion decision making. Here, and in the next few chapters, we will be concerned with overcoming the difficulties encountered by individuals.

In our earlier discussion of limits on rationality, we saw that individual decision makers encounter considerable difficulty in their attempts to identify and use the information relevant to a decision. The purpose of this chapter is to introduce a technique that increases a decision maker's ability to systematically obtain and use the information relevant for making choices in multicriterion decision situations. In the next chapter we will describe the step-by-step procedure that is used when employing the technique.

The technique makes use of *multiattribute utility models,* a fancy name for a simple idea. After describing the general nature of the technique the chapter moves on to describe how it has been used in two of its many applications.

MULTIATTRIBUTE UTILITY MODELS

What is meant by the term *multiattribute utility model?* To answer this, let us begin with the word "model." From both our discussion in Chapter 3 and our daily use of the term, we know that a model is a representation or abstraction of something. Thus the decision matrices shown in Figures 3–2 and 3–4 are models of decision situations. The block-and-arrow diagram of Figure 3–1 is a model that relates some of the factors involved in individual decision making. But what, specifically, do we mean by "utility model"?

First we note that the extent to which an alternative satisfies a criterion is called its *utility*. Other words and phrases that have essentially the same meaning include *worth, payoff, psychological value,* and *satisfactoriness.* Now we can define a utility model as a graphical or mathematical model that can be used to estimate the utility of an item or alternative. Essentially, a utility model transforms a description of an item or alternative into a numerical evaluation of the item or alternative. As an example, consider the case of a manager reviewing the backgrounds of prospective employees. If one of the important criteria is how much experience the prospective employee has had in similar positions, asking the manager a series of questions might enable us to draw the model shown in Figure 4–1. In general, we would expect such a model to be some shape other than a straight line, but for now we will stick with this simple example.

Figure 4–1 is a utility model. In particular it is a *graphical* utility model. The corresponding *verbal* utility model portraying this same situation is "the utility, expressed as a percent satisfaction, is equal to twenty times the experience, expressed in years." If we abbreviate ex-

Figure 4-1.   A Simple Utility Model

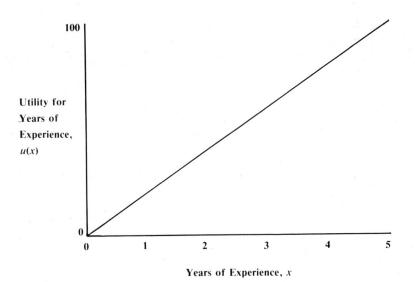

Years of Experience, *x*

perience as x and utility as u, then the *mathematical* utility model would state that the utility of experience, or $u(x)$, was equal to $20x$, or

Equation 4-1
$$u(x) = 20x.$$

Because mathematical equations are more efficient statements than sentences are, mathematical utility models are often used in place of verbal utility models.

What do we mean by *attribute?* An attribute is a characteristic or property of an item or alternative. For example, years of experience in certain types of employment is an attribute, or a characteristic or property, of prospective employees. Thus Figure 4–1 and Equation 4–1 are each single-attribute utility models. In contrast to them, a multiattribute utility model indicates or represents the overall utility derived from an item or alternative possessing more than one relevant attribute. Let us move on now from our discussion of single-attribute utility models to one of multiattribute models.

Multiattribute utility models (MAU models) are designed to obtain the utility of items or alternatives that have more than one valuable attribute; therefore, they must be evaluated on more than one criterion.[1] A MAU model essentially shows a decision maker how to aggregate the utility or satisfaction derived from each of the various attributes into a single measure of the overall utility of the multiattributed item or alternative.

An example of a MAU model is one used by coaching staffs of professional football teams to help make decisions during the annual college draft. The use of MAU model—in conjunction with a computer containing information on the college players eligible to play professionally—enables the decision makers to make a rough but systematic evaluation of hundreds of players in a matter of seconds. Some of the attributes used in this decision setting are the player's height, weight, and speed. A score—a $u(x)$ value—is developed for each attribute of each player and then weighted according to its importance. Finally, the weighted scores are added together to get an overall utility score for each player. This overall score can be used by the computer to identify potentially good football players and can be used as an input to the management's decision process. Other items of information, such as available scouting reports, are also used in the decision process.

---

[1]*In Chapter 5 we will make a distinction between an "attribute" and a "criterion." For the present we can use the terms interchangeably.*

It is important to realize that these systems do not provide substantially more information than available from the scouting reports. What the rating reports do provide is a means to rank the athletes in a consistent manner with most of the bias eliminated (each scout has a weighting factor specified by the coach of the team). (Ladany and Machol, 1977, p. 200)

Thus, in this decision situation, as in most, the model is used as an aid to judgment and not as a substitute for judgment.

The concept behind the use of MAU models is straightforward. We simply weight and aggregate the utilities derived from the individual attributes to get an overall utility for each alternative. Then, unless there is good reason not to, we choose the alternative with the highest overall utility score. The use of MAU models allows us to overcome the effect of some of our intellectual limitations by using an external memory, a carefully constructed model, and a step-by-step procedure for aggregating information.

Many applications of MAU models appear in the managerial and decision-making literature. Examples that demonstrate the diversity of their use include the budgeting decisions of public health officials, the job-choice decisions of job applicants, the student-admission decisions of universities, the plant-location decisions of corporate executives, the funding decisions of federal program administrators, the land-use decisions of regional planning groups, and the personnel-assignment decisions of various military services.

In the next few pages we will describe two actual cases where consultants used MAU models to assist decision makers. In one case the decision makers to be helped were high-level officials of the U.S. Department of Health, Education and Welfare. In the other, the decision makers were people selecting jobs.

We note in passing that the danger in looking at any one case is that the reader might not be able to relate to it and so reject the use of MAU models as not applicable to his or her job situation. This rejection would be unfortunate, not because MAU models are useful for solving *all* problems—as we will see they are not—but because the basic concepts of their use are applicable in any decision setting. This will become apparent as we work through the cases.

As we examine these cases we will observe that the MAU models were not used as substitutes for judgment but rather as aids to judgment. Specifically, the use of the models enables the managers and other decision makers to employ their judgment more systematically than they could if left to their own devices.

AN APPLICATION OF THE MAU MODEL
TECHNIQUE: HELPING JOB SEEKERS

Many public and private agencies use computers to help people find jobs. A few years ago, one of these agencies asked a consultant to help it deal with the following problem.

When the agency had its computer search on behalf of a job-seeking public school teacher, the computer would sometimes indicate that in its inventory of over 50,000 public school job openings, there were no appropriate jobs for the particular job seeker at hand. On other occasions, the computer would generate brief descriptions of hundreds of job openings, but would provide no information to indicate that each was not equally worthy of further investigation. The job seeker then had a mind-boggling sorting task.

The agency director was understandably concerned about these occurrences of less than satisfactory service. He summarized the situation with, "We'd like to be able to have the computer find the ten best jobs for any client. We don't want the output to be zero job openings or hundreds of job openings, but a number in between and under our control. We must be able to give the client something reasonable to work with. He or she can take it from there. And if the computer could rank order the job openings in terms of their satisfactoriness for the particular client, we could advise the clients where to interview first. That's important in terms of saving their time and maximizing their chances of getting a job."

The consultant brought in to help with this problem quickly determined that the computer relied entirely on constraints in its search of job openings. That is, an employment counselor asked each job applicant to identify the constraints or limits that he or she had for each of the five job attributes that the organization had found helpful in matching job-seeking teachers and job openings. For example, the applicant was asked, "What is the lowest salary that you think you would accept?" and "What are the regions of the country where you would not take a job?" The answers to these and related questions were then fed into the computer, which screened job openings as either satisfactory or unsatisfactory. It did not, however, develop any "goodness of fit" score.

When the answers caused the constraints (e.g., geographical preference) to be very "tight," then almost all job openings were screened out. When the answers caused all the constraints to be very "loose," then almost no job openings were screened out. There was also a lack of information in the system from which the computer could identify either potential matches that were just a bit off or really good matches that ought to receive the highest possible priority when setting up an interview.

It was clear that these difficulties could be reduced by patching up the existing system. For example, the computer could count how many of the five constraints were satisfied and in this way create some sort of goodness of fit score. On the other hand, both the agency and the consultant were interested in advancing the state of the art, and so it was decided to search for a more complete solution.

Their approach was to attempt to predict which evaluation scheme an individual job seeker would use to evaluate job openings. They put this information in a form that the computer could understand, had the computer use the information to evaluate each of its 50,000 openings on behalf of the job seeker, identify the ten or so best jobs, and rank these in terms of their utility. The process of setting up interviews could then be done with maximum efficiency.

The use of multiattribute utility models was a conspicuously available technique for this task. If a MAU model that predicted the client's evaluations of jobs could be developed for each client, then the computer could be programmed to use the model in a search on behalf of that particular client.

The first step was to identify the attributes to be used in the model. Normally this step would involve determining which job attributes the decision makers wanted to use in evaluating their alternatives. However, because the job openings in the computer were already described by a particular set of five attributes—which the agency had developed from its years of counseling job-seeking teachers—these attributes were accepted as the ones to be included in the MAU model. The attributes and their discriminating levels are shown in Table 4-1. It seemed reasonable to believe that these attributes would be appropriate for screening. When we later discuss the validation of the models, we will see that they were valid for predicting which jobs the applicants finally chose.

The second step was to determine the utility associated with each level of each attribute. This involved constructing a utility model for each of the five attributes. Because the consultant in this case was interested in satisfying the goals of individual decision makers, he had to obtain the five utility models of each individual job seeker. The information necessary to develop the model was obtained through a questionnaire. An example question was, "On a 0–100 point scale, where 0 means

TABLE 4-1.   Attributes Used in the Job Descriptions: Their Levels and Their Coding

Attributes	Attribute levels and their coding
1. Type of position, x_1	teaching (x_{11}), research (x_{12}), administrative (x_{13}), coaching (x_{14}), special services (x_{15}).
2. Type of school, x_2	elementary (x_{21}), junior high (x_{22}), high school (x_{23}).
3. Size of community, x_3	less than 10,000 (x_{31}), between 10,000–100,000 (x_{32}), between 100,000–400,000 (x_{33}), greater than 400,000 (x_{34}).
4. Location, x_4	region, state, section of state, and city different from desired (x_{41}); state, section of state, and city different from desired (x_{42}); section of state and city different from desired (x_{43}); section of state corresponds to desires, city may or may not (x_{44}).
5. Salary, x_5	\$6,000 to \$14,000 in \$2,000 increments (x_{51}, x_{52}, x_{53}, x_{54}, x_{55}).

that you would receive no satisfaction and where 100 means you would be completely satisfied, how satisfied would you be with a teaching position?" This was followed by similar questions concerning the job seeker's satisfaction for positions in research, administration, coaching, and special services. The answers to such questions allowed the consultant to construct the job seeker's utility model for each attribute. An example is shown in Figure 4–2. In this example, "teaching" would be called the "level" of the attribute, "type of position." The model indicates that "60" was the job seeker's response to the question concerning his or her relative satisfaction with a teaching position, as contrasted with an administrative position.

The third step was to have each job seeker rate the relative importance of the five attributes. This was done using a 0–100 point scale, where 100 was assigned to the most important attribute and other numbers between 100 and 0 were used to indicate the relative importance of the other attributes. Typical relative importance ratings (w_1, w_2, w_3, w_4, and w_5 for attributes x_1, x_2, x_3, x_4, and x_5 of Table 4–1) were 90, 60, 30, 100, and 70.

The fourth and final step was to have the computer estimate the job seeker's overall utility for each job in its memory. It did this by using

Figure 4–2.   A Utility Model for Type of Position

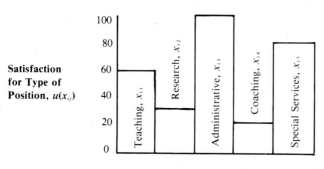

Type of Position, x_i

the job seeker's ratings of (1) the relative satisfaction with the level of the attribute, and (2) the relative importance of each attribute. In verbal form, the five-attribute utility model used by the computer was stated as "the extent to which a job seeker would be satisfied with a particular job opening is equal to the weighted combination of the satisfactions, or utilities, derived from the five job attributes as they occur in the particular job opening."

Were these MAU models valid? Did they really represent the model that the decision maker wanted to use in evaluating jobs? The evidence indicates that the answer to these questions was "yes."[2] For example, as part of the study, the consultant used questionnaires to develop the MAU models of thirty job seekers who applied for jobs through the agency in January. The models were then used to evaluate and rank the satisfactory job openings that the computer had provided to each applicant in February.[3] Finally, the consultant observed whether the job eventually taken by a particular person, usually in May or June, was in the top half of the ranking. If it was, this would demonstrate that the model had at least some validity.

For twenty-six out of the thirty job seekers, the job taken was in the top half of the twenty (on the average) satisfactory jobs that the ap-

[2]The details of how these models were developed and validated are described in G. P. Huber, R. Daneshgar, and D. L. Ford, "An Empirical Comparison of Five Utility Models for Predictive Job Preferences," Organizational Behavior and Human Performance 6 (May 1971): 267–282.

[3]The applicants were informed of only satisfactory jobs—those that satisfied all of the constraints or limits that the applicant had indicated he or she would use in screening jobs for acceptability.

plicant had been told about. Moreoever, for eighteen of these thirty job seekers, the job that the MAU model ranked number one in January was the job actually taken four or five months later. Clearly, these were "adequate" models, in terms of how much of the decision situation they encompassed. The step-by-step procedure used (i.e., the development and weighted addition of the utility scores) processed the information in a way that was useful in predicting the choices resulting from the decision maker's own processing of the relevant information.

DISCUSSION OF THE JOB-SEEKER APPLICATION

A number of questions might be, and sometimes should be, asked when applying MAU models in a situation such as this. One of these concerns whether or not simply adding the weighted utilities together is the most appropriate procedure or strategy for estimating the overall utility. Let us begin answering this question by examining the mathematical model that reflects the procedure. We must first introduce a few symbols to substitute for the words used in the verbal model.

We will use x_i to represent the ith attribute (e.g., from Table 4–1, we use x_1 to represent "type of position"). We will use x_{ij} to represent the jth level of the attribute (e.g., in Table 4–1, we use x_{11} to represent "teaching"). Finally, we will use $u(x_{ij})$ to represent the utility derived from an alternative's possessing the ith attribute to the jth level (e.g., using Table 4–1 and Figure 4–2, we see that the utility for a teaching position, $u(x_{11})$, is 60).

Now, if one of the job seekers had been considering a job that was in coaching (x_{14}), in a high school (x_{23}), in a community of 20,000 people (x_{32}), in the most desired section of the most desired state (x_{44}), and that offered a salary of $10,000/year ($x_{53}$), we see that we would be dealing with utilities $u(x_{14})$, $u(x_{23})$, $u(x_{32})$, $u(x_{44})$, and $u(x_{53})$. If, for this job seeker, these values were $u(x_{14}) = 80$, $u(x_{23}) = 100$, $u(x_{32}) = 20$, $u(x_{44}) = 100$, and $u(x_{53}) = 60$, then we would have had the computer calculate his or her overall utility for this job opening as a weighted combination of these five utility values.

If the job seeker's relative importance weights for the five attributes were $w_1 = 90$, $w_2 = 60$, $w_3 = 30$, $w_4 = 100$, and $w_5 = 70$, the computer would have multiplied $u(x_{14})$ by w_1, or 80 by 90, and gotten 7200, then multiplied $u(x_{23})$ by w_2, or 100 by 60, and gotten 6000, and so forth. Thus this job seeker's utility, U, for this job would have been

$$U = 90(80) + 60(100) + 30(20) + 100(100) + 70(60);$$

or

$$U = 28,000.$$

The general mathematical model appropriate to this particular job opening is

Equation 4–2
$$U = w_1u(x_{14}) + w_2u(x_{23}) + w_3u(x_{32}) + w_4u(x_{44}) + w_5u(x_{53}).$$

Equation 4–2 is a simple additive model. Is it possible that, in the mind of the decision maker, some of the attributes interact? For example, is the utility for different salaries affected by the type of position? Certainly this could be the case. If it were, a more complex model would be called for. In this application, the consultant did not look into the possibility. In many other applications and studies, however, the possibility of interactions has been examined and, almost without exception, the simple additive model has been found to be as predictive of decision-maker preferences as a more complex model that considered the interactions. When the exceptions did occur, the marginal increase in predictiveness was small.

Though more complex models are seldom more useful than simple additive models, a consultant might want to search for and deal with the presence of an interaction in a particularly important decision situation. The procedure for both identifying and dealing with such interactions will be discussed in Chapter 5.

A second question that might be asked when applying MAU models is whether there are other procedures for obtaining the relative importance weights besides that of direct questioning used in this application. The answer is "yes." One approach is for the consultant to describe for the decision maker a set of alternatives in terms of the levels to which each alternative possesses each of the attributes, and then have the decision maker make global, overall ratings of each of the alternatives. By correlating all of the ratings with the attribute levels that resulted from each rating, the consultant can work backwards to determine the single attribute utility models and the importance weights that the decision maker used to make the ratings. Computers and statistical techniques make this a relatively easy procedure.

What the consultant does in this procedure is build a descriptive MAU model that may reflect the conceptual model and information-processing strategy that the decision maker used when evaluating multiattributed items or alternatives. This model may not reflect the model or procedure that the decision maker would like to use. For example, research shows that when faced with the problem of evaluating multiattributed items without the help of models or other aids, our limited ability to process information forces us to focus on only a few attributes, and allows other important attributes to influence our judgments hardly at all.

Models developed by consultants or other observers using the working-backwards procedure just described are called *observer-derived* models. Models developed by having the decision maker alone explicate the model, as was done in the case of the job-seeking public school teachers, are called *self-explicated* models. Because they are derived from an analysis of choices, observer-derived models are especially useful in predicting choices, such as those of consumers. Because they are developed from statements about what the decision maker wants to do, self-explicated models are especially useful in improving choices, such as in helping decision makers do what they want to do despite their cognitive limitations. Because our purpose is to improve decisions, we will direct our attention to the development and use of self-explicated models.

The application of MAU models just described focused on helping individual decision makers achieve their individual goals. Let us turn now to an application that focused on helping organizational decision makers achieve organizational goals.

AN APPLICATION OF THE MAU MODEL TECHNIQUE: HELPING HEW EXECUTIVES

In 1973, Congress directed the U.S. Department of Health, Education and Welfare to support the development of health maintenance organizations, a type of health delivery organization with widely publicized potential for providing high-quality, comprehensive health care. It also required that priority in funding be directed toward areas with populations that were "medically underserved." Further, it required the department to inform Congress within three months of the procedure to be used to identify these areas and to inform Congress within twelve months as to exactly which areas it had designated as being medically underserved.

The HEW executives assigned this responsibility found themselves in a very difficult decision situation. The situation was difficult for three reasons. One was that they believed they would be under tremendous pressures from various special interest groups and elected officials to allocate the funds to the areas (counties and subcounty regions) represented by these groups and officials. The second reason was that there was no procedure for assessing "medical underservedness," the global criterion to be used in choosing the areas for funding. The third reason the situation was difficult was that the logistical tasks involved in assessing the medical and health conditions in the 3141 counties in the U.S. were enormous.

To aid them in this assignment, the executives sought the help of a group of consultants with experience in both decision making and the health field. The overall strategy agreed upon was to develop a multiattribute utility model that would transform a description of a county or subcounty region into a numerical score of medical underservedness for that county.[4] The following paragraphs give a brief overview of the procedure that was used.

As a first step, different panels of health experts from around the country were interviewed and then surveyed with a series of questionnaires. The consultants identified community attributes (e.g., "number of physicians per 1000 population") that they felt were related to the general concept of medical underservedness. Nine attributes seemed to receive consensus agreement, and data were available on seven.

The second step consisted of obtaining a utility model for each of the various attributes from each member of another panel of health experts. Each utility model essentially transformed a single-attribute description of an area into an estimate of the medical underservedness for the area. Of course, medical underservedness itself is not an attractive feature. In this case, though, it was the global concept used to indicate the utility of additional resources, and in this sense it was equivalent to utility.

Figure 4–3 shows one of these models. The models from the individual experts were averaged to obtain a single utility model for each attribute. The method used to obtain these models has been used and validated in many contexts and will be described in detail in the next chapter.

[4]*The details of the study and the rationale for the choice of this strategy are described in Health Services Research Group, "Development of the Index of Medical Underservice,"* Health Services Research *10 (Summer 1975): 168–180.*

Figure 4-3.   A Utility Model for Physicians per 1000 Population

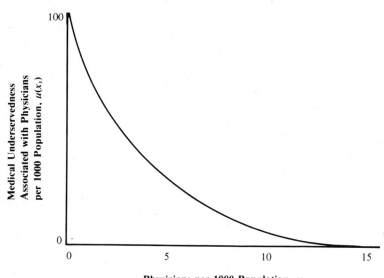

Physicians per 1000 Population, x_1

The third step consisted of having each expert assess the relative importance of each attribute as a measure of medical underservedness. The relative importance judgments from the individual experts were then averaged to obtain the relative importance weights used in aggregating the utilities derived from an area's possessing particular characteristics.

The fourth step consisted of validating the model. In developing a MAU model for as important an application as this, a great deal of care was taken to validate both the applicability of the procedures used and the resulting model itself. For example, medical underservedness scores for 62 areas were generated by the model and were compared to the medical-underservedness assessments made by various panels of local health experts personally familiar with these areas. These local experts made their assessments independent of one another. In all, 57 local experts provided a total of 1662 assessments. The estimates of these assessments, obtained with the MAU model, corresponded very closely to the actual assessments.[5]

[5]*The correlations between the means of the global, unaided assessments made by the local experts and the scores developed using the MAU model were typically above .8.*

Further study showed that a MAU model that included only the four most important attributes correlated with these local expert assessments about as well as the seven-attribute model. In verbal form, the four-attribute model stated that the extent to which an area is medically underserved was to be estimated with a weighted combination of four indicators:

1. $u(x_1)$, the medical underservedness indicated by the area's physicians per 1000 population
2. $u(x_2)$, the medical underservedness indicated by the percent of the area's population having family incomes of less than $5,000
3. $u(x_3)$, the medical underservedness indicated by the area's infant mortality rate
4. $u(x_4)$, the medical underservedness indicated by the percent of the area's population who are over 65 years old

Since the relative importance weights (the w_is) for these four attributes were, respectively, 28.7, 25.1, 26.0, and 20.2, the final model submitted to the HEW officials was

Equation 4–3
$$U = 28.7\ u(x_1) + 25.1\ u(x_2) + 26.0\ u(x_3) + 20.2\ u(x_4).$$

This model was adopted by HEW and used to evaluate the medical underservedness of thousands of counties and subcounty areas.

DISCUSSION OF THE HEW APPLICATION

There are a number of questions that might be asked when applying MAU models in a situation such as this. One of these concerns whether it is appropriate to substitute a decision maker's model for the decision maker. To answer this question, let us review the difficulties faced by the HEW officials and see if the use of the MAU model helped solve them.

The first difficulty concerned coping with the inevitable political pressures on resource controllers in organizations. The alternative approaches for assessing the medical underservedness in a local area—such as the use of site visit teams of HEW representatives or the use of hearings for each petition for funding—would have required both personal communication and subjective judgments specific to the local area. Either of these conditions would have opened the door to persuasions through the use of power and politics. In contrast, the publicly proclaimed and actual use of the model helped the HEW officials resist these political pressures.

The second difficulty was the lack of a defined procedure for assessing "medical underservedness." The model and the procedures associated with its development and use became that procedure and helped in resolving this difficulty as well. The third difficulty concerned the logistics of using site visits, hearings, or the unaided review of proposals to assess the medical underservedness of over 3000 locations. The use of the model reduced these logistics to a level just slightly higher than key punching the data associated with the four attributes contained in the model.

Though the HEW actually used the MAU model scores as only one input to their decision making (and probably continued to use their own discretion in many cases), the model was useful in minimizing the organizational difficulties in this decision situation. It also increased the consistency with which information about the four attributes affected the final evaluations. That is, it reduced the influence of factors that the decision makers did not want to have influence their judgments, such as fatigue or the happenstance order in which the information on the area attributes was encountered.

Altogether, these observations suggest that it is appropriate, in some cases, to substitute the model for the decision maker. But was this an actual substitution? Did the previous application, involving job seekers, comprise an actual substitution? The answer is "no." In both applications, the model was used to aid the decision maker. No options were eliminated through the use of the model. In these applications, the MAU model was used to score large numbers of alternatives so that the decision maker's time could be spent on those that were the most critical. In the job seeker application, the most critical alternatives were those that scored highest and probably deserved further investigation, perhaps in the form of an interview. In the HEW application, the most critical alternatives were those areas on the borderline between being funded or not being funded. We are left, then, with the conclusion stated earlier: MAU models are not best used as substitutes for judgment but rather as aids in making judgments.

Before moving on to the chapter summary, we should briefly introduce a principle that is often mentioned in the management and decision-making literature, although not always by name. This principle, sometimes called *the decomposition principle,* holds forth that in many cases we can more effectively deal with a complex problem by breaking the problem into its component parts, attacking these parts one at a time, and then synthesizing the results in a way that addresses the complexity of the original problem. As Professor Howard Raiffa of the Harvard Business School explains it, the idea behind the principle is to "divide and conquer: Decompose a complex problem into simpler problems, get one's thinking straight on these simpler problems, paste these analyses together with logical glue, and come out with a program for action" (Raiffa, 1968, p. 271).

In the job-seeker application, as an example, the "simpler problems" included not having assessments of the utility derived from each of the various job attributes. The "logical glue" consisted of the arithmetic relationships used to aggregate these incremental utilities once they were obtained from the questionnaires.

Research shows (cf. Armstrong, Denniston, and Gordon, 1975) that in many situations attacking a problem in this way (rather than attempting to swallow it all at once) leads to better solutions. Several of the decision-aiding techniques described in this book are, in essence, mechanisms for making the decomposition principle operational. In particular, one perspective on the MAU model technique is the view that it is a mechanism for applying the decomposition principle in decision situations where the source of the problem's complexity is the need to consider more than one criterion.

SUMMARY AND OVERVIEW

This chapter began by introducing the topic of multiattribute utility models and the idea that a decision-aiding technique employing such models could be helpful in overcoming some of the limits on rationality described in Chapter 3. It further noted that multiattribute utility models have been used to aid decision makers in a variety of multicriterion decision situations.

The chapter continued by describing and discussing two applications of what was called the "MAU model technique." The purpose of the first application was to help individual decision makers achieve their individual goals. The purpose of the second application was to help organizational decision makers achieve organizational goals. We noted that, in both applications, the MAU models were used as aids to judgment rather than as substitutes for judgment.

In both these applications, consultants were used to help decision makers. Can individual decision makers and their staffs use MAU models to help themselves? In the next chapter we will see that the answer is clearly "yes."

REFERENCES AND RELATED READINGS

Armstrong, J. S., W. B. Denniston, Jr., and M. M. Gordon. "The Use of the Decomposition Principle in Making Judgments." *Organizational Behavior and Human Performance* 14 (October 1975): 257–263.

Edwards, W. "How to Use Multi-Attribute Utility Measurement for Social Decision Making." *IEEE Transactions on Systems, Man, and Cybernetics* SMC–7 (May 1977): 326–340.

Health Services Research Group, University of Wisconsin–Madison. "Development of the Index of Medical Underservedness." *Health Services Research* 10 (Summer 1975): 168–180.

Huber, G. P., R. Daneshgar, and D. L. Ford. "An Empirical Comparison of Five Utility Models for Predicting Job Preferences." *Organizational Behavior and Human Performance* 6 (May 1971): 267–282.

Keeney, R. L. "Evaluation of Pumped Storage Sites." *Operations Research* 27 (January–February 1979): 48–64.

Ladany, S. P., and R. E. Machol. *Optimal Strategies in Sports.* New York: North–Holland Publishing Company, 1977.

Raiffa, H. *Decision Analysis.* Reading, Mass.: Addison-Wesley Publishing Company, Inc., 1968.

5

Improving Decisions Involving Multiple Goals: A Self-Help Procedure

In the previous chapter we saw how consultants used multi-attribute utility models to help decision makers faced with situations where several goals or criteria had to be considered. In this chapter we will show through a step-by-step procedure how individual managers and their staffs can use such models. The procedure can be applied both in situations where financial criteria are of major importance and in situations where they are of minor importance. But before looking at how the procedure employs MAU models, let us review the benefits that we can obtain by using MAU or similar models.

1. Developing and making explicit our view of the decision situation in the form of a model helps us identify the inadequacies in our implicit, mental model.[1]

[1]*On one occasion, I expressed some skepticism to an administrator concerning whether or not my MAU model for evaluating the multicriterion performance of several subordinate departments would really be of much use to him or his staff. The administrator replied, "Don't worry about that at all. We have gained so much insight into our thinking and our operations from having had to answer your questions about which factors were important around here, and just how important, that I would be more than satisfied with this project even if we never found the time to actually implement your model."*

61

2. The attributes contained in the model serve as reminders of the information that should be obtained about each alternative. This helps avoid the common practice of evaluating one alternative on Attributes A, B, and E, while evaluating another alternative on Attributes A, C, and D, simply because in one case one set of information was available while in the other a different set was at hand.

3. The information displays and graphical models that contain the information used in the mathematical model serve as organized external memories. Here we can efficiently record, analyze, and retrieve information, thus overcoming some of our limitations as processors of information.

4. The step-by-step procedure associated with the model enables us to aggregate large amounts of information in a prescribed and systematic manner, rather than in a manner determined by the order in which the information appears or by the limits of our intellect.

5. The information displays and procedure associated with the model increase the ability of managers to communicate with those advisors who might be asked to help with making the choice, with those superiors to whom they might have to justify the choice, or to those subordinates who might have to carry out the choice.

Let us turn to a description of the step-by-step procedure that causes these benefits to occur. The reader will undoubtedly recognize most of these steps as ones that he or she has carried out or participated in. The possible exceptions are those where a systematic approach is used to aid in making judgments that are usually made implicitly and haphazardly. Descriptions of some of the many decision settings where this procedure (or minor variations of it) has been used are contained in the review "Multiattribute Utility Models: A Review of Field and Fieldlike Studies" (Huber, 1974), and in the tutorial "How to Use Multiattribute Utility Measurement for Social Decision Making" (Edwards, 1977). As will be seen, this procedure helps the decision maker do what he or she wants to do; it clearly serves as an aid to rather than a substitute for judgment.

DEVELOPING AND USING MAU MODELS

In this section we describe each of the steps involved in using the MAU model technique. Generally they are carried out in the order shown. The exceptions are discussed in the last section of the chapter. In order to indicate the scope and nature of the individual steps, we will draw on diverse example applications. However, in order to show that the combined steps comprise a useful technique, we will also carry along one example application throughout the step-by-step procedure.

In examining the technique, the reader will see that it requires managers and their staffs to grapple with questions that by nature or habit they normally avoid. It also requires them to think systematically when the dynamic nature of their jobs often conditions them to be less than systematic. Clearly, such a demanding procedure cannot be used in every multigoal decision situation. In which situations should it be used?

This type of question is not uniquely applicable to the MAU model technique—it applies to any sophisticated decision-aiding technique. The answer to the question is that the MAU model technique and most other sophisticated decision-aiding procedures were designed to be used in important decision situations. This is where they have proven their worth.

The concepts behind such techniques are useful in thinking through almost any decision situation, but the techniques themselves are intended to be used when it is important that the correct decision be made. Newman and Warren expressed the idea as follows:

> In Western society, with its heavy emphasis on science and utilitarianism, we take for granted that the best decisions are made by *rational* choice. There are alternative ways of selecting a plan—intuition, precedent, voting, divine guidance—but in a purposeful organization such as a business firm, it is the rational decision that is widely believed to be the best.
>
> In spite of this very high regard for rationality, in our actual behavior there is a striking failure to follow the basic steps of rational decision making. Our personal plans typically are not fully rational, and managers often rely on other methods in making their plans. Unfortunately, rational decision making is hard work; and both skill and wisdom are required in its use. So as a practical matter we can use the rational process for only the more important decisions we make. (Newman and Warren, 1977, p. 227)

Let us now turn to an example application of the MAU model technique.

The carry-through example: Managerial selection

Mr. John Smith, director of personnel, has been appointed head of an ad hoc management committee assigned the task of seeking and screening applicants for the position of national sales manager for the XYZ Corporation.[2] After three weeks of recruiting through company sources, an executive search firm, and limited national advertising, thirty-two apparently qualified people had expressed an interest in the position. At that point Smith and the committee recognized that it would be necessary to use some systematic procedure to evaluate all of the candidates. Once this task was completed, the decision process would continue with interviews conducted by the top corporate officers and a final selection decision made by these same officers.[3]

Smith had learned of the MAU model technique in a professional journal and had later encountered it in a management development short course. Based on what he had learned, he felt that the committee could use the technique in screening the candidates. After Smith gave an explanation of the technique, the other committee members endorsed its use. Smith subsequently assigned a staff assistant from the personnel department to aid the committee in employing the technique.

We will elaborate upon this example case as we discuss the application of the MAU model technique to it. Let us move on now to an examination of the steps that comprise the technique. We will assume that the *problem exploration* and *alternative generation* phases of the problem-solving process have identified the alternatives that apply to the decision situation.

Step 1. Identify and list the relevant criteria and constraints • Most managers are familiar, by virtue of their training and experience, with the decision settings in which a particular choice situation might occur. Because of this, listing the relevant considerations (i.e., the criteria and constraints by which an alternative should be judged) is usually not a difficult task.

Our key concern in this step is to avoid allowing old habits, sloppy

---

[2]*Committees are often asked to undertake screening efforts such as the one described here. Although it will not be until we reach Chapters 9, 10, and especially 11 that we describe guidelines and techniques that enable committees and their chairpersons to accomplish such tasks with relative ease (even when differences of opinion are present), we choose to demonstrate the MAU model technique in this group setting in order to highlight its versatility.*

[3]*This example case is a simplified derivation from instances of executive selection in which the author and a colleague have been involved and in which the MAU model technique was employed. The confidential nature of executive selection precludes the use of an actual case.*

thinking, or lack of information result in our overlooking a critical consideration. In important or nonroutine decisions, extra effort and care at this step reduces the possibility of embarrassment later on. In any case, our overall goal is to improve our decisions, and lack of effort does not enhance our chances to do so. We should be intent on increasing the thoroughness of our thinking. It is for this reason that we list the considerations (the criteria and constraints), rather than simply mentally review them.

There are two approaches we can use to be more thorough in generating our list. One approach is to use *forced and partitioned thinking.* In this approach, we allot and use a certain amount of uninterrupted time to list first the primary (and generally more obvious) considerations and then to list the secondary considerations. Forcing ourselves to list the secondary considerations prevents us from suppressing a consideration because it does not seem, at this early stage, to compete in importance with some others. Forcing ourselves to use a ten-minute block of time prevents us from treating the exercise as trivial. This is important because a deeper insight can occur after the more obvious considerations have been listed but while the task of listing is still before us. This procedure will usually generate an extensive list which can later be culled and reduced. In the meantime, the list will have forced us to think more about our decision situation than we otherwise might have. This alone may be of considerable benefit to us.

The other approach to ensure that relevant considerations are not overlooked is to obtain the help of other people. In order not to lose our present focus on individual decision making, we will postpone our examination of this approach until we discuss group decision making. We might say here, however, that when faced with an unfamiliar or highly sensitive decision situation, the manager may be advised to ask someone with more experience, "Here's what I think should be considered. Can you think of anything I've overlooked?"

In the managerial-selection decision described above, Smith and the committee discussed the position of national sales manager with some of the top corporate officers and among themselves. After reviewing the relevant hiring policies, they decided to use the following criteria and related constraints in screening the candidates: (1) a record of successful sales management, (2) familiarity with the household products industry, and (3) willingness to travel extensively. The committee then addressed itself to the question of how to assess the extent to which these criteria are satisfied.

Up to this point we have used the words attribute and criterion interchangeably, but beginning with the next few paragraphs we will need to distinguish between them. At this point an attribute is defined as an observable characteristic or property of an alternative that allows us to assess the extent to which the alternative satisfies a criterion. Salary and commissions are examples of attributes with which to measure the extent to which a position would satisfy the criterion of providing an adequate income.

Step 2. Identify and list the relevant attributes • Since attributes are the measurable characteristics or properties with which we assess the extent to which an alternative satisfies the relevant criteria, it is clear that at some point in the decision process we must identify the appropriate attributes. This is generally a straightforward task, since for many criteria there will be one attribute that is obvious and encompassing of a single criterion. For example, there are many potential measures of the criterion "income derived from employment," but the "salary" measure was probably a sufficient attribute in the job-seeker application in Chapter 4. To take the other extreme, however, there could be many measures of the HEW funding allocation criterion "medical under-servedness," but as we saw in the example application, no one attribute would be sufficient individually.

In those cases where we can identify two or more attributes that relate to a particular criterion, we must judge whether the attributes are related or unrelated. If they are closely related, as are "rate of return on investment" and "years to recover investment," or "grade in school" and "student age," we should use only one—the one that best measures the degree to which the criterion is satisfied, or the one about which it is easiest to obtain the data. If the attributes are relatively unrelated, we should choose what appear to be the two or three most relevant.

In either case, identifying attributes, after having identified the criteria, is generally easily accomplished. If the manager is concerned about overlooking an appropriate attribute, either of the list-generating techniques discussed in Step 1 can be used.

Let us return to the managerial-selection decision. After using the *forced and partitioned thinking* process to generate a list of possible attributes, the committee members agreed on the following attributes:

1. A record of successful sales management is reflected by:
   a. the number of years of experience a person has had in sales management, and
   b. the average annual increase in salary of the person while serving as a sales manager.

2. Familiarity with household products is indicated by the number of years of experience the person has had in the household products industry.

3. Willingness to travel is indicated by an applicant's statement concerning the number of days per year that he or she is willing to travel on job-related business.[4]

With this done, the committee proceeded to Step 3.

Step 3. Determine the utilities for the various levels of each attribute • There are two cases to be considered. One is where the levels of the attribute are discrete or qualitatively different, as they were for the attribute "type of position" shown in Table 4–1. Another example could be the attribute "quality of local public access road," where the three levels might be "four-lane, two-lane with built-up shoulders, and two-lane without built-up shoulders." The procedure to use in this case is to (1) rank the levels in terms of their utility or satisfactoriness, (2) assign a value of 100 to the most satisfactory level, and (3) assign other values between 0 and 100 to the remaining levels that reflect their satisfactoriness relative to the most satisfactory level. If it seems worthwhile, a utility model such as that shown in Figure 4–2 can be drawn to help visualize the relative utility assigned to the various attribute levels.

The second case to be considered is where the attribute levels are continuous or quantitatively different, rather than qualitatively different. An example is the attribute "net profit" or "physicians per 1000 population."

One procedure to use in this case is to assign a value of 100 to the most satisfactory level and then sketch in the remainder of the graph so that the height of the curve (measured on a 0–100 scale) reflects at all points the relative satisfactoriness of the corresponding level of the attribute. This was done in Figure 4–3. The alternative procedure is to break the continuum into categories or discrete levels and then employ the procedure described in the previous paragraph for developing utility values for discrete attribute levels. An example result is shown in Figure 5–1. This second procedure is simpler to use, but sacrifices some degree of precision.

---

[4]*In most actual situations, such a list would be more extensive. The author was recently involved in a professional personnel selection case where eleven attributes were assessed from the information provided on the application. Six additional attributes were assessed from interviews conducted by the screening committee.*

Figure 5-1.   A Utility Model for Size of Community

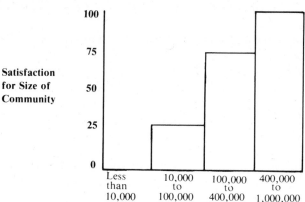

Size of Community–Population

In either of the above two cases, the most desirable level of those that will occur in the decision situation is assigned a value of 100. Saving the utility rating of 100 for levels that will not occur in the decision situation accomplishes nothing and confuses the issue.

To see just how utility estimates are obtained, let us listen in on an example utility elicitation session. Assume that the information services manager, Mr. Smith, has hired a consultant to help select a time-sharing computer system and that one of the criteria is how many terminals the system can support.

Consultant: Mr. Smith, you indicated that, with respect to the number of terminals that the system can support, you would be fully satisfied with the seventy-two terminals suggested by your "Needs Analysis Report." Let's assign a satisfaction (utility) score of 100 to this number of terminals. Now the issue is how satisfied you would be with lesser numbers of terminals. For example, relative to your satisfaction with seventy-two terminals, how satisfied would you be with sixty terminals?

Smith: Well, those last twelve would be nice, but they are certainly not as important as the first twelve, or even the fifth twelve, so I guess I would be 90% satisfied with sixty terminals. But I hope we get seventy-two.

Consultant: Okay, now how satisfied would you be with forty-eight terminals?

Smith: Well, now we're beginning to hurt, but I know that we could provide more than two thirds (or 48/72) of the services required, so I'll say not 66% but 75%.

Consultant: How about thirty-six terminals?

Smith: We're still ahead. I'll say 60%.

Consultant: How about twenty-four?

Smith: Now we're in trouble, because we'd have to do some of the production work with calculators and semiautomated procedures. That, I think, would cause a fair number of administrative problems. I'll assign a value of 40% satisfaction to the twenty-four terminals and, anticipating your next question, because the administrative problems associated with a twelve terminal system would be worse yet, I'll assign a value of 20%.

Using the information obtained in such an interview, the consultant could develop a utility curve such as that shown in Figure 5-2. This example was a simple one, so that we could move along to our review of the remaining steps. In a later section of the chapter we will discuss some of the finer points of the process for obtaining utility judgments and answer some questions that might follow from the use of a simple example, such as how to check the reliability of these judgments.

Figure 5-2. Utility Model for Number of Terminals

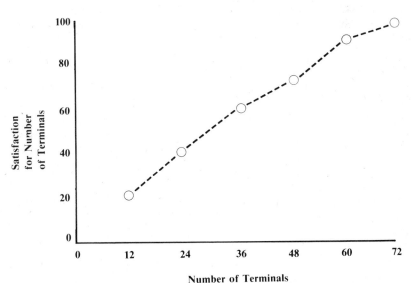

Number of Terminals

Returning again to the managerial-selection case, the committee members decided to have the staff assistant conduct a utility-elicitation session with each member and then average the resulting utility models to obtain a single *committee utility model* for each attribute. The committee utility model for the average annual increase in salary is shown in Figure 5-3. After having reviewed and agreed upon the utility models, the committee moved on to determine the relative importance of each of the criteria.

Step 4. Determine the relative importances or proportion weights of the criteria • This is an easy step. The procedure is to (1) rank the criteria in terms of their relative importance, (2) assign a value of 100 to the most important criterion, and (3) assign other values between 0 and 100 to the remaining criteria that reflect their importance relative to the most important criterion.

When performing this step, we must keep in mind that the importance weights for an attribute will vary depending on the range of the attribute levels. For example, "income from employment" might rank third among five job attributes if the salary range is $13,000–$16,000 per year. But what if the range is only $14,500–$15,000 or as much as $8500–$20,000? Would it still rank third? Probably not. It is because the importance of a criterion depends on the range of its attribute that we

Figure 5-3.   Average of Committee Members' Utilities for Various Average Annual Salary Increases

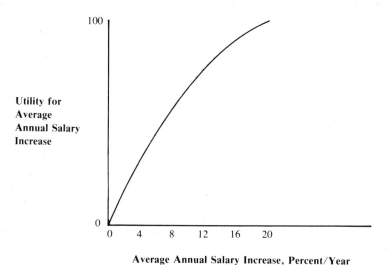

Average Annual Salary Increase, Percent/Year

should always obtain our importance weights after we have consciously worked through Steps 1, 2, and 3. The careful thinking that we force upon ourselves as we go through the processes of identifying criteria and attributes and of evaluating the utility derived from different levels of the attributes provides a basis for making the judgments required in this step.

In the next section we will describe methods for checking the reliability or consistency of our importance weights. We can mention at this point that additional insight into our own evaluation scheme can be obtained by transforming weights we have into *proportion* weights, weights that sum to 1.0. Proportion weights are obtained by dividing each of the relative importance weights by the sum of all of the importance weights. For example, if Criteria A, B, C, and D ranked B, C, D, and A in importance and received importance ratings of 20, 100, 50, and 30, then the proportion weight for B would be equal to 100 divided by 100 + 50 + 30 + 20, or .50. The sum of the proportion weights is, of course, equal to 1.00.

Proportion weights are often used in MAU models. In the HEW application, they were multiplied by 100 and converted to the percentage weights 28.7, 25.1, 26.0, and 20.2. Because they are more interpretable than importance weights, we will use proportion or percentage weights in our remaining examples.

In the managerial-selection case, the committee again had the staff assistant work with each member in assigning the criterion importance weights. The average of these was compiled as the *committee importance weights*. "Record of successful sales management" received an average score of 92, "familiarity with household products" received 75, and "willingness to travel" received an average score of 47. The staff assistant calculated the proportion weights shown in Table 5–1 from these importance values. After reviewing these, the committee members would then move on to determine the importance of the attributes selected in Step 2.

Step 5. Determine the proportion weights of the attributes • For those cases where there is only one attribute per criterion, we use the proportion weight for the criterion as the importance weight for the attribute. For cases where there is more than one attribute per criterion, we use a straightforward two-phase procedure. In Phase 1, for each multi-attributed criterion, we (1) rank the attributes in terms of their relative importance as measures of the criterion, (2) assign a value of 1.0 to the most relevant, reliable, or representative attribute, (3) assign values between 0 and 1.0 to the remaining attributes that reflect their relative im-

TABLE 5-1.   Weights for Relevant Criteria

Criterion	Importance	Proportion Weight	
1. Successful Record	92	$^{92}/_{214} =$	.43
2. Familiarity with household products	75	$^{75}/_{214} =$	.35
3. Willingness to travel	47	$^{47}/_{214} =$	.22
	214		1.0

portance, and (4) divide each of these values by the sum of all. These four steps result in a weight for each attribute that reflects its relative importance as a measure of the *criterion*. Thus in the HEW application, the proportion weights of .287, .251, .260, and .202 reflected the relative importance of the respective community attributes as measures of the criterion "medical underservedness."

In Phase 2 we take each of these weights and multiply it times the proportion weight of the respective superordinate criterion. The resulting values reflect the relative importance of the attributes in the decision situation and are used as the proportion weights in the MAU model.

A conceptual example is shown in Figure 5-4. The criterion whose proportion weight is .60 has two attributes. This weight must be distributed in accordance with the relative importances (.30 and .70) of the two attributes used to determine the extent to which the criterion is satisfied. Therefore .30 of the .60, or .18, is assigned as the proportion weight for the one attribute and .70 of the .60, or .42, is assigned as the proportion weight for the other. Since .18 and .42 sum to .60, the criterion retains its original influence. The MAU model would be

> *Equation 5.1*
> $$U = .18 \, u(x_{A_1}) + .42 \, u(x_{A_2}) + .40 \, u(x_B).$$

If in the HEW application the officials had wished to allocate funds according to two equally weighted (.50 and .50) criteria, "medical underservedness" and "quality of proposal requesting funds," then in the final five-attribute MAU model, the proportion weights for the four community attributes would have been $(.5)(.287) = .144$, $(.5)(.251) = .125$, $(.5)(.260) = .130$, and $(.5)(.202) = .101$. The proportion weight for proposal quality would have been .50. The first four values sum to .50, the original proportion weight for the medical-underservedness criterion.

Figure 5–4. Determining the Proportion Weights for Attributes

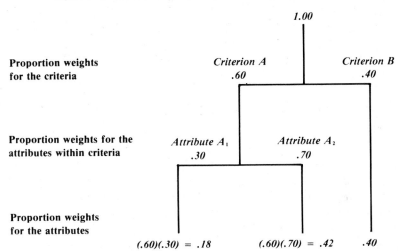

Let us return to the managerial-selection decision. Following the two-phase procedure discussed above, the committee members ranked the importance of the two attributes associated with a person's record of successful sales management. Years of experience in sales management was ranked first and year-to-year change in salary second. They then agreed that the attribute ranked second was about half as important and so the attributes were assigned importance scores of 1.0 and .5 respectively. Because the other two attributes were the sole measure of how well the respective criterion was satisfied, they received the same weight as the associated criterion. Table 5–2 shows the calculations of the staff assistant in each of the two phases. With the completion of Step 5, the committee had finished specification of the MAU Model.

In order to expedite the future step of computing overall utilities for each applicant, the staff assistant developed the performance table shown on the left-hand side of Figure 5–5 and the utility table shown on the right-hand side. The utility values corresponding to the "performances" were obtained using the committee utility models, such as in Figure 5–3. As an example, Figure 5–3 indicates that the utility of the 9 percent salary increase of applicant thirty is sixty.

As its next task, the committee used constraints to screen out unacceptable alternatives.

Step 6. Identify the constraints and screen out the unacceptable alternatives • As we noted earlier, unaided decision makers tend to use overly simplistic decision strategies that rely heavily on the use of con-

TABLE 5–2.   Weights for Attributes

Phase 1		
Attributes Within Successful Record Criterion	Relative Importance	Proportion Weights for Attributes Within Track Record Criterion
1a. Experience as sales manager	1.0	$1/1.5 = .67$
1b. Year-to-year change in salary	.5	$.5/1.5 = .33$
Phase 2		
Attributes for MAU Model	Proportion Weights to Be Used in MAU Model	
1a. Experience as sales manager (x_1)	$(.67)(.43) = .29$	
1b. Year-to-year change in salary (x_2)	$(.33)(.43) = .14$	
2. Willingness to travel (x_3)	$(1)(.22) = .22$	
3. Experience in household products (x_4)	$(1)(.35) = .35$	

straints. We will solve our problems more effectively, in the long run, if we do not use unnecessarily restrictive constraints to screen out alternatives that might possess compensating attributes. Thus, although the use of constraints is appropriate, constraints should be restricted to identifying those levels of attributes that cannot be tolerated or compensated for.

The use of constraints is a quick and dirty way of screening out alternatives. It saves us from having to give detailed consideration to those infeasible alternatives that would be unacceptable no matter what their overall MAU score was. Although we may not actually construct it, it may be useful to think in terms of a multiattribute performance table, such as the one shown in Figure 5–6. This table shows how each alternative performs with respect to each attribute. The entries in such a table are performance data or *payoffs* (to draw upon the terminology of

Figure 5-5. Applicant Performance and Utility Table

Applicant Performance Table

Applicants	x_1, Experience in sales management	x_2, Salary increase	x_3, Willingness to travel	x_4, Experience in household products
1	4 years	4%	45 days	8 years
2	2 years	10%	50 days	3 years
3	10 years	5%	35 days	15 years
4	15 years	3%	30 days	8 years
30	7 years	9%	40 days	5 years
31	11 years	6%	25 days	17 years
32	20 years	4%	30 days	25 years

Applicant Utility Table

Applicants	$u(x_1)$, Experience in sales management	$u(x_2)$, Salary increase	$u(x_3)$, Willingness to travel	$u(x_4)$, Experience in household products
1	0	30	90	100
2	0	65	95	0
3	100	35	60	100
4	40	25	60	100
30	60	60	90	70
31	100	40	20	100
32	40	30	60	100

Figure 5-6.   Performance Table for Various Second Office Locations

	Monthly rent	Minutes from main office	Square feet of space	Cost of redecorating
Office Site A	1000	30	15,000	2000
Office Site B	1200	10	17,000	500
Office Site C	1400	5	20,000	1000
Office Site D	1000	15	15,000	1500
Office Site E	900	10	12,000	1100
Constraints	1200 maximum	20 maximum	12,000 minimum	2000 maximum

Chapter 3). The information at the bottom of the table describes the constraints that are to be used in conjunction with the performance data to screen out infeasible alternatives.

As can be seen, the first constraint eliminates Site C, where the rent is beyond what we can afford. The second constraint screens out Site A, which is too far from our main office. The third and fourth constraints do not eliminate alternatives. Thus we are left with three sites that should be evaluated further.

When applying this step in the managerial-selection decision, Smith's committee decided that the only attribute which could not be compensated for by training or changing job duties was the applicant's experience as a sales manager. Three years of experience was determined as an absolute minimum. Applying this constraint eliminated ten applicants. The committee then had the staff assistant apply the MAU Model to the attribute values of the remaining twenty-two candidates.

Step 7. Apply the MAU model and computational procedure to the feasible alternatives, and identify the one (or two) with the greatest overall utility • It is useful in this step to summarize the information from Steps 1–6 in a multiattribute utility table, such as the one shown in Figure 5–7. The entries in the table are the single-attribute utilities cor-

Figure 5-7.   Utility Table for Various Second Office Locations

Alternatives \ Attributes	Monthly rent	Minutes from main office	Square feet of space	Cost of redecorating
Office Site B	0	100	100	100
Office Site D	50	70	90	0
Office Site E	100	100	50	40
Proportion weights	.40	.20	.30	.10

responding to the performance data of Figure 5–6. The information at the bottom of the table shows the weights to be used, in conjunction with the single-attribute utilities, to compute the MAU scores for these feasible alternatives.

The scores for the three alternatives are as follows:

1. Utility for Site B $= .40(0) + .20(100) + .30(100) + .10(100)$
   $= 60.$
2. Utility for Site D $= .40(50) + .20(70) + .30(90) + .10(0)$
   $= 61.$
3. Utility for Site E $= .40(100) + .20(100) + .30(50) + .10(40)$
   $= 79.$

In the managerial selection case, the staff assistant carried out this step using the proportion weights of .29, .14, .35, and .22 from Table 5–2 and the utilities from the right-hand side of Table 5–3. The scores for three of the applicants were calculated as follows:

1. Utility for Applicant 1 $= .29(0) + .14(30) + .22(90)$
   $+ .35(100) = 0 + 4.2 + 19.8 + 35 = 59.0.$

2. Utility for Applicant 3 $= .29(100) + .14(35) + .22(60)$
$+ .35(100) = 29 + 4.9 + 13.2 + 35 = 82.1.$
3. Utility for Applicant 30 $= .29(60) + .14(60) + .22(90)$
$+ .35(70) = 17.4 + 8.4 + 19.8 + 24.5 = 70.1.$

After reviewing the MAU scores, the committee decided that the five applicants with the highest scores were to be recommended to the top corporate officers for interviews. The last step in the MAU model technique is to consider both the criteria not included in the analysis and the possible adverse consequences of choosing the highest scoring alternative and then to make a choice. In this case, however, the committee decided not to implement any parts of this step, as it felt these matters could best be assessed by the corporate officers making the final selection.

Step 8. Consider both the criteria not included in the analysis and the possible adverse consequences of choosing the highest scoring alternative, and make the choice • Some decision situations will contain components that cannot be realistically captured in the MAU model. Sometimes these will be political—such as the expressed preference of some executive or union agent for Site D. On other occasions they will be probabilistic—such as the possibility that the building at Site E might be condemned for future highway construction.

Matters such as these are important and must be dealt with. An important positive consequence of having completed Step 7 is that we are in a better position to do this. Specifically, completion of Step 7 allows us to realistically portray the decision situation with a model that contains two alternatives (the highest scoring alternative and its conspicuous competitor) and two criteria (the numerical difference between the utility scores of these two alternatives and the criterion associated with the political or probabilistic component). Although such a decision situation is certainly not trivial, it is generally less complex than the original situation with its several alternatives and considerations—of which the political or probabilistic component is only one.

A summary listing of the steps just discussed is shown as Table 5–3.

The idea brought forth in Step 8—that our cognitive abilities are better able to deal with explicit trade-offs between two criteria than with implicit trade-offs among several criteria—moves us to a discussion of the *cost-benefit analysis technique* and *dollar-equivalent techniques.* These two techniques are very similar to the MAU model technique but have more of an economic focus.

TABLE 5-3.   Procedure for Using Multiattribute Utility Models

Step 1.	Identify and list the relevant criteria and constraints.
Step 2.	Identify and list the relevant attributes.
Step 3.	Determine the utilities for the various levels of each attribute.
Step 4.	Determine the relative importances or proportion weights of the criteria.
Step 5.	Determine the proportion weights of the attributes.
Step 6.	Identify the constraints and screen out the unacceptable alternatives.
Step 7.	Apply the MAU model and computational procedure to the feasible alternatives and identify the one that has the greatest overall utility.
Step 8.	Consider both the criteria not included in the analysis and the possible adverse consequences of choosing the highest scoring alternative, and make the choice.

THE COST-BENEFIT AND DOLLAR-EQUIVALENT TECHNIQUES

Both of these techniques are quite similar to the MAU model technique. Some people regard them as variations of it.

In *cost-benefit analyses,* the decision maker or the staff attempts to convert all of the benefits (payoffs and costs) from each alternative into their monetary equivalents by following standard economic or accounting practices, such as by employing the *rate of return* or *time value of money* concept. They then choose the alternative that provides the greatest net monetary benefit. For example, in the office site selection decision, the staff members would attempt to convert all payoffs to their respective monthly equivalents. With respect to the first attribute (see Figure 5-7), they already have the monthly cost associated with the rent. With respect to the fourth, they would distribute the cash outlay associated with the redecoration across the interval of time involved in redecorating. They would then add to the resultant monthly value the "cost" of not having that amount of money invested elsewhere and add the sum of these values to the monthly rent. The third attribute is the square feet of space. Here they use standard market parameters to assign a monthly dollar value to the space provided by each alternative. Finally they would turn to the second attribute—and cringe. If they stick solely to the use of economic techniques, they would attempt to assign a dollar value to the total man-hours lost each month by company personnel traveling between the two offices. This would require them to draw upon the kind of creative accounting for which chief accountants are known and feared.

The thrust of the *dollar-equivalent technique* is the same as for cost-benefit analysis. The difference is that the monetary equivalents are developed judgmentally when the standard economic techniques are stretched beyond their limits. For example, when dealing with the attribute of floor space, the analyst would develop a *trade-off model* such as the one shown in Figure 5–8. This is similar to a utility model and is developed by asking a series of questions such as "How much monthly rent are you willing to pay for 1200 square feet of floor space?" The values from the curve can then be used to determine the utilities, expressed in dollars, that the decision maker would derive from the space provided by various sizes of offices. As in the case of the MAU model technique, these dollar values—one from each attribute—are added together to obtain the overall utility for each alternative.

The dollar-equivalent technique would typically be employed in decision situations such as that of Jones, the bank operations manager described in Chapter 3. A simplified version of Jones' situation is shown in Figure 5–9. Somehow Jones must aggregate the payoffs (costs) on the

Figure 5–8.   Trade-off Graph: Monthly Rent versus Floor Space

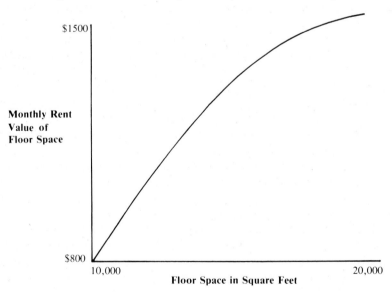

Figure 5-9.   Performance Table for Various Staffing Alternatives

Criteria/Attributes

Alternatives	Additional operating costs*	Additional waiting customers†
Make no changes	0	80 people
Draw on regular staff	– $500	20 people
Hire temporary employees	– $300	50 people

*Per day during holiday season   †Average number at any given time of day

two criteria. One approach is to construct a utility model for dollars and a utility model for waiting customers. These models could be used to convert dollars and waiting customers to units of utility and to aggregate these in a MAU model. Another approach is to construct a trade-off model that directly converts waiting customers to dollars. The question used to develop this model would be of the nature "How much are you willing to pay to reduce the number of additional customers waiting for service from twenty down to zero? If the answer was $200 (i.e., $600 when the question pertained to fifty customers and $1000 when the question pertained to eighty customers), then we could use these conversion values to replace Figure 5-9 with Figure 5-10.

If there were no important criteria or contingencies that were not included in the analysis, Jones would probably act on the analysis portrayed in Figure 5-10 and would choose to draw on regular staff when attempting to solve the bank's holiday workload increase.

Putting these three techniques in perspective, we see that the cost-benefit technique is a special case of the dollar-equivalent technique. The conversion of each payoff to some monetary equivalent can be made by following standard economic or accounting practices. In turn, the dollar-equivalent technique is a special case of the MAU model technique. Here the decision maker converts payoffs on all attributes to monetary values.

Figure 5–10.   Dollar Equivalent Table for Various Staffing Alternatives

Criteria/Attributes

Alternatives	Additional operating costs	Dollar equivalent of additional waiting customers	Overall costs
Make no changes	0	– $1000	– $1000
Draw on regular staff	– $500	– $200	– $700
Hire temporary employees	– $300	– $600	– $900

In some cases this conversion seems straightforward. In other cases, such as the HEW application, such a conversion seems awkward.[5]

When its conversions are defensible, the cost-benefit technique is preferred over the other two techniques because its conversions are more explicit. Therefore, it is open to examination and challenge. Not that the technique does not include the use of subjective judgments—it does—but the judgments are more describable. We have treated this technique briefly, not because it is not useful, but because its range of application is relatively narrow. It also is a special case of the more general and important cases of the dollar-equivalent and MAU model techniques.

When conversion of the payoffs on all attributes to dollar equivalents seems reasonable and defensible, the dollar-equivalent technique is preferred over the MAU model technique. This is a consequence of the fact that the single aggregate figure derived in dollars can be more easily compared to the levels of other criteria that were not included in the analysis. For example, in Step 8 of the procedure for applying the MAU model technique, we referred to the possibility of trading-off the 18 percent difference in satisfaction or utility for the endorsement of a choice by an executive or union agent. It is not as easy to make a comparison of this nature as it is to make a comparison between a

[5]*In many instances this awkwardness is a consequence of the fact that the different interested parties have different utilities for money. In others it is because many people feel uncomfortable about assigning dollar values to such variables as "infant mortality."*

monetary difference of, for example, $300 per month and the endorsement, or the level of some other unincluded criterion. Again, we have treated the technique only briefly because it is a special case of the more general and conceptually more important MAU model technique.

In this and the preceding section, we briefly described how to use the MAU model technique and two of its variants or special cases. In the next section we will expand on some of the points that were treated briefly here.

FURTHER DISCUSSION OF DECISION MAKING IN MULTIGOAL SITUATIONS

In order to give additional perspective on the use of MAU models, we will use these next few paragraphs to answer questions that might follow from the previous discussions.

Question 1: How accurate do the weights assigned to various attributes have to be?

The answer to this question is that minor inaccuracies do not have much of a practical effect. Consider, for example, the following two sets of proportion weights: .40, .30, .20, .10 versus .30, .30, .25, .15. For an alternative whose $u(x)$ scores were 70, 70, 70, and 70, each set of weights would give exactly the same overall utility score of 70. For an alternative whose $u(x)$ scores were 70, 60, 40, and 30, the first set of weights would give an overall utility score of 57 while the second would give a score of 53.5. As can be seen, this set of fairly large errors (.40 versus .30 is a 33 percent error) had a small impact even in the adverse case where the largest absolute error—the .40 − .30 = .10 error—was applied to the attribute with the highest score. Other examples could be used to highlight the important fact that inaccuracies in the attribute weights are most harmful when there are few criteria.

Question 2: How accurate do the single-attribute utility models have to be?

The answer is, again, that minor inaccuracies do not have much of a practical effect. For example, research results show that if utility curves do not change direction across levels of the attribute (i.e., if their

direction is continuously either increasing or decreasing, but not revers-
ing), the substitution of straight lines for curves often has a relatively
small effect on the single-attribute utility score. Perhaps this can be seen
by reviewing Figure 5–3. In this figure, for any given x the $u(x)$ value obtained by reading up to the curve and across is not much different from
the value obtained by reading up to a straight line and across. In addition, whatever error there may be in a $u(x)$ value is diluted per-
centagewise due to the presence of the other attributes. Even a 20 percent
error in an attribute having a proportion weight of .25 generates only a 5
percent error for the overall utility score ($.20 \times .25 = .05$). Because, as
these examples show, additive MAU models are fairly insensitive to
minor inaccuracies, they are said to be *robust*.

Question 3: Should I check the consistency of my utility and importance judgments?

This is a good question, and the answer is "yes." It is advisable, in
fact, to check the consistency of the judgments in each step before going
on to the next step.

There are two approaches we can use to check our consistency.
One is to sketch out a picture of our judgments. For example, instead of
merely obtaining and using the relative utility values obtained in Step 2,
we can draw the single-attribute utility model, such as Figure 5–2. Or, instead of merely stating the relative importances of the criteria, we can
prepare a graph such as Figure 5–11, where the height of each column
reflects and portrays the relative importance of the attributes. These
graphical displays add a visual dimension to our introspective analysis of
how to evaluate alternatives. We can look at them and ask ourselves

Figure 5-11.   Graph Showing Relative Importance of the Attributes

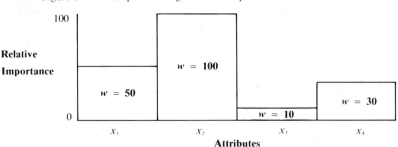

"Does this look like what I have in mind?" If the answer is "no," they indicate where some useful adjustments might be made.

The other approach for checking our consistency is to ask ourselves questions that compare our judgments. For example, we can say, "Now I've stated that Level B is 60 percent as satisfying as Level A and that Level E is 20 percent as satisfying as Level A. This must mean that Level B is 3 times as satisfying as Level E. Is this true?"[6] If the answer is "no" the necessary adjustments can be made so that the judgments are consistent with each other. As another example, we can say to ourselves, "I've given Attribute C a proportion weight of .30 and Attribute D a proportion weight of .20. Is it true that C is 50 percent more important than D?" Again, if the answer is "no" we can make the necessary adjustments.

Question 4: How do I handle the situation where the utilities associated with the levels of one attribute might depend on the levels of another attribute?

As an example, in the job-seeker application we might be concerned that the utility for different salaries could be affected by the type of position. The procedure for both identifying and dealing with this possible dependency or interaction is straightforward. We first develop the utility model for one attribute when the level of the second attribute is fixed at, say, level 1. Then we again develop the utility model for the first attribute, but with the level of the second attribute fixed at, say, level 2. For example, by asking a series of questions such as "On a 0–100 scale, what would be your relative satisfaction with a $10,000/year salary if you were in a teaching position?" we could construct the utility model for salary, given a teaching position. If we repeated the same series of salary-oriented questions, but in the context of a coaching position, we could construct the utility model for salary, given a coaching position. If the models were different looking, we would have identified a dependency. When we evaluated a particular alternative, we would use the model appropriate to the particular mix of levels that characterized that alternative.

[6] *Those familiar with mathematics will see here the virtue of having 0 in the utility scale correspond to the* natural origin *(the sometimes hypothetical level that provides no satisfaction at all) rather than having it correspond to the level of those present that provides the least satisfaction. Only when the 0 corresponds to the natural origin can we consider ratios, as we do when we use this approach to check the consistency of our judgments.*

Question 5: Should I first use the constraints to screen out alternatives, or should I first compute the utilities for all alternatives?

The answer to this question is a judgment that the manager must make in each decision situation. Early use of constraints to eliminate absurd alternatives is commonsensical and saves time. On the other hand, early use of constraints may eliminate an alternative that is so desirable, given its scores on its other attributes, that we may later wish that we had chosen it. We could have relaxed the constraints a bit or compensated in some other way for the existence of the deficiency or adverse attribute level.

Question 6: If an alternative possesses some attribute to such a small extent that the utility score on that attribute is zero, does this remove the attribute from further consideration?

The answer to this question is "no." Consider Alternative A that scores 60 on one attribute and 20 the other (equally important) attribute. Its overall utility is $.5(60) + .50(20) = 40$. If Alternative B scores 0 on one attribute and 90 on the other, its overall utility is $.5(0) + .5(90) = 45$, and it would be chosen over Alternative A.

There are, of course, instances when an alternative is removed from further consideration because of low performance on some attribute. This was the case in Figure 5–4 when some of the candidates for the national sales manager position were eliminated because of insufficient sales management experience. But these instances are associated with the use of constraints and are not the result of low utility scores.

SUMMARY AND OVERVIEW

In this chapter we examined a step-by-step procedure for using multiattribute utility models and asked and answered some questions concerning the use of MAU models.

At the beginning of the chapter, we identified and listed five specific benefits obtained when using MAU models. We then developed the information displays that are component parts of the overall MAU model procedure. As can be seen from the listing, the benefits from model building are obtained to a considerable degree even if the decision maker never actually undertakes the final step of computing an overall utility score. Models are aids to thinking; in complex decision situations, their development leads to insights and understandings that would not otherwise be available. This is true even if their development is of the most rudimentary form (e.g., the development of a checklist of criteria or constraints).

The development of a model representing the decision situation and the use of a step-by-step procedure for using the information captured in the model are, together, the application of a decision-aiding "technique." Thus in this chapter we have discussed the MAU model technique. Whether decision-aiding techniques make decision processes more satisfying or effective is a debatable question; it undoubtedly depends greatly on the nature of the decision maker and his or her circumstances. Nevertheless, the use of consideration of the strategies and models associated with decision-aiding techniques, besides achieving the five benefits noted earlier, does tend to make the processes more rational. Sometimes heightened rationality is a worthy goal in its own right. Allan Easton expresses the idea as follows:

> There is a definite belief in both scientific and administrative circles that rationality in decision making is preferred to nonrationality; that the use of judgment and intuition is undesirable except as a last resort. For rational decisions, the reasoning processes are capable of definition and explication; for intuitive decisions, the thinking processes are either imperfectly understood or completely unknown. Rational decisions are, therefore, easier to explain and defend even if they may really be no better than intuitive decisions.

> Thus, there are many circumstances, particularly in an organizational or political setting, where intuitive (or less communicable) processes are simply not admissible. In such cases, the ability to skilfully explicate a decision from beginning to end may be saving of lives, assets, reputations, prestige, and personal freedom, even if it should appear that judgment played a substantial part in the handling of the intangibles. (Easton, 1973, pp. 11–12)

These benefits of using decision-aiding techniques were noted in the context of a manager working his or her way through decision situations whose complexity is a consequence of the alternatives possessing more than one valuable attribute. As we will see in the next chapter, the same benefits are also obtained when such techniques are used as aids in decision situations whose complexity is a consequence of the fact that the manager does not know which possible future conditions will occur.

OPPORTUNITIES FOR FURTHER THOUGHT

1. Considering the example situations of this chapter and of Chapter 4, what characteristics of a decision situation would suggest to you that the MAU model technique could be useful in arriving at a choice?
2. Assume that you have been asked to use the MAU model technique to reduce a list of twenty-five well-qualified applicants, for the position of director of marketing of a medium-sized corporation, to a list of five. List the criteria, constraints, and relevant attributes that you would use in the model. Then choose the three most important attributes, draw utility models for them, assess their importance weights, and, finally, compute the overall utility for a hypothetical applicant.
3. Review Step 7 of this chapter's procedure for using the MAU model technique. In view of the ideas expressed in Chapter 3, do you think that Step 7 should be optional? Give one argument for making it optional and one argument for making it mandatory.

REFERENCES AND RELATED READINGS

Easton, A. *Complex Managerial Decisions Involving Multiple Objectives.* New York: John Wiley and Sons, Inc., 1973.

Edwards, W. "How to Use Multiattribute Utility Measurement for Social Decision Making." *IEEE Transactions on Systems, Man, and Cybernetics* SMC–7 (May 1977): 326–340.

Haveman, R. H. *The Economics of the Public Sector.* New York: John Wiley and Sons, Inc., 1976.

Huber, G. P. "Multiattribute Utility Models: A Review of Field and Fieldlike Studies." *Management Science* 20 (June 1974): 1393–1402.

Johnson, E. M. and G. P. Huber. "The Technology of Utility Assessment." *IEEE Transactions on Systems, Man, and Cybernetics* SMC-7 (May 1977): 311–325.

Keeney, R. L. "The Art of Assessing Multiattribute Utility Functions." *Organizational Behavior and Human Performance* 19 (August 1977): 267–310.

Keeney, R. L. and H. Raiffa. *Decisions with Multiple Objectives: Preferences and Value Tradeoffs.* New York: John Wiley and Sons, Inc., 1976.

Newman, William H. and E. Kirby Warren. *The Process of Management.* Englewood Cliffs, N.J.: Prentice-Hall, Inc., 1977.

6

Improving Decisions in Risky or Uncertain Situations: A Self-Help Procedure

This chapter is concerned with how a manager should make decisions in situations where the payoffs associated with a particular choice will vary with the conditions that occur after the chosen alternative is implemented. Such "risky" or "uncertain" situations are commonplace. Consider, as examples, the following:

1. *Introduction of a new product:* Whether or not it is advisable to introduce a new product depends on, among other things, what the sales are likely to be.
2. *Investments in real estate:* Whether or not a particular purchase is wise depends on, among other things, what the future population patterns are likely to be.
3. *Agricultural decisions:* Whether it will be more profitable to plant Crop A or Crop B depends on, among other things, what the future weather patterns and government price supports are likely to be.

In such situations, the decision maker should evaluate the alternatives and consider what might happen after the decision is made and implemented. It is also clear, from our discussion of limits on rationality, that unaided decision makers might have considerable difficulty in organizing and processing the information appropriate to the evaluation in a manner that will lead to decisions of high quality.

The purpose of this chapter is to describe a technique that managers and their staffs can use to reduce the difficulties encountered when using information relevant to making high-quality decisions in risky or uncertain situations. The technique concerns the use of a *decision matrix,* a fancy phrase for what we saw in Chapter 3 to be a simple idea. In the early parts of the chapter we will introduce the technique and then work through a small-scale demonstration of its use. In the later parts we will describe the step-by-step procedure that is used when employing the technique and will further discuss the nature of decision making in such situations. At the end of the chapter we will employ the step-by-step procedure in working through an example problem.

THE USE OF DECISION MATRICES: AN EXAMPLE

A decision matrix is a table that has "alternatives" for row headings and "future conditions" for column headings. Figure 6–1 is an example. As we recall from our earlier discussion, the cells in such a matrix are called *outcomes.* The values in the cells indicate the payoff (or utility) that would be obtained if the alternative associated with the cell were chosen and then the future condition associated with the cell were encountered.[1] In Figure 6–1, for example, the $50,000 of the upper central cell is the payoff (profit) that the owner of the "Souvenirs and Sporting Goods" store obtains if the inventory level chosen is "high" and the tourist season is "average."

Earlier we itemized the benefits derived from the use of information display models, such as that shown in Figure 6–1. One of these was that such displays "serve as organized and external memories where we can efficiently record, analyze, and retrieve information." Decision matrices in particular are frequently used to analyze the decision-related

[1]*Decision matrices are similar in appearance to utility tables, such as the one shown in Figure 5–7. This has led some to suggest that future conditions could be regarded as attributes of the decision situation. Others argue that viewing future conditions as simply another set of attributes is more confusing than helpful, especially in situations where there are both multiple criteria and uncertainty involved.*

Figure 6-1.   Decision Matrix for Inventory Investment Decision

		Future Conditions Nature of the Tourist Season		
		Good	*Average*	*Poor*
Alternative Preseason Inventory Levels	*High*	$80,000	$50,000	$20,000
	Moderately high	$65,000	$45,000	$30,000
	Moderately low	$55,000	$45,000	$35,000
	Low	$45,000	$35,000	$30,000

information. For example, borrowing a concept from the previous chapter on multiattribute decisions, we might ask if there are any minimum payoffs that should act as constraints on our options. For example, let us assume that the store owner's situation demanded a minimum profit of $25,000, and that there was no way around this constraint. This piece of information—which is not really part of the decision matrix but prompted by the information that is part of the matrix—causes us to eliminate the alternatives of investing in "high" inventory levels from further consideration.

As another example of how the matrix might help us analyze the information, Figure 6-1 shows that no matter which future condition occurs, "low" inventory level will not outperform "moderately low" inventory level. This allows us to eliminate "low" inventory level from further consideration. It may have been possible, in a small scale problem such as this, for the decision maker to see the inappropriateness of this alternative without the use of the display. In a larger scale problem, this would not be the case.

Elimination of the low inventory level alternative was an application of a commonsense idea that is formally called the *principle of dominance.* This principle states that:

Any alternative whose payoffs, when compared to any other feasible alternative, are inferior for at least one future condition and superior for no future conditions, is said to be dominated and can be eliminated from consideration without affecting the final choice.

Further inspection of Figure 6–1 shows that, no matter which of the remaining alternative inventory levels we choose to invest in, our payoff will be the same if we encounter an average tourist season. Another commonsense idea called the *principle of irrelevant conditions* might be used to eliminate this column of data from further examination. This principle states that:

> Any condition whose payoffs are equal for all alternatives being considered is said to be irrelevant and can be eliminated from further analyses without affecting the final choice.[2]

Use of these three commonsense ideas—employment of constraints and application of the principles of dominance and irrelevant conditions—allows us to reduce the size of the information package relevant to our choice. In this instance we were able to reduce the decision matrix to that shown in Figure 6–2. Close scrutiny of what we now see to be the relevant information suggests that, unless a poor tourist season is quite a bit more likely than a good one, we should invest in a moderately high inventory level.

Figure 6-2. Reduced Deicision Matrix for Inventory Investment Decision

Nature of the Tourist Season

	F_1, Good	F_2, Poor
A_1, Moderately high	$65,000	$30,000
A_2, Moderately low	$55,000	$35,000

Inventory Level

In this example, the use of the decision matrix and our common sense allowed us to cut the problem down to a manageable size. What should we do when this is not the case (i.e., what decision rule should we use when we are faced with a decision situation where the number of feasible alternatives or the number of future conditions remains large)? This question is addressed in the next few pages.

[2]*An exception is discussed in Step 5 of a later section of this chapter.*

MAXIMIZE EXPECTED UTILITY AS A DECISION RULE

There are several decision rules that we can use to choose among alternatives in risky or uncertain situations. Some of them were developed by people who were more interested in exploring the nature of decision rules than they were in developing good decision rules. These rules tend to have little practical value, but because they might help sharpen our overall understanding of choice making in uncertain situations, we will review them toward the end of the chapter.

At this point, however, we will focus our attention on the decision rule that is universally recommended by decision scientists. It is called the *Maximize Expected Utility* (MEU) decision rule. The logic of the rule is that we should make each choice in a way such that, if we made all of our choices in this way, we would maximize our overall utility. In order to see how the decision rule is used, let us apply it to the decision matrix of Figure 6-3. For the sake of simplicity, we will use the dollar values associated with the outcomes as estimates of the outcome utilities. Thus, in this case we are using the *Maximize Expected Value* (MEV) decision rule. The circumstances where direct payoffs are usable as estimates of the corresponding utilities will be discussed later in the chapter.

Using the information contained in this matrix, let us consider the average payoff that we will achieve if we choose to buy Land Site A_1. If

Figure 6-3.   Decision Matrix for Real Estate Purchase Decision

Future Conditions

Alternatives	F_1, Industrial park locates on east side of town	F_2, Industrial park locates on west side of town
Buy Land Site A_1	$50,000	$30,000
Buy Land Site A_2	$20,000	$60,000

we buy A_1 and if Condition F_1 occurs, we will make a profit of $50,000. If F_2 occurs, we will make a profit of $30,000. If our analysis of the political and economic situations leads us to believe that F_1 is more likely than F_2, and if we think F_1 has a 60 percent chance of occurring and F_2 has a 40 percent chance of occurring, then in order to determine the appropriate *weighted average* or expected payoff, we should weight the possible payoff of $50,000 by .6 and the possible profit of $30,000 by .4. More specifically, we should multiply $50,000 by .6 and get $30,000, multiply $30,000 by .4 and get $12,000, and then add these two numbers together to get the expected profit of $42,000. The values .6 and .4 are, of course, the probability or likelihoods of the two possible future conditions F_1 and F_2.

Expected Payoff for A_1 = .6(50,000) + .4(30,000) = $42,000.
Similarly,
Expected Payoff for A_2 = .6(20,000) + .4(60,000) = $36,000.

Common sense, aided by the computations associated with the MEU decision rule, suggests that unless there are $42,000 − $36,000 = $6,000 worth of reasons not to do so, we should choose Land Site A_2.

In both this example problem and the previous one we made use of information concerning the probability of different future conditions arising. Decision makers do this all the time, although they seldom make their judgments concerning future conditions so explicit. More likely, if they are asked to think aloud while they make their decision, they will make statements such as "Well, that is not very likely so I won't give it much weight." This statement shows that the simplistic strategies that unaided decision makers use do not provoke them to seek explicit probability values. They would most likely not know what to do with them if they had them.

In those situations where the payoffs vary significantly across future conditions, the use of more simplistic decision rules generally leads to choices of lower quality than those that would have evolved using the MEU decision rule. Unfortunately, a lack of knowledge about how to obtain and use probability estimates limits many decision makers to the use of simplistic decision rules. Recognition of this fact has led to applications-oriented research concerning methods for developing probability estimates. In the next few pages we draw on this research for a practical and proven approach to developing probability estimates by making use of expert judgments.

OBTAINING PROBABILITY ESTIMATES

There are many decision situations where the historical data normally used to develop probability estimates are either (1) of unacceptable quality, (2) known to be unrepresentative of future conditions, or (3) unavailable. It may be that the majority of important decisions fit into one or more of these categories. Certainly Downs' study of decision making in bureaucracies suggests that this is the case. Recall our earlier quotes from his book to the effect that

> The amount of information initially available to every decision maker about each problem is only a small fraction of all information potentially available on the subject. Additional information . . . can usually be procured, but the costs of procurement and utilization may rise rapidly as the amount of data increases.

and that

> Important aspects of many problems involve information that cannot be procured at all, especially concerning future events; hence many decisions must be made in the face of some ineradicable uncertainty. (Downs, 1966, p. 75)

In situations such as these, it is reasonable to turn to knowledgeable experts for estimates of the probabilities of the future events or outcomes.[3]

Many decision situations have been described in the managerial and decision science literature where probability estimates have played an important role in the final choice. They include situations as diverse as product development, hurricane seeding, corporate facilities expansion, wildfire prevention strategies, and product pricing.[4]

Of course, explicit probability estimates are not applicable to all decision situations. They are applicable when the payoffs vary significantly across future conditions and when there are no objective or data-based probabilities that are both appropriate to the particular deci-

---

[3]*Such estimates are sometimes called* subjective probabilities.
[4]*A number of case studies of decision situations where subjective probabilities played an important role in the final choice are included in Decision Analysis Group,* Readings in Decision Analysis, *Menlo Park, Calif. Stanford Research Institute, 1976.*

sion and obtainable at a reasonable cost. Indeed, under such conditions there is really no sensible alternative to the elicitation of probability estimates from the people most knowledgeable about the problem area. Sometimes, of course, the decision maker, as the most knowledgeable person, can best provide these estimates.

Research studies indicate that probability estimates obtained from experts by means of the technique introduced in the next paragraph are adequate for solving many managerial problems. On occasion, they are more predictive than estimates obtained through elaborate statistical techniques. Studies also indicate that people either follow or very nearly follow the axioms of mathematical probability theory when they make their estimates. Finally, studies from still another stream of research suggest that the use of unstated probabilities in informal models results in evaluations that are less accurate than the use of explicitly stated probabilities in the prescriptive and formal models developed by decision scientists.

There is a variety of methods available for obtaining estimates of probabilities.[5] Most of them have been used, in various contexts, for some time. Until recently, however, there were very few published studies that could be used for examining the real-world workability and relative merit of these models. It now appears that the method that provides the most accurate estimates across the largest range of decision situations is the *direct estimation method*. This approach involves having the decision maker or other expert make direct estimates of the probabilities of the various future conditions. As an example use of this method, let us listen in on an elicitation session.

Consultant: Ms. Johnson (the decision maker, an experienced retail sales manager), you indicated that the sales levels could usefully be categorized as "less than 1100," "1100–1200," "1200–1300," and "over 1300." Which of these sales levels do you feel is least likely to occur?[6]

Johnson: Well, I'd say it is least likely that sales will exceed 1300.

[5]*A review of alternative methods for obtaining subjective probability estimates and of the accuracy of these estimates is contained in G. P. Huber, "Methods for Quantifying Subjective Probabilities and Multiattribute Utilities."* Decision Sciences 5 (July 1974): 430–458.

[6]*We avoid a preliminary ranking, and begin with the least likely event to offset the tendency—well-documented by the many studies in this area—for people to overestimate the probabilities of the more likely outcomes and to underestimate the probabilities of the less likely outcomes. Beginning with the less likely outcomes tends to give them more prominence.*

Consultant: Okay, now how likely is that outcome? What probability would you assign it?

Johnson: Oh, about 10%, about one chance in ten.

Consultant: Now, holding aside for the moment that the interval "over 1300" has a probability of 10%, which of the remaining sales levels is least likely, and what do you think its probability is?

Johnson: Well, that's a hard one. I think that "less than 1100" and "1200–1300" are about the same, and that either is quite a bit more likely than "over 1300." I'll say that they each have a probability of about 25%.

Consultant: Okay, given these probabilities, what is the probability of the outcome "1100–1200"?

Johnson: Well, I can see that it should be 40%, but that does seem a little low.

Consultant: Okay, let's go on. Right now, your estimates of "less than 1100" and "1200–1300" are exactly equal. Is this what you mean to say?

Johnson: After thinking about it, I don't believe that "less than 1100" is quite as likely as the other. Maybe it should be 20% and then "1100–1200" could be 45%. I like that, because "1100–1200" is almost as probable as everything else put together, but not quite.

Consultant: Is "less than 1000" twice as likely as "over 1300"?

Johnson: Yes, I think it is, and anticipating your next question, I think that "1100–1200" is almost but not quite two times as probable as "1200–1300." I guess that I'm comfortable with the values 20%, 45%, 25%, and 10%.

This example captures the essence of the procedure for obtaining probability estimates. The results of an elicitation session such as this can be graphed for further scrutiny and discussion, as is shown in Figure 6–4. In the figure, the percent values have been replaced by the equivalent probabilities.

In the previous chapter we summarized the benefits that can be obtained by using MAU or other, similar models. Clearly these same benefits, most of which have to do with overcoming our limited capabilities as decision makers, apply to the use of decision matrices as well as to the use of MAU models. Let us turn now to a step-by-step description of how the procedure is employed when using decision matrices in combination with the Maximize Expected Utility (MEU) decision rule. This procedure helps the decision makers do what they want to do; therefore, it serves as an aid to judgment rather than as a substitute for judgment.

Figure 6–4.   Graph Showing Johnson's Probability Estimates

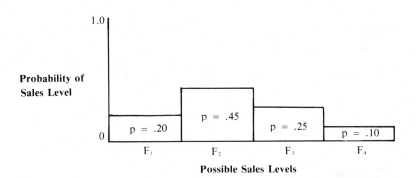

USING DECISION MATRICES AND THE MAXI-MIZE EXPECTED UTILITY DECISION RULE: THE MEU TECHNIQUE

In this section we describe the step-by-step procedure to be followed when using decision matrices and expected utility models. We will label the procedure as the *MEU technique* and will note that it has a number of similarities to the MAU model technique of the previous chapter.

In order to indicate the scope and nature of the individual steps, we will draw upon diverse examples. In order to show that together these steps do comprise a useful technique, we will also carry along one example application throughout the procedure.

The carry-through example: A bidding problem

Let us consider again the bidding problem presented in Chapter 3. In this situation, a construction company had the opportunity to bid on building a small apartment complex. The decision matrix shown in Figure 6–5 captures the essence of the problem. In Chapter 3, we assumed that the probability estimates for F_1, F_2, and F_3 were .50, .50, and 0 respectively. This made our decision an easy one, as we could inspect the equally likely F_1 and F_2 columns of the matrix and see that bidding $1 million was clearly the best alternative.

There are many situations where a simple visual inspection with a qualitative judgment is not a sufficient analysis of the information con-

Figure 6–5. Decision Matrix for Bidding Problem

Alternatives	Future Conditions: F_1, Lowest competitor bid is less than $1 million	F_2, Lowest competitor bid is about $1.1 million	F_3, Lowest competitor bid is more than $1.2 million
A_1, Do not bid	0	0	0
A_2, Bid $1 million	– $5000*	$95,000	$95,000
A_3, Bid $1.2 million	– $5000	– $5000	$295,000

*Recall from Chapter 3 that the cost of developing and submitting a bid was $5000.

tained in the matrix. This is especially true if there are many alternatives or if there are many possible future conditions. For our present purpose, however, this is a fairly simple example.

Let us move on now to a description of the step-by-step procedure and of how Mr. John Stevens, the executive in charge of analyzing the apartment construction project, might work through it. We will assume that the *problem exploration* and *alternative generation* phases of the problem-solving process have identified the alternatives that apply to the decision situation.

Step 1. Identify and list the relevant future conditions • Because most managers are familiar with the decision settings in which a particular choice situation might occur, listing possible future conditions or events is usually not a difficult task. On the other hand, particularly with respect to future events such as "competitor takes us to court" or "state revises its tax laws," overlooking certain outcomes or conditions can be disastrous.

As a consequence, it is common practice for managers to obtain the help of other people in identifying future conditions and in assessing the likelihood that these conditions might occur. In order not to lose our focus on individual decision making, we will postpone our examination of this approach until we discuss group decision making. We might say, however, that when faced with an unfamiliar decision situation, it is often useful for the manager to discuss the matter with someone who is more experienced.

In the bidding problem portrayed in Figure 6-5, we see the three future conditions that Stevens thought were appropriate for the analysis of the situation.

Step 2. Determine the payoff or utility for each outcome • Payoffs for a given outcome (e.g., profits given a particular sales volume) are usually readily available from accounting data. If the relationship between the payoffs and the utilities for these payoffs is that of a straight or nearly straight line, such as that shown in Figure 4-1, then we can use the payoffs as proxies for the utilities. If the utilities associated with the payoffs or outcomes are required (i.e., if there is not a straight line relationship between the utilities and the payoffs), then the utilities should be obtained using the method described in Chapter 5.

In many situations, there are one or more unlikely but possible outcomes that have a highly negative payoff, such as "union strikes at all locations." If the maximize expected utility decision rule is applied in these situations, it invariably leads to conservative choices. One realistic and often used strategy is to develop a separate contingency plan for dealing with the adverse outcome, and then substitute the cost of implementing this contingency plan for the cost of the highly negative outcome. For example, if the decision concerned pricing and if the highly negative outcome were that customers would stop using our products or that clients would stop using our services, we could employ the contingency plan of quickly returning to our original pricing schedule and thereby incur a relatively small loss. We will discuss the use of contingency plans in more detail later in the chapter.

In the example problem, the payoffs shown in Figure 6-5 followed from a rough estimate indicating that the construction cost would be $900,000 and that the cost of developing and submitting a detailed bid would be $5000. Thus Stevens developed the payoff for the center cell by first subtracting the $900,000 construction cost from the $1,000,000 price that was asked in the bid. Then he subtracted from this $100,000 gross profit the $5000 cost of achieving the bid.[7] We will assume that the construction company has a number of projects under way and that, as a consequence, its utility for the dollar values shown in Figure 6-5 is strictly proportional to the dollar values themselves.

Step 3. Identify the constraints and screen out the unacceptable alternatives • As we noted earlier, unaided decision makers tend to use overly simplistic strategies—such as the "satisficing" strategy of Chapter 3—that rely heavily on the use of constraints. As we saw in the inventory investment example, the use of constraints saves us from having to give detailed consideration to infeasible alternatives—alternatives that in-

[7] *All of these values could be reduced, if desired, to account for the effect of corporate income taxes.*

clude outcomes that are unacceptable no matter how attractive other outcomes associated with the alternative are. On the other hand, we will make better decisions in the long run if we do not casually use constraints, as we may be screening out good alternatives that could be salvaged if a contingency plan were developed to deal with the highly negative outcome.

In the bidding example, Stevens and the construction company could face a number of constraints that might affect the decision, but none of these seem likely. For example, he might not have the time or staff to prepare a detailed bid and so would have to choose the "do not bid" alternative. Or he might have a minimum allowed rate of return on such a project, perhaps 15 percent. That would disallow the alternative "bid $1 million," since this alternative provides a before-tax rate of return of just over 10 percent.

Step 4. Determine the probability of each outcome or future condition • If appropriate historical data are economically available, we should use them to develop estimates of the probabilities of the various outcomes or conditions. If such data are not available, we should obtain estimates of the probabilities from whomever is most knowledgeable. In obtaining the estimates, we should use a question and answer format similar to that used in the previous example dealing with the likelihood of various sales levels.

Research shows that appropriately obtained group estimates of probabilities are invariably better than the estimates from the average member. In fact, they are often better than the estimates of the most accurate member. We will discuss why this is so and which are the best approaches for obtaining group judgments in later chapters.

Let us return to Stevens' decision situation. Although he recognized that an argument could be made for obtaining probability estimates for each outcome in this matrix, Stevens believed that competitors' decisions would be largely independent of his own, as all possible steps were being taken to keep the company's interest and analysis confidential. Thus, at least for the purposes of the preliminary analysis, the probabilities of future conditions could be considered as independent of the alternatives in the matrix. Using this assumption allowed Stevens to seek probability estimates for only the future conditions, rather than for each outcome.

Employing the probability estimation procedure described earlier in the chapter on both himself and on an experienced associate, Stevens took the average of the estimates and arrived at the following probability estimates: $P(F_1) = .3$; $P(F_2) = .5$; and $P(F_3) = .2$. Using these estimates, Stevens turned to applying the MEV decision rule.

Step 5. Apply the Maximize Expected Utility decision rule and computational procedure to the feasible alternatives and identify the one (or two) with the largest expected utility • As an example application of this step, let us review the computations associated with the real estate investment decision modeled in Figure 6–5. As we saw in the related discussion, we multiply the payoff or utility associated with each outcome by the probability of the outcome. We then sum these products as the expected utility of the alternative. If this value does not satisfy a constraint, such as a minimum expected rate of return on an investment, the alternative is eliminated from consideration. Finally, we identify from the alternatives that satisfy our constraints the one that provides the largest expected utility. Unless factors not included in the model dictate otherwise, we choose it for implementation.

As a second example, let us consider Stevens' application of the step to the payoffs in Figure 6–5 and the probability estimates obtained in Step 4. A particular case in point is Alternative A_3. Stevens knew that the three payoffs that might follow from adopting A_3 were $-\$5000$, $-\$5000$, and $\$295,000$. He felt that it made sense to consider them in aggregate by weighting them according to how likely it was that each would occur. Accordingly he multiplied the $-\$5000$ corresponding to F_1 by .3 (as this was the best estimate of the probability that F_1 would occur), then multiplied the $-\$5000$ corresponding to F_2 by .5, multiplied the $\$295,000$ by .2, and then added the three products, as shown below.

Expected Value for A_3 = .3($-5,000$) + .5($-5,000$)
+ .2(295,000) = $-1500 - 2500 + 59,000 = \$55,000$.
Expected Value for A_2 = .3($-5,000$) + .5(95,000) + .2(95,000)
= $-1500 + 47,500 + 19,000 = \$65,000$.
Expected Value for A_1 = .3(0) + .5(0) + .2(0) = \$0$.

Step 6. Consider both the criteria not included in the analysis and the possible adverse consequences of choosing the highest scoring alternative, and make the choice • As we discussed under Step 8 in the preceding chapter, in some situations, there will be criteria and potentially adverse consequences that cannot be realistically captured in the decision model. In such a situation and in this step, we ask ourselves if the nonincluded criterion or potentially adverse consequence is important enough to offset the apparent marginal advantage of the aggregate of the information included in the model. For example, in the decision situation associated with Figure 6–3, we found that the information included in the model suggested that Alternative A_1 has an advantage of $6000. At this point in the application of the decision matrix and MEU decision rule, we would ask ourselves if there were nonincluded criteria or potentially adverse consequences that were contrary to the indicated choice of Alternative A_1. If not, we would choose A_1. If there were, we would attempt to determine if they were serious enough to offset the advantage of A_1 for $6000.

An important advantage of using the matrix and MEU technique to aggregate the information in the decision matrix is that the aggregation provides us with a single number against which we can compare the value of nonincluded facts or criteria. In Stevens' situation, if the company has the resources to undertake the construction project, if the alternatives are really limited to the three shown, and if the estimates of the payoffs and probabilities are thought to be accurate (i.e., if Figure 6–5 really portrays all of the relevant information), then it is reasonable to choose A_2 and put in a bid for $1 million.

FURTHER DISCUSSION OF DECISION MAKING IN RISKY OR UNCERTAIN SITUATIONS

In order to provide some additional perspective on the use of decision matrices and the maximize expected utility (MEU) decision rule, we will use these next few paragraphs to answer some questions that follow from the earlier discussions.

Question 1: How accurate do the probabilities have to be?

The answer to this question is similar to that given in the case of criterion and attribute weights. The MEU decision rule takes the form of an additive model, identical in form to an additive MAU model. Because such models are fairly insensitive to minor inaccuracies, we do not have to rule out their use when we are uncertain about the estimates of the values included in them.

As a practical matter, it is advisable to obtain the best possible estimates of the probabilities, apply the MEU rule to make a selection, and then experiment with other probability values to see if they cause the selection to be changed. The purpose of this strategy is to identify the *switchover values,* those probability values that dictate a switching of choices. If our probability estimates are far from the switchover values, we have little motivation to seek information with which to enhance their accuracy. On the other hand, if the estimates are near the switchover values—and if the expected payoff for the alternative that would be switched to is very different from the alternative that would be switched from—then we should seek more information to determine the accuracy of our current probability estimates.[8]

Trial and error computations show that the switchover values for the situation portrayed in Figure 6–3 are $P(F_1) = .5$ and $P(F_2) = .5$. At these values, the expected payoff for A_1 and A_2 are equal. Thus as the probability of F_1 declines from .6 toward .5, our inclination toward choosing A_1 should decline. If the probability falls below .5, we should switch our choice from A_1 to A_2. This process of determining how sensitive our choices are to the probabilities used in making these choices is called *sensitivity analysis*.

Question 2: Should I check the consistency of my probability estimates?

As in the case of utility and importance judgments, it is advisable to check the consistency of probability estimates. One approach is to prepare a graph such as Figure 6–4, where the height of each column portrays the likelihood of the state of nature or competitor strategy. If we ask ourselves, "Does this look right?" and find that the answer is "no," then we can make adjustments until it does look right. We must keep in mind that the probabilities must add up to 1.00.

Another useful approach is to ask ourselves questions that compare our judgments. For example, we can say, "Now I've stated that a client demand of between 100 and 125 per day has a 40 percent chance of occurring and that a demand of between 125 and 150 per day has a 20 percent chance of occurring. Do I really think that the first case is twice as likely as the second?"

We note here that research shows that people's estimates of probability values for likely events tend to be greater than the actual

---

[8]*The switchover values can be identified with a few experimental calculations. We first substitute into our expected utility model some new set of probability values that tend to decrease the expected utility of the alternative presently having the highest expected utility. We then recompute the expected utility for this and all other alternatives. The probabilities that, after a sufficient incremental adjustment, finally cause the expected utilities for the two top ranked alternatives to be the same are the switchover values; any further change would cause us to switch our choice.*

probabilities. Similarly, values estimated for less likely events tend to be smaller than real probability values. Some decision scientists have interpreted this as an *overconfidence* bias. Others have interpreted it as *focus* bias, a bias reflecting a tendency to focus on more available or representative events. Awareness of this bias is important to us as we observe discrepancies in our estimates and attempt to resolve them. Based on the research evidence, we will resolve discrepancies in the direction opposite our bias.

Question 3: Are there other decision rules, besides maximizing the expected utility, that can be used to make decisions in uncertain situations?

The answer to this question is "yes," but as we noted earlier, most of the other rules have not been seriously considered for use in important decision settings. The reason for this is that these other decision rules employ the assumption that the decision maker has no information on the probabilities that the various possible future conditions will occur. Because organizations do not delegate important decisions to people who either have no information about the matter or cannot obtain such information, this assumption is hardly ever valid in real decision settings.

Although these decision rules have found little formal application, they are useful in sharpening our overall understanding of decision making in uncertain situations.[9] As a consequence, we will briefly review them and attempt to describe decision settings where they might help clarify the nature of the decision situation that the manager is facing. Let us review them in the context of the decision matrix portrayed in Figure 6-6.

The *maximax* decision rule states that we should choose the alternative that gives us a chance of obtaining the largest payoff in the matrix. Basically it says that we should choose so as to *max*imize the *max*imum possible payoff. Applying this decision rule to Figure 6-6, we would choose A_1 in order to obtain the \$34.

If the decision maker is an incurable optimist, he will use this decision rule, as would anyone who had total control over future conditions.

---

[9] *It is conventional practice among decision scientists to refer to the hypothetical case where the decision maker wishes to act as if he is totally ignorant about the probabilities of the future conditions as "decision making under uncertainty," and to refer to the case where he wishes to use probability estimates as "decision making under risk."*

Figure 6-6.   Decision Matrix Without Probabilities

Future Conditions

		F_1	F_2	F_3
	A_1	$34	-$18	-$4
Alternatives	A_2	$12	-$6	$10
	A_3	$2	$2	$2

Of course, if we had total control over future conditions, we would not be dealing with a decision under uncertainty. Consideration of the rule dramatizes the use of the decision matrix as a tool for determining which future condition should be sought if advertising, bargaining, cloud seeding, or other tactics are available for manipulating the probabilities of the future conditions.

The *maximin* decision rule states that we should choose the alternative that would give us the best payoff if the worst condition occurred. Basically it says that we should choose so as to *max*imize the *min*imum possible gain. Applying this decision rule to Figure 6–6 would cause us to choose A_3, as the minimum possible payoff would be $2. For any other alternative, the minimum possible would be less than $2.

If the decision maker is an incurable pessimist or believes that his selection will be known before his competitor chooses her strategy, he will use this decision rule. The rule dramatizes the use of a decision matrix as a tool for choosing an alternative when faced with a competitor who will have information about what our choice will be before having to make his or her choice. The rule may also have merit when our overriding concern is to come out of the decision situation "with at least something to show." This conservative strategy might be useful if the payoffs could be used to ensure our later participation (perhaps in a poker game or in the stock market) when conditions were more favorable. Thus the rule may be appropriate during economic, military, or meteorological disasters when we might want to choose the alternative with the best payoff under the worst possible condition.

The *minimize regret* decision rule states that we should choose the alternative that, whatever the future condition, would cause us the least regret at having not chosen another alternative. For example, in Figure 6–6 we can see that if we choose A_3 and if F_1 occurs, we will regret having missed out on the $34. Of course we will obtain $2, so our potential regret is only $32. If we select A_3, this $32 is our largest regret, no matter which condition occurs. If we select A_2, our largest possible regret is $22, and is obtained if F_1 occurs. If F_2 occurs, we would have only an $8 regret, as we would incur a $6 loss while foregoing a $2 gain for not having chosen A_3. If F_3 occurs, we will have no regret, as we have obtained the maximum possible payoff. Further examination of the matrix shows that if we choose A_1, maximum possible regret will be for the $20 difference between encountering an $18 loss and foregoing a $2 gain.

As can be seen, this decision rule focuses entirely on the psychological dissatisfaction or regret related to missed opportunities. It is most easily applied in conjunction with a *regret matrix.* Figure 6-7 is a regret matrix whose entries are determined by computing the difference between the payoffs in the cell and the best possible payoff in the column. The decision rule instructs us to choose the alternative that will minimize the maximum regret. In this case, we would choose A_1—as our maximum regret would be $20 with A_1, but would be $22 if we choose A_2 and $32 if we choose A_3.

A decision rule that has received some attention in the field of economics but little attention in the field of management states that we should choose the alternative that is least risky, the alternative whose outcomes are least variable. This is a reasonable rule when predictability is important, as it is when the outcomes of one choice (e.g., expenses or elapsed times) are integral to a coordinated effort (e.g., an overall project budget or schedule).

Figure 6-7.   Regret Matrix Derived from Figure 6-6.

Future Conditions

	F_1	F_2	F_3
A_1	$0	$20	$14
A_2	$22	$8	$0
A_3	$32	$0	$8

Alternatives

Before leaving this discussion of alternative formal decision rules, we should remember that a common managerial strategy for making choices in risky or uncertain situations is to choose the alternative that allows the greatest flexibility for adapting to future events. Within the context of applying the MEU technique, the manager can explicitly consider this strategy in either Step 2 or Step 6. For example, if one alternative would allow the manager to withdraw some of the committed resources if an adverse outcome developed, he or she could regard this alternative as having a contingency plan. The approach would be to adjust the payoff matrix (at Step 2) to reflect the lower costs associated with implementing the contingency plan rather than the higher costs associated with maintaining full commitment to the original plan. An alternative approach would be to weigh (at Step 6) the advantage of adopting the more flexible alternative against the loss in utility associated with adopting the alternative having the greatest expected utility.

Question 4: What should I do if the probabilities of future conditions depend on which alternative I choose?

In an earlier discussion we mentioned that the probabilities of future conditions can be affected by our own actions. For example, the probabilities of different sales volumes are affected by our advertising and packaging decisions, and the probability of finding oil or water or whatever is affected by how deeply we drill. The procedures for making rational choices in such a situation are the same as those discussed in the earlier parts of the section. For example, let us apply the MEU rule to the decision matrix shown in Figure 6-8, where the entry in the upper left hand corner of each outcome cell is the probability of that outcome. In this decision situation, $100,000 is at stake, and manipulative strategies cost $10,000 each.

1. Expected utility for A_1 = $.30(-\$120,000) + .70(-\$20,000) = -\$50,000$.
2. Expected utility for A_2 = $.40(-\$110,000) + .60(-\$10,000) = -\$50,000$.
3. Expected utility for A_3 = $.50(-\$110,000) + .50(-\$10,000) = -\$60,000$.
4. Expected utility for A_4 = $.60(-\$100,000) + .40(0) = -\$60,000$.

Figure 6–8.   Decision Matrix for Political Action Decision

	F_1, Legislative bill becomes law		F_2, Legislative bill does not become law	
A₁, Lobby aggressively and mount mail campaign	.30		.70	
		− $120,000		− $20,000
A₂, Mount mail campaign only	.40		.60	
		− $110,000		− $10,000
A₃, Lobby only	.50		.50	
		− $110,000		− $10,000
A₄, Do nothing	.60		.40	
		− $100,000		0

The analysis suggests that we should certainly mount a mail campaign and should also consider adding a lobbying effort, depending on whether the other factors not captured by the model do or do not favor this additional effort.

Question 5: What should I do if one or more of the possible outcomes in the decision matrix would be so disastrous that I am tempted to adopt a conservative alternative even if it does not maximize my expected payoff?

There are two possibilities. One is to develop a *contingency plan* that could be implemented to cut losses if the worst occurred. An example plan would involve a reallocation of the personnel and materials associated with a new product in case a competitor came out with a superior product when ours was being introduced into the market. The use of a contingency plan is a common strategy and usually allows us to insert a much smaller loss in the "disaster cell" of the decision matrix. Thus, we continue to apply the MEV decision rule.

The second possibility is to convert all of the payoffs in the decision matrix into utilities, or the losses into *disutilities* (negative utilities). Then we apply the MEU decision rule to this new matrix. This approach allows us to capture the real nature of the disastrous outcome while still applying a systematic procedure to the data captured in the decision matrix model. These approaches can be used simultaneously.

SUMMARY PROBLEM: NEW PRODUCT INTRODUCTION

Mr. Sam Wilson, director of marketing for QRS Company, learned how to use the matrix and MEU technique while attending a managerial short course. He decided to apply the ideas when next making a "preliminary" analysis of the advisability of introducing a new product.[10] Since he had two new products available but could finance the introduction of only one product during the next year, he decided to work with the following alternatives: (1) introduce Product A; (2) introduce Product B; and (3) do not introduce a new product.

In undertaking Step 1, *identifying and listing the relevant future conditions,* Wilson concluded from previous experience and from the results of marketing research data that the actions of the company's major competitor were the key conditions in determining the payoffs for both of the products. With this in mind, Wilson decided that, for this preliminary analysis, the relevant future conditions to consider were:

1. F_1. Competitor introduces superior product.
2. F_2. Competitor introduces equivalent product.
3. F_3. Competitor introduces inferior product.
4. F_4. Competitor does not introduce similar product.

His next step was to determine the payoff or utility to QRS that would occur for each combination of an implemented alternative and a future condition.

In order to simplify his preliminary analysis, when *determining the payoff or utility of each outcome,* Wilson chose to use dollar payoffs

---

[10] *We emphasize the word "preliminary" here because, while the use of the decision matrix and MEU technique is an entirely correct approach to analyzing Wilson's decision situation, the decision tree technique of the next chapter will be seen to be even more appropriate for doing the "final" analysis.*

instead of utilities in constructing the decision matrix. Based on the information from the accounting department and on sales estimates, Wilson calculated the payoffs shown in Figure 6-9. The values in parentheses in the cells of the first column are the losses that would occur if QRS stuck with the new product in the face of the competitor's superior product. The other values in the cells of the first column represent the losses that would occur if QRS adopted Wilson's contingency plan. This plan consisted of diverting the resources associated with the new product to other QRS products in the event that the competitor introduced a superior product.

As he turned to *identifying the constraints and screening out the unacceptable alternatives,* Wilson faced a common situation. Although he knew that QRS Company could not afford any large losses, he also knew that a possible loss of $1,200,000 was well within the range of losses that the company was prepared to absorb when marketing new products. Wilson therefore eliminated no alternatives through the application of constraints as a screening device. He next turned his atten-

Figure 6-9.   Decision Matrix for New Product Introduction Decision

Future Conditions

Alternatives		F_1, Competitor introduces superior product	F_2, Competitor introduces equivalent product	F_3, Competitor introduces inferior product	F_4, Competitor does not introduce similar product
	A_1, Introduce Product A	−$1,200,000 (−$1,800,000)	$1,000,000	$3,800,000	$6,250,000
	A_2, Introduce Product B	−$600,000 (−$950,000)	$1,250,000	$3,600,000	$6,950,000
	A_3, Do not introduce new product	0	0	0	0

tion to determining the probabilities of the various outcomes or future conditions.

When undertaking Step 4, *determining the probability of each outcome or future condition,* Wilson felt that, for the purposes of this preliminary analysis, the probabilities of his competitors' actions could be considered as independent from QRS' alternatives. This seemed reasonable since it was thought the extent of the company's progress in developing Products A and B had been successfully kept a secret. Thus probabilities were estimated for each of the future conditions rather than for each of the outcomes. The result of his using the probability estimation procedure described earlier on both himself and the market research manager and then discussing the two sets of estimates until a consensus was reached were $P(F_1) = .2$, $P(F_2) = .25$, $P(F_3) = .4$, and $P(F_4) = .15$.

When *applying the expected payoff model and computational procedure* to the alternative of introducing Product A, Wilson saw that there were four possible outcomes and payoffs: (1) QRS will incur an $1,200,000 loss if the major competitor introduces a superior product. This has a 20 percent chance of occurring; (2) QRS will incur a $1,000,000 gain if the major competitor introduces an equivalent product. This has a 25 percent chance of occurring; (3) QRS can incur a $3,800,000 gain. This has a 40 percent chance of occurring; and (4) QRS can incur a $6,250,000 gain. This has a 15 percent chance of occurring.

By multiplying the payoffs of the related probability estimates and then summing, Wilson got the following results:

Expected value if
QRS introduces Product A = (.2)(−1,200,000)
+ (.25)(1,000,000) + (.4)(3,800,000)
+ (.15)(6,250,000) = −240,000
+ 250,000 + 1,520,000 + 937,500
= 2,467,500.

Expected value if
QRS introduces Product B = (.2)(−600,000)
+ (.25)(1,250,000) + (.4)(3,600,000)
+ (.15)(6,950,000) = −120,000
+ 312,500 + 1,440,000 + 1,042,500
= 2,675,000.

Expected value if
QRS does not introduce a new product = (.2)(0) + (.25)(0)
+ (.4)(0) + (.15)(0) = 0.

At this point, Wilson saw that the information captured in this model led to the conclusion that QRS should introduce Product B. Since the principal fact not included in the model—the fact that Product B was more useful than Product A in filling out QRS' product line—led to the same conclusion as the MEU analysis, Wilson made a tentative decision to introduce Product B into the market.

SUMMARY AND OVERVIEW

In this chapter we have reviewed a technique that can be of considerable help to a manager in identifying and using the information that is relevant to making a decision in a risky or uncertain situation. Early in the chapter we introduced the use of decision matrices as a model for helping managers make decisions in risky or uncertain situations. Then we introduced the use of the Maximize Expected Utility decision rule as a decision strategy that could lead to further improvements in the quality of decisions made in such situations. Later in the chapter we examined the step-by-step procedure for using decision matrices and the MEU decision rule in combination, referring to this combination as the MEU technique. Toward the end of the chapter we discussed the nature of decision making in uncertain situations.

In many risky or uncertain situations we have the opportunity to obtain more information for reducing some of the uncertainties involved. Such opportunities pose the question, "Should we incur the expense or delay necessary to obtain this information?" The answer depends on the value of the information relative to its cost. In the next chapter we will examine techniques for determining whether or not to search for additional information before making a decision.

OPPORTUNITIES FOR FURTHER THOUGHT

1. List three arguments against the explicit estimation of probabilities and three arguments in favor of explicit estimation.
2. List three arguments against the modeling of decision situations with a decision matrix and three arguments in favor of such modeling.

3. Compute the expected payoff for an alternative that, if chosen, can encounter one of three future conditions. The first condition provides a payoff of $1000 and occurs with a probability of .3. The second provides a payoff of $2000 and occurs with a probability of .45. The third condition provides a payoff of $3000.
4. Think of a decision situation that you could model with a decision matrix. Apply the MEU or MEV decision rule to the information in the matrix and see if the result makes sense in light of what you know about the situation. If the result does not make sense, explain why not and what you would do about the incongruity between the logic of the model and decision rule and your own feeling about what the choice should be. In particular, consider whether Step 6 of the step-by-step procedure could be useful.

REFERENCES AND RELATED READINGS

Brown, R. V., A. S. Kahr, and C. Peterson. *Decision Analysis for the Manager.* New York: Holt, Rinehart and Winston, 1974.

Decision Analysis Group. *Readings in Decision Analysis.* Menlo Park, Calif.: Stanford Research Institute, 1976.

Downs, A. *Inside Bureaucracy.* Boston: Little, Brown and Company, 1966.

Huber, G. P. "Methods for Quantifying Subjective Probabilities and Multiattribute Utilities." *Decision Sciences* (July, 1974): 430–458.

Keeney, R. L. and H. Raiffa. *Decisions with Multiple Objectives: Preferences and Value Tradeoffs.* New York: John Wiley and Sons, Inc., 1976.

Seaver, D. A., D. V. Winterfeldt, and W. Edwards. "Eliciting Subjective Probability Distributions on Continuous Variables." *Organizational Behavior and Human Performance* 21 (June 1978): 379–392.

Tversky, A. and D. Kahneman. "Judgement Under Uncertainty: Heuristics and Biases." *Science* 185 (1974): 1124–1131.

7

How to Decide When to Decide: A Self-Help Procedure

Important managerial decisions are rarely made the very moment a problem appears. In many cases, time and other resources are used to search for additional information about the problem and the decision situation. Of course, managers do not always immediately undertake an information search. Instead they sometimes think about whether or not such a search is justified; associated delays can be costly and data gathered are not always as informative as was hoped. In essence, managers make a separate decision concerning when they should decide—immediately with the available information or later after obtaining more information.

This chapter describes a technique for determining whether a decision should be made with the information at hand or whether additional information should be sought. Example situations where the technique is useful include the following:

> *Introduction of a new product or service:* Whether or not to introduce a new product or service is a decision where the chances of making the correct choice might be improved if additional in-

116

formation about probable customer reaction were obtained (as through a survey or test market effort). But such information is costly and imperfect. Should the organization expend the resources necessary to obtain it?

Sale or purchase of property: Whether or not to purchase a resort, a ranch, or common stocks is a decision where the chances of making a correct choice might be improved if additional information were obtained about future conditions concerning, for example, government purchase of adjacent lands, support of beef prices, or tax policy toward the industry. But again, such information is costly and not totally reliable. Is it worth the price of purchase?

In situations such as these, the manager must make a sequence of decisions. The early decision, concerning whether to obtain more information, should be made with respect to how useful the information might be when the original decision situation is eventually addressed. A closely related type of situation includes one where the manager is reluctant to make a large resource commitment in the face of uncertainty and sees as one option the strategy of implementing a low-cost alternative while waiting for the decision situation to become clearer.

This strategy is a popular one and is reflected in statements such as "Let's keep our options open" and "Let's do what we can to maintain our flexibility." It is a commonsensical approach to decision making, but it can sometimes be costly. For example, building a small plant and then later adding to it may be more expensive, given the conversion and lost opportunity costs, than building the large plant to begin with. In such situations, the manager is dealing with a sequence of decisions (e.g., which plant to build now and whether to add on later). As before, the first decision should be made with respect to what the second decision might be. In fact, the alternative of implementing a lower cost solution, while allowing time to provide information about the desirability of a higher cost solution, is conceptually identical to implementing an *active search for information* alternative. As a consequence, we need not treat the two types of decision situations separately. In either of the two cases, when the costs and payoffs associated with the decisions are large, the situation deserves formal analysis.

The next two sections of the chapter describe and demonstrate a formal technique that can be used to analyze sequential decision situations such as those described. The technique has been successfully applied in many business and public sector organizations.[1] It involves the use of a model called a *decision tree* and is very similar to the decision matrix technique of the previous chapter.

The first of these sections describes the *fundamental* use of a decision tree (i.e., its use as a device for reducing the cognitive difficulties of individuals and the communication difficulties of groups). Here the focus will be on using the tree to help structure the decision situation. That this is the fundamental use is suggested by Rex Brown, a well-known writer and consultant in the field, whose belief is that the "contribution (of decision trees) to the quality of decision making seems to come more from forcing meaningful structure on informal reasoning than from supplanting it by formal analysis" (Brown, 1970, p. 88). This is also suggested by the executive quoted in the *Harvard Business Review* who reported "We argued for 45 minutes about what we should do right now and what it would cost to postpone a decision, but it wasn't until we put a decision tree on the board that people began to realize that we had all been talking about different problems!" (Hayes, 1969, p. 109). The second of the two sections describes the *unique* use of a decision tree (i.e., its use as an aid in the formal analysis of the value of additional information to the decision maker). Let us move on to discussing the fundamental use of decision trees.

DECISION TREES FOR STRUCTURING DECISIONS

A decision tree is a graphical model that displays the sequence of decisions and the events that comprise a sequential decision situation. We will introduce it by considering a simple example situation—a manager in the cosmetics industry who has before her a proposal for a large promotional effort that will, ideally, reach a previously untapped market.

As the subordinates present the situation, it seems to have two alternatives ("promotion" or "no promotion") and three possible future

[1] *For detailed descriptions of a number of corporate and public agency decisions where the decision tree technique has been applied, see Decision Analysis Group,* Readings in Decision Analysis *(Menlo Park, Calif.: Stanford Research Institute, 1976), and V. M. Rao Tummala and Richard C. Henshaw, eds.,* Concepts and Applications of Modern Decision Models *(East Lansing, Mich.: Michigan State University Business Studies, 1976).*

Figure 7-1.   Decision Tree for Promotion Decision as Initially Presented

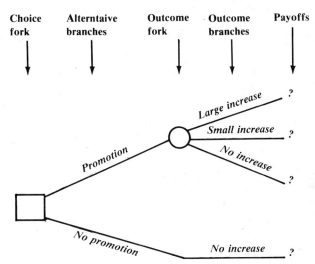

conditions or outcomes ("large market," "small market," or "no market"). We could use a decision matrix to model this problem, but for reasons that will become apparent, it will be more useful to start by modeling it with the small decision tree shown in Figure 7-1.

In constructing this model, we begin at the left with a *choice fork* from which our *alternative branches* project. At the end of the promotion branch is an *outcome fork* from which our *outcome branches* project. Each outcome branch, or outcome, has a payoff associated with it, as did the outcomes of the decision matrices of Chapter 6. Since such models generally portray only those outcomes that are consequences of choices, the outcomes of "large increase" and "small increase" are not shown as outcome branches when the "no promotion" alternative is the choice.

Figure 7-1 is a simple model of a simplified decision situation. As the manager begins to think about the matter, the implicit model that subordinates seem to be using may appear inadequate. Let us listen in as the manager reflects on the proposal.

"The decision put before me is whether to invest in this promotion or whether to let this opportunity pass by. Of course, if the large market is really out there, we will make a good deal of money, but the proposed promotion would cost about half of what we'd make. I'm not as certain as most people around here that the large market actually exists. In fact, I'd say the chances that we encounter a large market are fifty-fifty, no more. I am sure of one thing—I wouldn't mind looking at ideas for reducing the risk.

"All of us do agree that at least a small market exists. But if this is the only market available, it would be stupid to invest in the proposed promotion. We simply couldn't get our money back. Maybe we should try a smaller scale promotion. Of course, with the smaller promotion we wouldn't be able to exploit the large market, if it were there, but we couldn't lose as much either. I think I'll consider this idea of a small promotion as a third alternative.

"Now that I think about it, maybe I should have the marketing department conduct a formal study, a survey or something that will assess the size of the market. That would cost some money, but at least we'd have some better information for deciding what to do about the special promotion. Let's see, is this a fourth alternative, or is it a separate decision? This is getting complicated.

"It must be a separate decision though, because the outcomes of the study would be estimates of market size rather than actual sales resulting from the promotion. It seems like I have a series of decisions, first, 'whether to have a market study' and second 'what to do about the promotion.' This is really getting messy. Maybe I'd better draw a picture."

This manager is ready for a decision-tree model. She has recognized that the complexity of the situation is beyond her ability to mentally portray it. Let us assume that she decided to overcome her cognitive limitations by first sketching out the decision situation she would face if she did not commission the market study (i.e., the decision involving just the issue of the promotion). After a few false starts and a little help, the manager would probably develop a decision tree similar to that shown in Figure 7–2.

We repeat here, for emphasis, that a principal payoff we receive from drawing a decision tree is an increase in our understanding of the decision situation. Such an increase in insight is a consequence of first thinking through the structure of the tree, then identifying the relevant information, and finally aggregating that information. These three tasks are easily carried out if we adhere to the following three-phase procedure.

Figure 7-2. Decision Tree for Choosing Among Promotions*

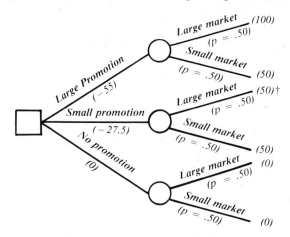

*All costs and payoffs shown represent thousands of dollars.

†Recall that the small promotion could not exploit the large market, thus the payoff is limited to that of the small, exploitable market.

Phase 1. Constructing a decision tree: Drawing the branches

When constructing a decision tree, begin at the left side of the diagram (see Figure 7-2), and progress to the right.

Step 1.1   Lay out the alternatives as branches from a choice fork ● Beginning at the left, the manager laid out as branches the basic alternatives of a large promotion, a small promotion, or no promotion. The square from which the three branches originate is called a *choice fork.*

Step 1.2   At the end of each alternative branch, lay out the possible outcomes as branches from an outcome fork ● The choice of an alternative can result in various outcomes. The manager recognized this fact by drawing a circle at the end of each alternative branch. The manager then drew a new set of branches corresponding to the outcomes of a large market and a small market. Such circles are called *outcome forks.*

For the sake of retaining a simple example, we will not include more alternatives (e.g., "medium-scale promotion") or more outcomes (e.g., "no market"). Completing this first phase amounts to explicitly and succinctly defining the decision situation.

Phase 2. Constructing a decision tree: Inserting the leaves

The next three steps help incorporate more decision-relevant information into the model. Through them we use the model to remind ourselves of the types of information elements that are relevant and to portray these elements on the external memory that the tree provides.

Step 2.1   For each alternative, indicate the cost of implementation • The cost values of −$55,000, −$27,500, and $0 are shown in the parentheses adjacent to the respective alternative branches.[2]

Step 2.2   For each outcome, indicate the probability of its occurrence • The probability values of .50 and .50 are shown in the parentheses adjacent to the respective outcome branches. In this case and at this stage, they would be subjective probability estimates developed in accord with the elicitation procedure described in Chapter 6. Eventually they might be modified by the arrival of more information, such as the results of the market study.

Step 2.3   For each outcome, indicate the gross payoff that it provides • The payoff values of $100,000, $50,000, and $0 are shown in the parentheses at the tips of the respective outcome branches.

We will expand this tree in the next section, but for the purpose of demonstration, let us use it as the manager might—to help analyze the relative desirability of the three alternatives of large promotion, small promotion, and no promotion. Assuming that she wants to utilize the Maximize Expected Value decision rule from Chapter 6, the manager should apply the following step-by-step procedure.

Phases 1 and 2 involve identifying and acquiring the information relevant to the decision situation. Completing the next and last phase helps us make systematic use of this information.

Phase 3. Pruning the decision tree: Aggregating information

Step 3.1   Compute the net expected value at each outcome fork • As an example, we see that if the manager chooses to implement the large promotion, she will first pay out $55,000. She will then receive

[2]*In this example we will use monetary costs and payoffs as estimates of the utilities involved. If the utility for money were not directly proportional to the amount of money, a utility curve for money could be constructed using the methods of Chapter 5. The utilities would then be used as leaves in the decision tree.*

either \$100,000 with a probability of .50 or \$50,000 with a probability of .50. Thus the net expected value (NEV) at the outcome fork is

$$NEV = -55,000 + .50(100,000) + .50(50,000) = \$20,000.$$

Similarly, the NEV at the outcome fork associated with implementing the small promotion is

$$NEV = -27,500 + .50(50,000) + .50(50,000) = \$22,500.$$

The NEV associated with implementing no promotion is 0.

　　Step 3.2　Replace each outcome fork with the net expected value at that fork ● Figure 7–3 shows graphically that with these two steps the manager has computed the net expected value associated with each alternative and *pruned* off the branches whose values have been aggregated in the NEV computations. Completing these two steps helps the manager see two things: (1) unless the probability and payoff estimates are inaccurate, she should choose to implement the "small promotion" alternative, and (2) without the market study, the expected payoff *at the choice fork* of Figure 7–2 should be \$22,500.

Figure 7–3.　Decision Tree After Information Aggregation

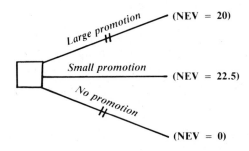

　　If the manager experiments with the NEV calculations, it is clear that the choice between the two better alternatives is sensitive to errors in the probability estimates. For example, if the probability that the large sales market exists is actually .60 rather than .50, then the large promotion would be favored and would reverse the presently indicated choice. This is shown in the following computations.

$$NEV \text{ (large promotion)} = -55,000 + .60(100,000)$$
$$+ .40(50,000) = 25,000.$$

$$\text{NEV (small promotion)} = -27,500 + .40(50,000)$$
$$+ .60(50,000) = 22,500.$$

Thus, if she had not been convinced before of the usefulness of a market test, she probably would be now. Even small changes in the present probability estimates could change the apparently preferable alternative.

Because the complexity of the decision situation increases when the alternative of a market study is considered, the manager might attempt to model the situation more completely with the decision tree shown in Figure 7-4. Inspection of Figure 7-4 shows that the manager has correctly determined that she should first decide whether to purchase the market study, and then decide what to do about running the promotion.[3] The figure also shows that, perhaps as a result of the calculations leading to Figure 7-3, the manager has decided to drop consideration of the alternative of no promotion.

Steps 1.1-3.2 pertain to decision situations with only one sequence of decisions (i.e., with one decision concerning the purchase of information followed by one decision concerning the choice of a strategy for solving the problem). The step-by-step procedure for using a decision tree that contains a sequence of two or more decisions is shown as Steps 1.1-3.4 of Table 7-1. It is an elaboration of the procedure described earlier.[4]

By applying Phase 1 of the procedure in Table 7-1 to the decision situation of Figure 7-4, we see that the first time Step 1.2 is completed, the "optimistic" and "pessimistic" outcome branches lead to the choice forks of "large promotion" and "small promotion," rather than to direct monetary payoffs. Therefore, Steps 1.3 and 1.4 were carried out, and Steps 1.1 and 1.2 were repeated. The second time Steps 1.1 and 1.2 were carried out, beginning at the "large promotion" versus "small promotion" choice fork, they provided market outcome branches that resulted

---

[3]*Discussions in the next two sections will explain how the probability values of Figure 7-4 were determined.*

[4]*We note here that the steps in Table 7-1 describe the development and use of decision trees, rather than the steps to be followed in making a decision. For example, in making the actual choice, the manager would undoubtedly implement Step 6 of the step-by-step decision-making procedure described in Chapter 6 (i.e., would "consider both the criteria not included in the analysis and the possible adverse consequences of choosing the highest scoring alternative"). A comparison of Chapter 6's step-by-step procedure for making decisions in uncertain situations and Table 7-1's step-by-step procedure for using decision trees shows that the procedure in Table 7-1 is one approach to carrying out Step 5 of Chapter 6. It is a particularly effective approach when the decision situation requires making a sequence of decisions.*

Figure 7-4. Decision Tree for Analyzing the Sequence of Decisions

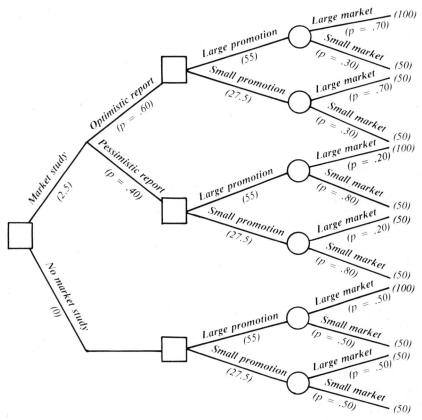

in payoffs rather than additional choice forks. The key feature of Steps 1.1-1.4, then, is that they guide the construction of a model for portraying decision situations where a sequence of choices or decisions is called for.

The example discussed on these last few pages demonstrates that decision trees, like other models, are useful aids in overcoming our cognitive limitations. It is much easier for managers and staffs to use the graphic portrayal of Figure 7-4 as an external memory than it is for them to deal with this decision situation while attempting to hold the same information in their heads. It is also apparent that Figure 7-4 is useful as an aid in communicating with others about various aspects of the decision situation. Thus, decision trees provide the same benefits as other

TABLE 7-1.   Procedure for Using a Decision Tree

Phase 1—Constructing a Decision Tree: Drawing the Branches
      Step 1.1   Lay out the alternatives as branches from a choice fork.
      Step 1.2   At the end of each alternative branch, lay out the possible
                  outcomes as branches from an outcome fork. (If all of these
                  outcomes results in direct payoffs rather than alternatives, go
                  to Phase 2.)
      Step 1.3   At the end of each outcome branch, lay out the alternatives
                  as branches from a choice fork.
      Step 1.4   Repeat Steps 1.1, 1.2, and 1.3 until the end of each outcome
                  branch results in a payoff rather than a choice fork.
Phase 2—Constructing a Decision Tree: Inserting the Leaves
      Step 2.1   For each alternative, indicate the cost of implementation.
      Step 2.2   For each outcome, indicate the probability of its occurrence.
      Step 2.3   Indicate the gross payoff provided by each of the rightmost
                  outcome branches.
Phase 3—Pruning the Decision Tree: Aggregating Information
      Step 3.1   Compute the net expected value at each of the rightmost out-
                  come forks.
      Step 3.2   Replace each of the rightmost outcome forks with the net ex-
                  pected value at that fork.
      Step 3.3   At each of the rightmost choice forks, eliminate each alter-
                  native branch except the one with the largest of the net ex-
                  pected values computed in Step 3.2, and treat the largest
                  NEV as the payoff for the outcome branch preceding the
                  choice fork.
      Step 3.4   Repeat Steps 3.1, 3.2, and 3.3 until the net expected value at
                  each alternative branch of the leftmost choice fork is com-
                  puted.

---

models. Their unique use, however, is yet to be discussed. Let us move
on to this discussion.

DECISION TREES AND THE VALUE OF INFORMATION

Earlier we mentioned that the unique contribution of decision
trees was as an aid in formally analyzing sequential decision situations
where earlier decisions were concerned with whether or not to search for
additional information. This section explains how to use decision trees in

conducting such analyses. Specifically, it explains how to use decision trees to calculate the value of information.

We begin by recalling that the manager's net expected payoff without the market study was $22,500. The use of the decision tree of Figure 7–4 can help determine what the net expected payoff would be with the market study. This is a very valuable figure to have; by comparing it with the NEV without the study, the manager can determine the value of the information provided by the market study. Stated more formally:

> The *value of information* is equal to the difference between the net expected payoff from the decision made without the information and the net expected payoff from the decision made with the information.

Computation of the value of information, in this case the market study, is a three-phase process. The first is to lay out or draw the basic structure of the tree. This phase (Phase 1) was described in the previous section and resulted in Figure 7–4. The second phase is as follows:

Phase 2. Constructing a decision tree: Inserting the leaves

Step 2.1   For each alternative, indicate the cost of implementation • As shown in Figure 7–4, the $2500 quoted cost of the market study and the $55,000 and $27,500 budgets for the large and small promotions are inserted.

Step 2.2   For each outcome, indicate the probability of its occurrence • Inspection of Figure 7–4 shows that there are three sets of probabilities to be determined. The first set consists of those probabilities estimated without an information search. In this case they are the .50 and .50 values that appear on the lower right branches of the decision tree. Because these values are determined prior to acquisitions of information gathered through search, they are called *prior probabilities*.

The second set of probabilities is associated with the outcomes of the search process. In this case they are the .6 and .4 values that appear below the two market study outcomes. Although they can be determined analytically, as shown in the appendix to this chapter, they can also be developed using the subjective probability elicitation procedure of Chapter 6. In either case they should reflect previous company experience with studies of this type.

Let us look at an example of how the values of .6 and .4 might follow from the use of managerial judgment. Assume that previous experience indicates that when a large market is available, marketing department studies will correctly indicate that this is so 90 percent of the time (p = .9). They will incorrectly indicate a small market 10 percent of the time (p = .1). On the other hand, when a small market is available the studies will incorrectly indicate a large market 30 percent of the time and a small market 70 percent of the time. Thus, in this example case, the market studies tend to be optimistic. The manager who knows this might reasonably estimate that if the actual probability of a large market is .50, the marketing department's studies will be optimistic (i.e., indicate a large market 60 percent of the time). She would therefore assign p = .60 as the probability estimate for receiving an optimistic report and p = .40 as that for receiving a pessimistic report.

The third set of probabilities that must be determined are those that reflect changes or revisions in prior probabilities. In other words, these probabilities are based on prior beliefs but reflect new information provided by the search, in this case the information provided by the market study. In Figure 7–4 the probabilities appear on the upper right branches of the decision tree. Although these values can be determined analytically, as shown in the chapter appendix, they can also be developed using the probability estimation procedure of Chatper 6. In either case, they should reflect both the manager's prior opinions and the possible market study results. For example, as shown in the decision situation portrayed in Figure 7–4, the manager decided that if the market study did indicate a potentially large sales increase, she would revise the probability estimates from .50 and .50 to .70 and .30. Knowing that the marketing studies were usually optimistic, she decided to revise the probabilities more radically if the result were pessimistic and determined to move from .50 and .50 to .20 and .80.

Step 2.3 Indicate the gross payoff provided by each of the rightmost outcome branches.

The third and final phase of the process that will determine whether to purchase the market study proceeds as follows:

Phase 3. Pruning the decision tree: Aggregating information

When aggregating information, we always aggregate at the rightmost forks first and proceed to the left.

Step 3.1   *Compute the net expected value at each of the right-most outcome forks.*

Step 3.2   *Replace each of the rightmost outcome forks with the net expected value at that fork* ● As an example, we see that the net expected value at the upper-right outcome fork is

NEV = − 55 + .70(100) + .30(50) = 30.

Figure 7–5 shows the results of carrying out these two steps for the rightmost set of outcome forks.

The next step recognizes that the manager is applying the MEV decision rule and at each choice fork will select the alternative with the highest net expected payoff.

Step 3.3   *At each of the rightmost choice forks, eliminate each alternative branch except the one with the largest of the net expected values computed in Step 3.2, and treat the largest NEV as the payoff for the outcome branch preceding the choice fork* ● The slash marks in certain of the branches of Figure 7–5 indicate which alternatives would be eliminated if the results of the market study were those shown in Figure 7–4 and if Step 3.3 were carried out. As an example, we see from Figure 7–5 that if the outcome of the market study were a pessimistic report, the manager's best choice would be to implement the small promotion.

Figure 7–5.   Decision Tree After Applying Steps 3.1 and 3.2 of the Pruning Procedure

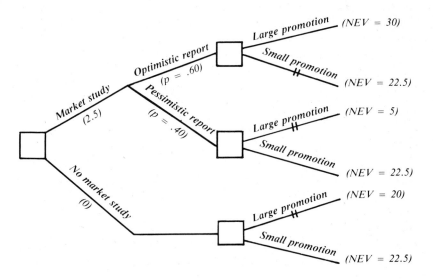

Figure 7-6 shows the result of this step. In actual practice, the pruning of the decision trees is often done by using an eraser or by scratching out, rather by drawing the pruned trees.

Step 4. Repeat Steps 3.1, 3.2, and 3.3 until the net expected value at each alternative branch of the leftmost choice fork is computed • From Figure 7-6 we see that the net expected value associated with purchasing the market study is

$$NEV = -2.50 + .60(30) + .40(22.5) = 24.50.$$

Since this value is greater than the NEV of 22.5 associated with the alternative of not purchasing the study, application of the MEV decision rule indicates that the manager should commission the study (i.e., should purchase the information).

Another way to decide whether to purchase the information is to think in terms of the "value of information" as it was defined earlier. In our example, the manager's expected payoff with the study is .60(30) + .40(22.5), or 27. The expected payoff without the study is 22.5. Therefore, the contribution or value of the study to the decision is 4.5 or $4500. Because in this case the price of information (2.5) is less than its value, the manager should make the purchase.

SUMMARY AND OVERVIEW

This chapter described how to develop and use a decision tree. The step-by-step procedure for doing so is summarized in Table 7-1.

Decision trees are the most sophisticated of the analytic decision aids that we have discussed and consequently involve the most computation. We made a distinction between a decision tree's use as an external memory and communication aid and its use as a guide in applying the MEV or MEU decision rules to decisions involving the possible purchase of additional information. Anyone can benefit from the first of these two uses. If the circumstances are appropriate and if the manager or the staff has a bent for arithmetic, he or she may also benefit from the second.

In Chapter 3 we pointed out that individual decision making, as it actually happens, produces decisions that are lower in quality than we would wish. This is in large part a consequence of our limited ability to identify and use the relevant information. Two approaches were noted as

Figure 7-6. Decision Tree After Applying Step 3.3 of the Pruning Procedure

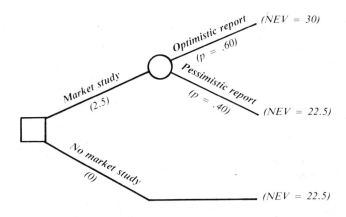

useful in overcoming this unfortunate state of affairs. One was for the manager to sharpen his or her thinking by applying one of the decision-aiding techniques that have been developed for identifying and using decision-related information. In this part of the book we have described a number of techniques that have proven themselves useful in this regard. The benefits derived from the use of these techniques include the following:

1. Developing and making explicit our view of the decision situation in the form of a model can help us identify the inadequacies in our implicit, mental model.

2. The attributes contained in the model serve as reminders of the information that should be obtained about each alternative. This helps avoid the common practice of evaluating one alternative on Attributes A, B, and E, while evaluating another alternative on Attributes A, C, and D, simply because in the one case one set of information was available while in the other a different set was at hand.

3. The information displays and graphical models that contain the information used in the mathematical model serve as organized external memories. Here we can efficiently record, analyze, and retrieve information, thus overcoming some of our limitations as processors of information.

4. The step-by-step procedure associated with the model enables us to aggregate large amounts of information in a

prescribed and systematic manner, rather than in a manner determined by the order in which the information appears or by the limits of our intellect.

5. The information displays and procedures associated with the model dramatically increase the ability of managers to communicate with those advisors who might be asked to help with the choice, with those superiors to whom they might have to justify the choice, or to those subordinates who might have to carry out the choice.

The second approach that was noted as useful for overcoming the manager's difficulties in identifying and using decision-relevant information was to extend intellectual and other resources through the use of decision-aiding groups. In the next and last part of the book we describe a number of techniques that are helpful in making groups effective aids to managers.

Before moving from analytic techniques to group-management techniques, it is important to note that all of the benefits that individual decision makers derive from the use of models are also derived by the individual members of a group. Perhaps the benefits are even greater, since the constant communication that goes on in a group intensifies the cognitive limitations of the individual participants. As a consequence, managers who involve groups in their decision-making efforts are advised to seriously consider using models to aid the reasoning, as well as the communications, of the group members.

APPENDIX

The purpose of this appendix is to describe the relationships that should apply among the probabilities in a decision tree. These relationships will be easier to understand if we base them on some definitions.

Definitions

Thoughtful review of the matter will show that there are four types of probabilities that play roles in the use of decision trees. One is a *prior probability*. A prior probability represents our degree of belief, prior to acquiring information directly related to the probability of a particular outcome, about how probable it is that the outcome will occur. Thus the two probabilities of .50 and .50 that appear in the lower right outcome fork of Figure 7–4 would be called prior probabilities because they were estimated prior to the acquisition of additional information (e.g., the market study). In this appendix we will denote the prior probability of the outcome "large market" as $P(O_l)$ and the prior probability of the outcome "small market" as $P(O_s)$.

Another of the four types of probabilities is called a *compound likelihood*.[5] A compound likelihood represents our degree of belief that a particular outcome (e.g., optimistic report) will occur. Thus the .60 and .40 values in Figure 7–4 would be called compound likelihoods, as would be any probabilities corresponding to the data outcomes of an information search effort. In this appendix we will denote the compound likelihood of the datum "optimistic report" as $P(D_o)$ and the compound likelihood of the datum "pessimistic report" as $P(D_p)$.

The third type of probability is called a *conditional likelihood*. A conditional likelihood represents our degree of belief about how probable it is that some outcome (e.g., optimistic report) will occur, given or assuming the existence of some other outcome (e.g., small market exists). Thus the .90 that we mentioned earlier as reflecting the probability that a report would be optimistic, given the outcome that a large market really existed, would be called a conditional likelihood. In the same paragraph we mentioned .30 as the conditional likelihood of the data of an optimistic report assuming the outcome of a small market.

In this appendix we will note the conditional likelihood of the datum "optimistic report" given the outcome "large market" as $P(D_o/O_l)$ and the likelihood of the datum "pessimistic report" given the outcome "small market" as $P(D_p/O_s)$.

The fourth and last type of probability is called a *posterior probability*. A posterior probability represents our degree of belief, after we modify the associated prior probability in light of any additional information, about how probable it is that an outcome will occur. Thus, the two probabilities of .70 and .30 in the upper right choice fork of Figure 7–4 would be called posterior probabilities. They indicate a revision of the prior beliefs about the existence of the markets, a revision based on the additional information provided by the market study.

In this appendix we will denote the posterior probability of the outcome "small market," given the datum "pessimistic report," as $P(O_s/D_p)$.

[5] *The adjective "compound" is somewhat superfluous and often not used. Its meaning will become clear later in this appendix.*

With these definitions in mind, let us return to the subject of the relationships that should apply among the probabilities.

Relationships

There are three relationships. One of these is the relationship among the probabilities at an outcome fork. It states that:

> At any outcome fork, the probabilities of the outcomes shown must sum to 1.00, or, if there are N outcomes,
> $P(O_1) + P(O_2) + \ldots + P(O_N) = 1.0.$

For example, in Figure 7-4, the two probabilities at the lower right outcome fork are .50 and .50 and sum to 1.00.

The second relationship associates the conditional likelihoods and the compound likelihoods. It is basically a definition which states that:

> The probability of any datum is a compound likelihood—a value equal to the weighted sum of the conditional likelihoods of that datum—where the weights are the probabilities of the outcomes that the conditional likelihoods depend upon.

This is truly a challenging definition, especially given the necessary but unfamiliar terminology. Fortunately, the relationship is more easily demonstrated than defined. Take, for example, the compound likelihood of .60 that represents the probability of encountering the datum "optimistic report." The datum "optimistic report," (D_o) can occur two ways. One way is for a large market (O_l) to exist. In this case the likelihood of an optimistic report is .90 (i.e., $P(D_o/O_l) = .90$). The other way is for a small market (O_s) to exist. In this case the likelihood of an optimistic report is .30 (i.e., $P(D_o/O_s) = .30$). According to the definition, the compound likelihood of the datum "optimistic report" is a weighted combination of .90 and .30, where the weights are the prior probabilities associated with the outcomes O_l and O_s. We, of course, have these two values. According to our present knowledge, the prior probability of the large market outcome is .50 (i.e., $P(O_l) = .50$).

The likelihood of .30 assumes the other outcome, a small market, which also had prior probability of .50 (i.e., $P(O_s) = .50$). Thus we have, following the relationship, the probability of the datum "optimistic report" as being equal to

$$P(D_o) = .60 = .90(.50) + .30(.50).$$

Moving from the use of these example numbers to the use of the definition, we see that the compound likelihood is equal to the weighted combination of the conditional likelihoods, as shown below.

$$P(D_o) = P(D_o/O_l)P(O_l) + P(D_o/O_s)P(O_s).$$

The probability of a pessimistic report can be computed in a similar manner. Common sense tells us that if the probability of an optimistic report, given a large market, is .90, then the probability of a pessimistic report, given a large market, is $1.00 - .90 = .10$. Similarly, the probability of a pessimistic report given a small market is $1.00 - .30 = .70$. Thus the overall probability of a pessimistic report is

$$P(D_p) = P(D_p/O_l)P(O_l) + P(D_p/O_s)P(O_s) = .10(.50) + .70(.50)$$
$$= .40.$$

We see in these examples that the probabilities of the various search outcomes in a decision tree can be obtained either by direct estimation, as they were in the chapter, or by computation. In either case they reflect experience (e.g., the .90 and .30 values were derived from observations of past events) and judgment (e.g., the prior probabilities of the assumed outcomes were based on the manager's judgments which themselves were based on experience).

The third relationship associates posterior probabilities with the other three types of probabilities.[6] It is called Bayes theorem, after Sir Thomas Bayes, the man who developed it. Basically it states that:

> The posterior probability of an outcome, given some datum, is equal to the prior probability of the outcome multiplied by the ratio of the conditional likelihood of the datum given the outcome to the compound likelihood of the datum.

The definition is again more easily demonstrated than defined. Take, for example, the posterior probability of a large market outcome given an optimistic report, or $P(O_l/D_o)$. Common sense tells us to revise

[6]For a discussion of Bayes theorem, see W. Edwards, Hays Phillips, and B. C. Goodman, "Probabilistic Information Processing Systems: Design Evaluation," IEEE Transactions on Systems and Cybernetics SSC-4 (Sept. 1968): 248–265.

our prior probability of a large market outcome, $P(O_l) = .50$, upwards because of the optimistic report. The question is, "How far upwards should we revise it?" The answer from the relationship stated above is, "as much as is indicated by the ratio of the conditional likelihood, $P(D_o/O_l) = .90$, to the unconditional likelihood, $P(D_o) = .60$." Thus

$$P(O_l/D_o) = P(O_l) \frac{P(D_o/O_l)}{P(D_o)} = .50 \frac{.90}{.60} = .75.$$

We see that the manager's own logic, described in the chapters, led to a revision of prior opinions in the right direction. These revisions did not go far enough, however.[7] Research shows that this conservative approach to probability revision, referred to as reflecting the bias of *conservatism* is rather pervasive.

There are four posterior probabilities in Figure 7–4. We have already computed the correct magnitude of one, $P(O_l/D_o)$. The others would be computed as follows.

$$P(O_s/D_o) = P(O_s) \frac{P(D_o/O_s)}{P(D_o)} = .50 \frac{.30}{.60} = .25.$$

Given an optimistic report for both, this probability of a small market added to the probability of a large market must sum to 1.00, according to the first of the three relationships described earlier in the appendix.

$$P(O_l/D_p) = P(O_l) \frac{P(D_p/O_l)}{P(D_p)} = .50 \frac{.10}{.40} = .125.$$

Here, too, we see conservatism being manifested, as the manager did not revise quite far enough from the prior probability of .50.

$$P(O_s/D_p) = P(O_s) \frac{P(D_p/O_s)}{P(D_p)} = .50 \frac{.70}{.40} = .875.$$

These last two probabilities also must sum to 1.00, as they do.

---

[7] *Recall that it was revised upwards to .60.*

OPPORTUNITIES FOR FURTHER THOUGHT

1. Lay out the branches and insert the leaves of a decision tree that represents a single choice situation, such as that of Figure 7–2, rather than a sequential choice situation.
2. Apply the MEU decision rule to the tree you just drew.
3. Describe a decision situation that could be more effectively modeled with a decision tree than with a decision matrix. Explain why a decision tree would be the more effective.
4. Lay out the branches of the decision tree corresponding to the decision situation you just described.
5. Use the posterior probabilities developed in the appendix in place of those shown in Figure 7–4 to determine the value of the market study.
6. Lay out the branches and insert the leaves of a decision tree that represents a sequential choice situation, such as that of Figure 7–4. Use what you think are reasonable estimates of the probabilities involved.
7. Use the relationships described in the appendix of the chapter to check the reasonableness of the above estimates. Do not check them in terms of their accuracy but in terms of their consistency as defined by the rules of probability and Bayes theorem.

REFERENCES AND RELATED READINGS

Brown, Rex V. "Do Managers Find Decision Theory Useful?" *Harvard Business Review*, (May–June 1970): 78–89.

Brown, R. V., A. S. Kahr, and C. Peterson. *Decision Analysis for the Manager.* New York: Holt, Rinehart and Winston, 1974.

Decision Analysis Group. *Readings in Decision Analysis.* Menlo Park, Calif.: Stanford Research Institute, 1976.

Edwards, W., H. Phillips, and B. C. Goodman. "Probabilistic Information Processing Systems: Design Evaluation." *IEEE Transactions on Systems and Cybernetics* SSC–4 (Sept. 1968): 248–265.

Hayes, Robert H. "Qualitative Insights From Quantitative Methods." *Harvard Business Review* (July–August 1969): 108–117.

Keeney, R. L. and H. Raiffa. *Decisions with Multiple Objectives:*

Preferences and Value Tradeoffs. New York: John Wiley and Sons, Inc., 1976.

Tummala, V. M. Rao, and Richard C. Henshaw, eds. *Concepts and Applications of Modern Decision Models.* East Lansing, Mich.: Michigan State University Business Studies, 1976.

Part Three
Group Decision Making

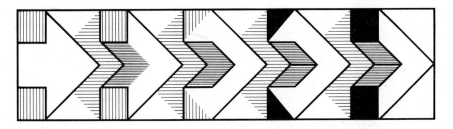

8

How to Decide Who Should Decide: Groups as Aids to Decision Makers

Committees, review panels, study teams, task forces, and other groups are a familiar fact of organizational life. They are frequently an important component of the overall organizational decision-making process. Because the manager who knows when and how to use such groups will be more successful than one who does not, this and the next several chapters describe and discuss procedures, guidelines, and techniques for determining when and how to use groups in the overall decision-making process. In particular, the purpose of Chapters 9–11 is to help managers increase the effectiveness of the groups they choose to include in their decision-making efforts. The purpose of this chapter is to help managers decide when to include groups in decision-making efforts.

In most instances, the following discussion uses the word "group" to refer to an interacting face-to-face assemblage of people. When this is not the case, and the word takes on a special meaning, we note the fact and define what we mean more precisely.

There are four main sections in the chapter. The first is introductory and includes a description of the decision-related tasks that managers frequently delegate to groups. The second examines the advantages of using groups to carry out such tasks, and the third examines the disadvantages. The fourth section presents guidelines for deciding when to use groups as aids in the managerial decision-making process.

WHY USE GROUPS?

Our everyday observations remind us that managers often use groups to help them in their decision-making efforts. There are two major reasons for this. One concerns the limited personal resources that any individual manager can bring to bear on any particular decision. From our earlier discussion of the limits on rationality, we know that an individual manager's decision-making ability is quite constrained by his or her cognitive limitations, time availability, and information accessibility. The intelligent use of a decision-aiding group, however, enables the manager to supplement resources by increasing the amount of information and information processing that can be used in the decision-making task. In this way, the group becomes an extension of the manager.

The second major reason managers involve groups is that the effectiveness of decision implementation is considerably affected by whether the decision is accepted by decision implementors. Early research by decision scientists demonstrated that most people were more willing to accept decisions that they had participated in making. This research found its way into management literature and management courses. It is now an accepted part of managerial thinking and practice.

There are many situations where one or both of these reasons cause managers to use groups as aids in their decision making. The following is a brief listing of tasks that are typically assigned to decision-aiding groups.

1. *Analyzing the problem.* Groups are often directed to identify and define a problem and to diagnose its causes.

2. *Identifying components of the decision situation.* This task is largely associated with developing the three basic types of information used in decision making (i.e., with identifying alternatives, criteria, and future conditions). However, it is also associated with identifying problem symptoms and unfulfilled goals during the problem-exploration step that was discussed in Chapter 2.

3. *Estimating components of the decision situation.* One of the tasks that managers frequently delegate is the development

of estimates. For example, groups are typically directed to estimate the probabilities of various outcomes, the payoffs associated with various outcomes, or the specific magnitudes of certain constraints (e.g., the time available to complete a specific project).

4. *Designing alternatives.* This task generally involves a high level of interaction among group members. Its purpose is to create a new alternative, presumably superior to any other. Examples include a complex allocation of funds among projects, a schedule of target completion times for a group of interrelated construction activities, or a set of decision rules and contingency plans for dealing with a military situation.

5. *Choosing an alternative.* Under some circumstances, to be discussed later, managers may direct groups to make the final choice. In others, the groups are made responsible for only one of the tasks just discussed and are not involved in making a final choice among alternatives. On the other hand, choosing the constraints or the probability estimates to be used in choice making are group tasks that involve the same type of evaluation efforts as making the final choice does. Thus, in many situations, decision-aiding groups are also decision-making groups.

Although the primary focus of this chapter and this book is the use of groups that are aids to, responsible to, and subordinate to individual managers, we should not lose sight of the fact that many groups in our organizations and our communities have a great deal of autonomy. They also address decision situations of their own choosing, and are clearly involved in decision making as contrasted with decision aiding. Examples include governing boards in both the private and public sectors, legislatures and legislative committees, university departmental faculties, standing committees in various organizations (such as grievance committees), and ad hoc groups created by their members to attack a common problem.

In many respects, autonomous groups such as these are similar to those groups that are subordinate to individual managers. For example, just as a manager—or the person appointed as group leader—engages in planning, organizing, staffing, directing, and controlling, for and with respect to the group, so too must a more autonomous group—or the person it chooses as its leader—engage in these managerial functions. As another example of the similarity, we can see that the five group tasks listed are not the exclusive domain of subordinate groups but are carried out by autonomous groups as well.

Because these two types of groups are so similar, and because managers, as leaders in their organizations and communities are called upon to be members and leaders of both types, our discussion will refer to both subordinate and autonomous groups. Thus, to facilitate our discussions (unless the context prohibits it), we use the term *decision group* to mean either a subordinate or an autonomous group—a group with either decision-aiding or decision-making responsibilities.

Let us turn to a discussion of the advantages and disadvantages of decision groups as contrasted with individual decision makers.

ADVANTAGES OF USING DECISION GROUPS

The use of a decision group can have three benefits to a manager:

1. The group might make better decisions than any one individual—including the manager.
2. The group may later be more effective in implementing decisions if the members participated in making the decisions.
3. Participation in the decision process may be a useful technique for training and developing subordinates.

Let us look more specifically at the reasoning that supports these conclusions.

One supporting argument is that *groups have more information and knowledge.* In situations where necessary information is not readily available (as is the case where a novel idea or little-known fact is critical to solving a problem), the likelihood that the information exists in a group is much higher than the likelihood that it exists in the mind of any one member. In situations where the critical need is for knowledge about how to put all the information together, it is more likely that previous experience in aggregating such information will exist within a group than it is that such an experience will be in the background of an individual.

Another reason why groups can sometimes make better decisions than individuals is that *groups make fewer errors in using information.* Because group members do have different viewpoints and backgrounds, it is less likely that an information-processing error will go unnoticed in a group setting than in a setting where one person works alone. Information usage errors range from a simple error in arithmetic to a political error in misreading the views of some influential person.

A particularly common error made by individual problem solvers is that they get into a rut in their approach to solving a problem or class of problems. Perhaps they overlearned from some previous instance where a particular solution worked well, or perhaps they were never exposed to some of the available alternative solutions. For example, in attempting to increase savings deposits, a marketing manager might be overly influenced by a single experience with a similar problem where radio advertising resulted in a large increase in the number of new depositers. Actually, newspaper advertising or a phone call campaign to increase the amount deposited by current depositers might be more effective approaches. Or, for example, in attempting to reduce the loss of life due to a given disease, one expert may focus on cures when actually immunization or improved sanitation might be more useful. If multiple experts were to attack these problems, it is more likely that these other approaches would surface and be considered.

The fact that groups generally have more information and a greater ability to use it correctly gives them an important advantage over individual decision makers. This has been demonstrated both mathematically and experimentally. It is particularly true when the decision problem is difficult, but is most easily demonstrated when the problem is simple, as in estimating the date of some future occurrence. The random errors that individual experts might make in arriving at such an estimate tend, in the long run, to cancel each other out. For example, the sales estimates from four sales managers might be 800, 750, 700, and 650. If the correct answer is actually found to be 710, the average error obtained by using the estimate from any one of these supposedly equivalent experts would have been 50, but the error obtained when using the group estimate of $725 = (800 + 750 + 700 + 650)/4$ would have been much less. This tendency for group averages to be more accurate is statistical in nature, but it has also been demonstrated in the small group laboratory.

As we noted earlier, members of a group will generally be more effective in implementing a decision if they are involved in making the decision. One reason for this is the fact that *participation in decision making increases acceptance of the decision.* In many cases, implementation of a plan or decision must be carried out by people who could be involved in the planning or decision-making process itself. Aside from the fact that their participation might increase the quality of the decision, it will very likely increase their acceptance of the decision and their enthusiasm for seeing it through. This motivational aspect of participation is important because if a manager makes a decision, he or she has the additional task of persuading others to carry it out. However, if several of these "others" participate in making the decision, it follows that there are both fewer people to persuade and more people to help with the persuading.

A second reason that people tend to be more effective in implementing decisions in which they have been involved is that *participation in decision making increases understanding of the decision.* Decisions made by an individual must be communicated to others. It is impossible for this communication to contain all of the information that led to the particular choice. Yet this information could be critical to those implementing the decision. If these implementors participate in making the decision, they not only better understand the solution because they see it develop, but they are also aware of the other alternatives under consideration and the reasons why they are discarded. In addition, they are more aware of the assumptions used in making the choice and of the way in which the choice is intended to meet the various organizational goals and constraints. Finally, the information and social exchange that takes place in the decision-making effort tends to facilitate later communications among those who must work together in the implementation phase of the overall problem-solving effort.

The third benefit obtained from group decision making is that *participation in decision making increases the information and skills that the group members may need for future organizational assignments.* For example, in order to increase a junior manager's understanding of the issues and considerations important to other organizational units or other managerial levels, a manager might assign this person to a problem-solving task force that included members from these other units or levels. Or, in order to increase the interpersonal or decision-making skills of some newly employed subordinate, a manager might assign him or her to a committee where these skills would likely be demonstrated by other committee members and would be required of the subordinate. It is common knowledge that information and skills are best learned by firsthand observation and application. Participation in problem-solving groups and committees is often an effective way to provide such a learning environment.

To summarize the advantages of group decision making, we can say that: (1) the availability and processing of information tend to be more complete when the decision-making unit is a group rather than an individual; (2) the acceptance and understanding of the decision by those involved in implementing it tend to be more complete when these people are also involved in making it; and (3) the information and skills available to subordinates can be increased by including them in the decision process.

Because these advantages are important ones, and because participation in decision making is a rather widespread expectation in our society, it is easy to conclude that almost all organizational decisions are or should be made in a group context. Before accepting this point of view, however, we should consider the disadvantages of group decision making.

DISADVANTAGES OF USING DECISION GROUPS

There are four disadvantages to a manager's involvement of groups in his or her decision-making process:

1. Groups tend to consume more personnel time in making a decision than does an individual.

2. Groups sometimes make decisions that are not in keeping with the goals of higher organizational levels.

3. Organizational members may come to expect that they will be involved in all decisions. They may then resist subsequent decisions that are appropriately but unilaterally handed down from higher organizational levels.

4. Disagreements among the members may result in the group's being unable to reach a decision, thus delaying progress on solving the problem and leading to ill will among the group members.

When the time of potential group members is a scarce organizational resource, it is reasonable for the manager, or perhaps some other person, to make some decisions alone. This saves others the time and trouble of joining in the decision-making process. The goals and decisions of higher organizational levels may also be more likely to be in keeping with the composite demands of clients, customers, special interest groups, the public at large, and governing agencies than are the goals and decisions of the lower levels. It is then reasonable for higher organizational levels—perhaps a single executive—to make the decisions.

Let us look now at some of these disadvantages of group decision making in more detail. With regard to the fact that *groups tend to consume more personnel time in making a decision,* we must remind ourselves that besides spending time exchanging task-related information, group members spend time in traveling to and from the meeting. Group leaders and their assistants spend time in arranging the meeting. In addition, the results of research studies remind us that before members fully devote themselves to the assigned task, they take some time to acquaint or reacquaint themselves with each other and to develop a set of interpersonal relationships. In some cases the marginal advantage gained by using a group may not compensate for these losses in the personnel time expended. In other cases, the deadline for making the decision may not allow time to free the potential group members from their other responsibilities.

Turning now to the problem that *groups sometimes make decisions that are not in keeping with the goals of higher organizational levels,* we note as an example that the decisions to integrate minorities into blue collar workforces have been made at the top organizational levels, where the demands of governmental and social action groups are most frequently directed. These demands, pressures, and social concerns result in participation in the decision process being restricted to those who would accept as paramount the goal of satisfying these demands, as opposed to a goal of maintaining a workforce of persons with similar cultural heritages and norms. As a further example, salary and promotion decisions are frequently made at higher organizational levels because it is believed that not all subordinate groups would use contribution to the organization as their principal decision-making criterion. Although this belief may not be justified, it is perpetuated by the demand of organized employee groups that a principal decision criterion be length of tenure in the organization and by the inclination of the public to elect movie stars, astronauts, and sports figures to public offices.

With respect to the possibility that the frequent use of *group decision making may cause organizational members to resist decisions made without their participation,* we remind ourselves of what we commonly observe. Organizational members tend to rely heavily on tradition and precedent as guides in shaping their expectations of what the organizational decision processes will and should be. This is as true of staff members expecting to be involved in business policy as it is of children expecting to be involved in family decisions about dining out. College professors accustomed to participating in university governance are resentful when administrators unilaterally decide to drop a field of study due to low student enrollment. Those unaccustomed to participating regard such decisions as natural.

Finally, we must consider the possibility that *disagreement among the members may result in the group's being unable to reach a decision.* Such an impass may result from disagreement about either how the group should proceed or what its choice should be. Although an intervention by the manager, perhaps even a dismissal of the group, can be used to resolve the difficulty, the possibility of this occurrence is certainly a disadvantage to be noted.

To summarize these disadvantages we can say that:

1. A greater amount of personnel time tends to be consumed in group decision making.

2. Goals other than those considered most important by top management are more likely to be involved in group decision making.

3. Unwanted expectations that future decisions will involve group participation may be a consequence of previous group participation.

4. Disagreement among members may result in the group's being unable to reach a decision.

Let us turn from this overview of the advantages and disadvantages of using decision groups to a more specific examination of guidelines for deciding when to use groups as aids in the managerial decision-making process.

GUIDELINES FOR DECIDING WHEN TO USE DECISION GROUPS

When should managers use groups to aid in decision making? This is a complex question. Fortunately, it can be broken down into four more manageable questions:

1. When should we involve others in our decision making?

2. When should we direct those involved, our advisors, to work as a group?

3. When should we include ourselves in the group?

4. When should we delegate final decision-making authority to the group?

The answers to the first two questions are, in combination, the answer to when we should use groups to help us in our decision making. The answers to the second two questions respond to a closely related issue—the manner in which we use such groups.

Figure 8-1 portrays the relationships among these questions and the outcomes that follow from the answers. Let us move on to some guidelines for arriving at the correct answers. We begin with the first question.

When should we involve others in our decision making?

This question is relatively easy to answer in most decision situations. Managers tend to answer it by determining how the previously discussed advantages and disadvantages of using groups apply to the decision situation with which they are currently faced. Note that we are not yet addressing the question of whether the manager should use groups (interacting members), but rather we are simply determining whether it would be useful to involve others, regardless of whether their involvement is as individual advisors or as members of an appointed decision group.

Drawing on our earlier discussion of the advantages and disadvantages of using groups, we can offer the following guidelines:

1. If increased availability or processing of information would increase the quality of the decision, then we should involve those who could be helpful in providing or processing this information.

2. If acceptance or understanding of the decision might be an issue, then we should involve those whose acceptance and understanding is important.

3. If developmentally useful information or skills would result from involvement in the decision process, then we should involve those whose development is important and who would profit from the resulting information and skill-building activity.

The fact that these conditions are commonplace may explain why many of the decisions made on behalf of organizations are made, not by individual managers, but by groups or managers who have involved their subordinates, peers, or superiors.

Still, there are situations where the manager might choose not to involve people who (on the basis of the three guidelines listed above) we

Figure 8–1. A Procedure for Deciding Who Should Decide

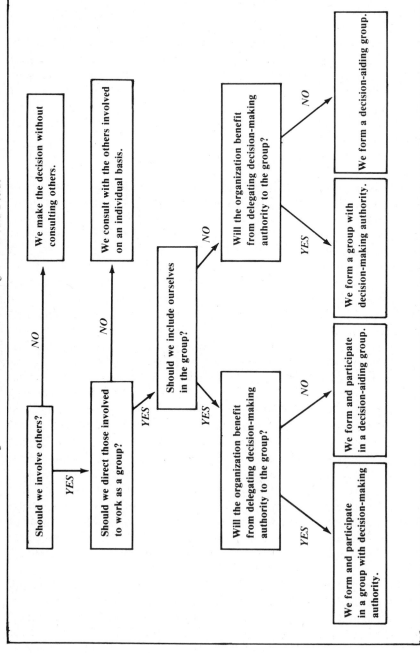

might expect to see involved. In many of these situations we would find that the following commonsense guideline had been applied.

> 4. If it appears that the time necessary to involve certain individuals or groups would not be justified by the advantages gained from the involvement, then we should avoid the involvement.

Of course the "time" we speak of could be either the time of the others, our own time, or both.

This guideline follows directly from the first of the three disadvantages of decision-making groups that we examined earlier. The second disadvantage—that the other people involved might make decisions not in keeping with the manager's goals—is more applicable to the issue of delegation of authority and will be addressed when we discuss that issue. The third disadvantage—that organizational members may expect that they will be involved in all decisions—is seldom really an issue. It can generally be circumvented by making clear that the prerogative of involving others will remain with the manager and that the current involvement is not to be viewed as establishing a precedent.

The fifth and last of the guidelines is not often applicable, but is important when it is applicable. If the decision is an unpopular one, those involved may lose the respect, liking, or future cooperation of their coworkers. Managers tend not to suffer these consequences; their positions and the recognized need for them to make some decision, even an unpopular one, protects them to a considerable extent. This is not true of subordinates, however. As a consequence, a manager may choose in some instances to protect subordinates by not involving them in a decision process that is likely to lead to an unpopular choice. The following guideline may be employed:

> 5. If it appears that the final decision will be an unpopular one, and if it appears that the consequent damage to a subordinate's relationship with his or her peers would not be justified by the advantages to be gained from his or her involvement, then we should avoid the involvement if possible.

The "if possible" qualifier is a recognition of the fact that job responsibilities of certain subordinates may require their involvement. If this is the case, the negative feedback from their coworkers is then part of the price of holding their job. On the other hand, if we see that the ultimate choice is likely to be unpopular, then endangering a subordinate's relationship with coworkers because his or her involvement might be marginally useful or would lend support to the decision would be viewed by many as shortsighted and, perhaps, uncourageous.

These five guidelines, rephrased as considerations in Section A of Table 8-1, have focused on the question of whether to involve others in the decision-making process. Assuming that we do decide to involve others, the next question concerns whether we should draw upon them as individuals—perhaps in a series of one-on-one briefings—or whether we should direct them to work as a decision group and submit a collective report. If we decide to use others as advisors, another question arises.

When should we direct our advisors to work as a group?

Note that in addressing this question we are not asking whether the manager should be included in the group. We are asking whether it

TABLE 8-1.   Considerations in Deciding When to Use Decision Groups

A. Considerations in Deciding Whether to Involve Others
    1. Would involvement increase quality?
    2. Would involvement increase acceptance or understanding?
    3. Would involvement develop personnel?
    4. Would involvement waste time?
    5. Would involvement damage subordinates' relationships?
B. Considerations in Deciding Whether a Group Should Be Formed
    1. Would interaction help quality?
    2. Would interaction increase motivation?
    3. Would disagreement be useful or damaging?
    4. Would interaction conserve or waste time?
C. Considerations in Deciding Whether to Include Ourselves
    1. Can anyone else provide sufficiently strong leadership?
    2. Can anyone else answer unanticipated questions?
    3. Would our participation inhibit the surfacing of sensitive (but important) information?
D. Considerations in Deciding Whether to Delegate Final Decision-Making Authority
    1. Would delegation save time?
    2. Would delegation increase motivation?
    3. Could the goals or abilities of the group members lead to a choice of less than adequate quality?

would be most useful for him or her to receive a single group-determined input or separate inputs from each of the individuals involved.

There are four guidelines that can be used to help answer this question. The first refers back to our earlier discussions of the cognitive limits on our rationality and acknowledges the fact that managerial decision situations typically require information-processing capabilities that are beyond any one person. If the decision situation is highly structured, then we can use the models and techniques of previous sections as aids in our information-processing efforts. If, on the other hand, the situation is unstructured, we will often find that it can be advantageously structured through the collective and interactive efforts of a number of people. For example, people exchanging information in a group may be able to sort out contingencies and trade-offs that individuals working separately could not. Thus, one guideline for determining whether to use groups is:

> 1. If the decision situation is at present unstructured and if it appears that interaction among our advisors would be helpful in structuring it, then we should involve these advisors as a group.

The second guideline follows from the fact that individuals working in the presence of others are often more productive than when working alone. There are exceptions, of course, as when some group members disrupt the thinking of other group members. Generally speaking, however, one of two motivating forces will be present and lead to greater performance: (1) the mildly competitive environment that is frequently observed when people attempt tasks in the presence of others, or (2) the possibility of group approval for unusually helpful contributions. Thus the second guideline is:

> 2. If increased motivation is likely to result from interaction within the group, then we should involve our advisors as a group.

What are the arguments against involving our advisors as a group? One is that disagreements among the group members, concerning, for example, how to proceed or what the group should recommend, can result in the group's being unable to function. Good group management practices, like those to be discussed in Chapter 10, will eventually overcome this problem. However, we cannot always count on either good group management practices being present or on the time being available for them to work if they are. On the other hand, experience shows that disagreement often causes people to see and understand issues that they had not recognized before. In addition, disagreement often results in the development of more creative alternatives. These ideas suggest that we consider the third and fourth guidelines:

> 3. If disagreements among the group members are likely to result in the group's being unable to carry out its assignment, then we should not involve our advisors as a group.
> 4. If disagreement is likely to result in increased understanding or more creative solutions, we should involve our advisors as a group.

The last guideline concerned with using decision groups, as opposed to individual advisors, is an attempt to deal simultaneously with two facts. One of these is that interviews with a series of advisors will often provide redundant information and thus reduce the efficiency of the overall information-gathering process. For example, the time involved in having a series of meetings with individual advisors may be greater than the time involved in having one meeting with all. If the information generated is the same in either case, then the single meeting is the more efficient procedure. Also, as we noted earlier, there are time losses within group meetings as the members attempt to relate to one another and manage their group. These time expenditures are necessary for the group to function but do not directly contribute to the group carrying out its assignment.

Since these two facts, both concerning the issue of time utilization, lead to different conclusions, the resulting guideline is:

> 5. If all else is equal, advisors should be involved in the way that minimizes the cost of the time expended.

Put in this way, we can see that the time of both the manager and his subordinates must be considered. These guidelines are rephrased as considerations in Section B of Table 8–1.

If we do decide to direct our advisors to function as a group, another question follows.

When should we include ourselves in the group?

In order to answer this question, it will be useful to first comment on the closely related matter of leadership. The manager who creates a group to help make decisions has the ultimate responsibility of carrying out the managerial functions for the group. The manager must do the initial *planning,* as well as the *organizing, staffing, directing,* and *controlling.* Although the functions of planning, organizing, or staffing are seldom delegated, those of directing and controlling are. The person who carries out these latter two functions is the *group leader.* Sometimes the group leader is the manager. Other times it is the manager's appointee. Sometimes leadership is shared; different group members may take the lead at various points in a given meeting.

Most decision groups have formally appointed or elected leaders. The widespread use of leaders follows from recognition of the fact that groups without formal leaders sometimes encounter leadership voids—periods where they flounder for lack of direction and control. On other occasions, little or no progress is made when two or more members compete to become the leader. In addition, if the formal leader sees the need for shared leadership at some particular point in the proceedings, he or she can always choose to exert little or no control. This creates the opportunity for shared leadership to evolve.

As a consequence of these considerations, it seems that in the great majority of instances and for the sake of maximizing the group's effectiveness, the manager who creates a decision group should either appoint a formal leader or require that the group appoint one. In view of this observation and the fact that most decision groups do have formal leaders, we will proceed with the rest of our discussion as if the decision groups to which we refer have formal leaders.

Now let us return to the basic question of when we should include ourselves in the group. The answers and guidelines are, individually, not complex.

> 1. If it seems that no one else could provide sufficiently strong leadership, then we should include ourselves as the group leader.

An example of such a situation is one where we expect a good deal of conflict and disagreement and have no one we could appoint as leader who has the influence and ability to deal with these conditions.

> 2. If it seems that the group will, from time to time, have an unanticipated need for information that only we can provide, then we should include ourselves in the group.

An example of such a situation is where the decision group is to explore a problem and only we know the background of certain of the problem symptoms. Another example is where the group is attempting to design a solution to the problem and only we can make judgments as to the rigidity of the constraints.

The next guideline suggests that we should not include ourselves.

> 3. If it seems that our presence would inhibit the surfacing of sensitive and important information, then we should not include ourselves.

An example of such a situation is the case where we wanted the group to provide an analysis that was independent of what its members thought we might want to hear.

These three guidelines are rephrased as considerations in Section C of Table 8–1. They address the question, "Can the group complete its assignment more effectively without our participation?" If the answer is "yes," then we should not include ourselves. By not participating we will save our time and thus fulfill the purpose of using the group.

Let us turn now to the last of our four questions.

When should we delegate final decision-making authority to the group?

There are two reasons for delegating decision-making authority. One is to save ourselves the effort of reviewing the group's decision when we know in advance that we will be relatively indifferent to whatever the decision may be. The other is to motivate the group members to work harder on making the decision and to be more accepting and enthusiastic about its implementation. These two reasons lead to the following three guidelines.

> 1. If it appears that delegating final authority would save our time, then we should delegate this authority.
> 2. If it appears that delegating final authority would result in increased motivation, then we should delegate this authority.

The disadvantage of delegating final authority is, of course, that we could not alter what we might know to be a poor choice. Thus the third guideline is the following.

> 3. If it appears that either the goals or the ability of the group members could lead to choices that we would judge to be of poor

quality, and if it is important that the final choice be of moderate or better quality, then we should not delegate final decision-making authority.

These guidelines are rephrased as considerations in the Section D of Table 8-1.

SUMMARY AND OVERVIEW

In this chapter we examined the question of how to decide who should decide. Specifically we looked at how to decide when and in what manner to use groups in decision making. We began by reviewing five tasks that decision groups frequently engage in (i.e., the tasks of analyzing the problem, identifying the components of the decision situation, estimating these components, designing alternatives, and choosing among alternatives). We then examined the advantages and disadvantages of using decision groups as contrasted with carrying out these five tasks ourselves. Finally, we reviewed sets of guidelines for answering four questions that, in total, respond to the original question of how to decide who should decide.

Let us turn now to a new set of questions. If we decide to use groups, how should we use them? More particularly, how should we manage them? What preparations should we make before the group actually is directed to function? How should individual meetings be directed and controlled? These and similar questions are answered in the next three chapters. We begin, in the next chapter, by describing how to plan for, organize, and staff a decision group.

OPPORTUNITIES FOR FURTHER THOUGHT

1. Recall the situation of a decision-aiding group of which you were a member. What was its specific assignment? Explain why you think it was wise or unwise for the group to be given this assignment.
2. Consider a decision that you or another manager made with respect to the use of groups. Using the guidelines associated with those of the four questions that apply, see if you replicate the

decision that was made. If you do not, explain why you think
you do not.

3.   Think of a decision that you will have to make concerning the
use of groups. Using the guidelines associated with those of the
four questions that apply, arrive at a decision about who should
participate. Does it agree with your intuitive feelings about the
matter? If it does not, explain why you think it does not.

4.   Jane Smith has been the manager of the Customer Complaints
Department of a large retailing company for the past three years.
During that period, the number of complaints received by the
company has increased very slowly, but the backlog of unpro-
cessed complaints has increased almost 50 percent. At present the
average time to process a complaint is more than twenty working
days. Smith is becoming increasingly concerned about this situation and has decided to explore this problem situation. She is
presently deciding if and how to involve her staff in finding the
cause of the problem and, if necessary, in making the changes
necessary to solve it.

What would you suggest is an appropriate procedure in this decision situation? Base your answer on the questions and guidelines
in this chapter.

REFERENCES AND RELATED READINGS

Maier, N. F. *Problem Solving and Creativity in Individuals and Groups.*
       Belmont, Calif.: Brooks/Cole Publishing Company, 1970.
Stumpf, S. A., D. E. Zand, and R. D. Freedman. "Designing Groups for
       Judgmental Decisions." *The Academy of Management Review*
       4 (Oct. 1979): 589–600.
Vroom, V. H. and P. W. Yetton. *Leadership and Decision Making.*
       Pittsburgh: University of Pittsburgh Press, 1973.

9

Group Decision Making and the Management of Committees: Planning, Organizing, and Staffing

This chapter and the next describe guidelines, tactics, and step-by-step procedures that will enable the manager to more effectively manage committees, task forces, and other forms of decision groups. Employment of these aids will both improve group performance and increase the satisfaction of group members.

This chapter describes what the manager in charge of a decision group needs to do before the group begins to function. The chapter's guidelines refer to the *planning, organizing,* and *staffing* functions associated with activating a decision group. The following chapter describes what a manager should do before and during individual group meetings. Its guidelines refer to the *directing* and *controlling* functions associated with managing a decision group. Both chapters are oriented toward managing the familiar face-to-face interacting group, as contrasted with brainstorming groups, nominal groups, and Delphi groups. The management of these less traditional and specially designed and directed groups will be discussed in Chapter 11.

We will make no distinction in the following discussion between the manager who creates a group to aid his or her decision making and the manager who is appointed as the leader of a group created by some-

159

one else. The guidelines and procedures presented are applicable and useful in either case. We will simply refer to "the manager," and mean by this the person who, because of either hierarchal authority or temporary assignment, is responsible for the group's results.

This chapter is divided into three main sections, each dealing with a separate task. The first concerns *defining the group's assignment.* This involves getting answers to the fundamental questions about the group's purpose, responsibility, and needs. The second section concerns *planning the overall group effort* in terms of completion dates, resources needed, and coordination with other groups. The third section concerns *organizing and staffing the group.* This includes choosing the group members and assigning them roles if this is desirable (e.g., choosing the group leader).

DEFINING THE GROUP'S ASSIGNMENT

To explain what is involved in defining the group's assignment, let us consider the three questions that the manager must eventually answer.

1. What is the issue the group must deal with? • What is its nature? Is the issue, for example, concerned with reducing absenteeism or with improving employee morale? What is its scope? Will the group be concerned with reducing absenteeism in Department A or in the whole organization?

Although answering issue-oriented questions such as these is not always easy (especially if organizational factions have different views on the nature of the problem that should be solved), it is certainly necessary. If the manager does not make the issue explicit, the group will. The result will occasionally be a distortion of the issue and will often occur only after a time-consuming and divisive discussion. In some cases, the group itself may sharpen the definition of the issue, but in any case, ambiguity about the nature and scope of the issue will slow the group's progress and foster disagreement and conflict.

2. What is the group's responsibility? • Is the group responsible for making a decision, as would be the case for a political caucus or board of directors? Is it responsible for giving advice with respect to some action a manager should take, as would be the case for a study team or staff group? Or is it responsible for a collective decision having to do with the activities of its members, as would be the case for a project management team, or a curriculum planning committee in a school or university?

Perhaps this topic of responsibility deserves elaboration. Recall that we are concerned with decision groups and not, for example, with groups assembled so that the manager can announce the decision. We are concerned with groups that are actually part of the decision process. There are three responsibilities that might be assigned to such groups.

a. *Decision-making groups.* These groups have the responsibility and authority to make decisions on matters brought before them. In some cases, they have original authority, as do juries, boards of directors, and legislatures. In others they have delegated authority, as might the groups that an executive creates to make certain decisions while he or she tends to other matters.

Executives, boards of directors, and legislators aid their own decision making by using another type of decision group—the advisory or study group.

b. *Advisory or study groups.* These groups generate some of the information used in decision making (i.e., they construct part of the decision model). For example, they might generate alternative plans or candidates for a manager to choose from, or they might perform analyses that would indicate the payoff associated with some outcome. After such study they often go further and advise the manager which alternative should be chosen.

c. *Coordinating groups.* In coordinating groups the individual members exchange information that helps them fulfill their individual or joint assignments. In actual practice these groups are created because of dependencies among the units represented by the group members, and they often make decisions to deal with these dependencies. For example, the managers of units involved in fulfilling a large production contract may meet periodically, as might the directors of various aspects of a political candidate's election campaign. The fact that many of the difficulties arising from the dependencies among these units are resolved through decisions made in a group setting causes us to include these groups in our discussion of group decision making.

Let us turn now to the third of the three questions that must be answered in order to define the group's assignment.

3. What are the requirements the group must meet? ● When must the group's responsibilities be fulfilled? Is there a need for intermediate reports? What should be the format of the group output—a written report or an oral presentation? Obtaining and communicating the information concerning the requirements will reduce the group's uncertainty and will minimize the chances that an individual meeting might be stagnated while answers are sought or debated.

Together, the answers to the three fundamental questions concerning the issue, the responsibility, and the requirements comprise the group's "assignment." An example of an assignment is "Identify the four most qualified candidates for the position of vice president of finance. Submit their names and resumes to me by March 15."

Preferably the issue, the group's responsibility, and the group's requirements should each be stated in writing. In any case, they should be referred to frequently so that the group's efforts will not be dissipated on peripheral issues. As the group progresses, it may obtain information or insight suggesting that the issue should be redefined. When this occurs, the group should obtain the agreement of the manager, or others to whom the group is responsible, to address what seems to be the more appropriate issue.

Group managers will do a great service if at the first meeting they describe the group's assignment in some detail. By so doing they reduce the chances that the group will head in the wrong direction and increase the chances for effective communication and understanding. Beforehand, it is useful for managers to summarize the assignment in the letter or phone call that appoints the group members. This minimizes the chances that incorrect assumptions or expectations will develop before the group even assembles.

Turning now from the manager's first task of defining the group's assignment, let us move on to the second task—planning the overall group effort.

PLANNING THE OVERALL GROUP EFFORT

The assignments given to decision groups are generally complex (i.e., they deal with complex issues, responsibilities, or constraints). Perhaps this is because the less complex assignments are either handled by the manager alone or delegated to an individual. In any case, it is useful to break the complex assignment into more manageable parts. A useful way of doing this is to divide the overall assignment into the problem-solving steps outlined in Chapter 2, especially Table 2-1.

Dividing the overall assignment into smaller parts, such as the problem-solving steps, serves two purposes. First, by focusing on individual steps, we overcome the psychological hurdle of attacking what may appear to be an overwhelming assignment. People are reluctant to undertake an exceedingly difficult or impossible assignment. Demonstrating, through this division into separate phases, that the overall assignment can be accomplished by fulfilling a series of not-so-difficult tasks motivates both group managers and group members.

The second purpose served by dealing with individual steps is that the manager can more accurately develop the time and other resource estimates needed to plan for the completion of the overall assignment. Because he or she can deal with smaller and more easily visualized tasks, estimates of the time necessary to complete the individual phases will be more accurate than a global estimate of the time necessary to complete the overall assignment. By using these estimates as guideposts, the manager avoids a last minute crash effort to complete the overall project and the poorer quality outcomes that often accompany such efforts.

Building on these ideas, we can state the first two steps in developing a plan for completing the group's assignment.

Step 1. Divide the group's overall assignment into parts.

Step 2. Estimate the time and other resources needed to complete each part of the assignment and the overall assignment • With respect to the second step, "other resources" might include items such as travel funds or staff support. Of course the key resource is the group members, but it is such a key resource that we will treat it separately in our discussion of organizing and staffing.

The third step follows from the second.

Step 3. Determine the time and other resources available, and take appropriate actions to reduce any differences between what is needed and what is available • For example, if the overall assignment really were to "identify the four most highly qualified candidates and submit their names and resumes by March 15," the manager might find that it was logistically impossible to meet both the implied requirement of searching all possible candidates for the top four and the stated requirement of doing this by March 15. He or she would then have to take some appropriate actions. This might involve getting the deadline extended, or rewording the assignment to "qualified" rather than "the most qualified."

Now, with the assignment defined and a plan for completion of the assignment developed, let us consider the manager's third task—organizing and staffing the decision group.

ORGANIZING AND STAFFING THE DECISION GROUP

In some situations, a manager may have almost complete control over who the members of a committee are, as when appointing subordinates to a committee of his or her own making. In other situations, the manager may have little or no say in choosing the group members. For example, he or she may be appointed chairperson of a committee by a higher level executive. In those instances where the manager has the opportunity to choose or recommend who should be included in the group, much thought should be given to handling the opportunity. Both research and our own experience tell us that the group's composition is a major determinant of the quality and thrust of its outputs. In the next few paragraphs we review five guidelines for deciding whom to include in decision-making groups.

1. Make sure that key information is available.

Groups are often formed so that different elements of information can be brought to bear simultaneously. The information can be made available in different ways. For example, if in the choice-making step the group will need information from a particular expert, we can provide this expertise in at least three ways: (1) we can appoint the expert as a continuing group member; (2) we can appoint the expert as a member in this step only; or (3) we can appoint the expert as a consultant to the group when it reaches this step.

This example shows the need to identify the informational resources required as part of the earlier planning task. In the organizing process, these informational requirements are translated into membership requirements. In situations of even moderate complexity, it is useful for the manager to list the necessary elements of information and the member or procedure that is expected to provide them. Not having key information available causes groups to get bogged down in the short run and to make poor decisions in the long run.

2. *Make sure that those who will be affected get to participate.*

Adherence to this guideline is perhaps the best-known strategy for minimizing the possibility of later resistance to a decision. There are two circumstances under which this guideline is most applicable. The first is when the group assignment deals with the allocation of resources among different units or factions. The second is when the cooperation of the affected units or factions is likely to depend on their satisfaction with the decision group's processes or outputs. As we noted earlier, participation in decision groups reduces resistance to the consequent decisions and increases cooperation at the implementation phase. This should be a strong motivation to the manager to include representatives of the affected units or factions as members of the decision group. In addition, representatives of such units or factions may be able to provide information (e.g., the relative importance of various criteria) that is not otherwise reliably obtainable.

On the other hand, it is not always possible to include representatives of every unit or faction. In these cases, procedures can be established that will allow at least some degree of involvement. For example, interviews or hearings that involve both members of the decision group and members of the affected group may be useful.

3. *Do not allow past practices to dictate group membership.*

Although previous organizational practices might be useful guides in deciding whom to include in the group, they should be reviewed and questioned for applicability in the current situation. Allowing past practices to dictate group membership should be avoided. Among the reasons for this are the following:

a. While it is important to include members who are experienced with the issue, new members bring a fresh perspective. They alert holdover members to the fact that the current issue is not exactly the same as the issues dealt with on previous occasions. Turnover on committees reduces the chance that a committee will use a previously successful but inappropriate model in visualizing a new decision situation.

b. Different issues require different perspectives and different types of expertise. Research indicates that the less successful organizations are those that use the same group to deal with all types of decisions. More successful organizations are those that use different decision groups to deal with different types of decision situations.

c. Participation in decision groups is a developmental and morale building experience. Occasionally appointing junior people, or people who have not been central to the organization, to a decision group tends to provide them with knowledge and interactions that can increase their future productivity and involvement.

These first three guidelines focused primarily on the staffing function. Because the characteristics of people determine how effectively they can fill certain roles (such as those of the group leader or the group's expert on taxes), staffing determines organization to some extent. Conversely, our ideas about how the group might best be organized (e.g., what types of experts are required) determines what people should be included. Thus, in the design of decision groups, organizing and staffing are so intertwined that they are often treated as a single function. The fourth guideline focuses on the organizing function as well as the staffing function.

4. Appoint a leader who is group oriented yet willing and able to exert control.

Management selection is a topic well beyond the scope of this book. Our purpose in including this guideline is to emphasize two important ideas. The first is that the advantages obtained from the use of decision groups will occur to a greater degree if the group leader focuses on facilitating the group's efforts to carry out its assignment, rather than imposing his or her views of what the group's output should be. If the group leader, whether ourselves or our appointee, already possesses the appropriate output (e.g., the problem diagnosis or the required decision), there is not a meaningful assignment for the group. That is, there is no need for a decision group to address the issue. If the group members see this, they will resent being manipulated into the position of endorsing the leader's conclusions and will either rebel or withdraw. This is not to say that managers should never assemble people to convince them of the merits of a decision, but such an audience is not a decision group. Nor is it to say that managers should not use a group to critically examine their thinking. But if this is the purpose, then they should focus on facilitating the group's efforts to carry out this assignment rather than on surreptitiously attempting to win an endorsement. Research results show that groups whose leaders use their position to help the group are more successful in fulfilling their assignments than are groups whose leaders attempt to use their positions to dictate the group's product.

The second purpose in including this guideline is to emphasize that, in general, groups managed by a strong controlling leader are more effective in accomplishing their assignments and in providing their members with a high degree of satisfaction. (We note here what we mean by a strong controlling leader. A strong leader is one who has the ability to control the behavior of the group and its members when he or she chooses to. A controlling leader is one who employs this ability to guide the group's efforts.)

There are three exceptions: (1) the case where the leader attempts to control the group by using unapproved methods or by moving towards goals that group members do not sanction; (2) the case where the group expects and favors a low degree of control, and (3) the case where the group is unconvinced that the appointed leader should, in fact, be the group's leader.

Sensitivity and common sense, if applied, can overcome the problems posed by these exceptions. An awareness of the group's norms helps circumvent problems associated with the first case (using unapproved methods or moving toward unapproved goals). Similarly, for the second case, an awareness that the group might expect a low degree of control can enable the leader to focus on the role of facilitator rather than manipulator. Finally, with respect to the third case, any manager appointing a group leader should seek to choose a person who will be viewed as appropriate by the group members. The manager should then communicate, either overtly or subtly, those characteristics of the appointee that make him or her an appropriate choice. This last step, of legitimating the appointed leader, is quite important. Resistance to the leadership of a person who is viewed as inappropriate for a designated position can result in chaos.

The role of the group leader as a person who both facilitates and controls the group's efforts to complete its assignment will become clearer when we discuss how to manage individual group meetings. At this point, the task is to identify, enlist, and appoint a person who has the ability to fill that role.

The fifth and last guideline also focuses on both the organizing and staffing functions.

5. Consider having different members participate in different parts of the overall assignment.

This guideline basically calls for efficiency in the use of personnel resources. As an example, let us discuss the possibility of using different members in the different steps of the problem-solving process. It is difficult to argue that any one person would be equally helpful in every step. In fact, it is reasonable to believe that the perspective, expertise, or interests of some member might match the activities associated with one problem-solving step much better than those of other steps. Should such a person participate to the same degree in all of the steps? Probably not, if other means of maintaining coordination across steps are available. For example, have only a subgroup of the people involved in one step participate in the next. Causing people who might be central to the tasks of a particular step to participate in steps where they are decidedly noncentral is a time-wasting practice.

Some examples might clarify this idea. Consider the situation where an employee has left the organization. We might decide on our own that the opened position is important, properly defined, and should be filled. Thus we would have, as the manager, completed the step of *exploring the problem*. We might delegate the task of *generating alternatives* to a search committee of some sort, or to the personnel department. We might, by ourselves, complete the step of *choosing among alternatives,* perhaps with consultation from the person who will supervise the new employee. Finally, we might delegate the steps of *implementing the solution* and *controlling the solution program* to the person who will supervise the new employee. Varying the membership of the decision group according to the phase of the problem-solving process can be a device for making efficient use of managerial resources.

As a more complex example, let us assume that we are upper-level sales managers of a company faced with declining sales in one of its product lines. We have decided to create groups to help us with this issue.

In the first step, *exploring the problem,* we are attempting to identify, define, and diagnose the problem. Here we should give priority to appointing as group members: (a) people who have observed the problem symptoms, such as a salesperson and a product manager, (b) people who have analyzed such issues before, such as a general sales manager, and (c) people whose expertise qualifies them to explore the nature of the problem, such as a market analyst.

If we are at the point of *generating alternatives* for solving the problem, we should give priority to appointing as group members (a) people who have dealt with such problems before, such as a general sales manager, and (b) people who are especially trained to deal with such problems, such as product designers and advertising managers.

If we are at the point of *choosing among alternatives,* then we should give priority to involving: (a) people who are expert at modeling or analyzing choice situations, such as operations researchers or decision-science consultants, (b) people who will be affected by the choice, such as the production manager, or the personnel manager if the alternative is to discontinue the product line, and (c) people who will be responsible for carrying out the choice, such as a higher level executive if the best alternative appears to be to discontinue the product line.

In this hypothetical case we see that two groups involving subordinates might have counseled the general sales manager, one by exploring the problem and the other by generating alternatives. At the choice step, however, the manager's advisors were not necessarily involved as members of a group. The principle that a given part of the overall process might be accomplished more effectively with different participants participating in different ways applies throughout the problem-solving process. On some occasions—on the basis of information that we have but do not feel free to share, or for the sake of making a quick response to at least part of a large problem—we ourselves might want to define the problem to be addressed, without adhering to the modifications or interpretations introduced by others.

This principle is also the basis for one of the most useful approaches to enhancing group efficiency—the use of committee staff or committee subgroups to handle tasks that need not be undertaken by the whole group. For example, the drafting of intermediate or final reports can usually be done more efficiently by one or a few people and then reviewed by the group as a whole. Similarly, debating what the facts are is often a time-wasting group activity that can be replaced by assigning one or more group members to obtain the necessary information before the next meeting.

Because the last two steps of the problem-solving process, *implementing the choice* and *controlling the solution program,* move

beyond the realm of decision making to the realm of decision implementation, we will not take the time to discuss the issue of group membership
in these phases. We note again, however, that it would generally be
useful to involve some of the people who will later be involved in decision
implementation in the decision-making step. Combined with the fact that
not everyone involved in the implementation can be involved in the decision making, this idea reminds us that time overlap of group members involved in the different steps is useful as a coordinating mechanism. Exact
duplication in membership often results in the wasteful allocation of the
time of key personnel.

The above considerations are summarized in Table 9-1 as a
checklist of guidelines for planning for, organizing, and staffing a decision group.

In setting forth these several guidelines we have not addressed two
familiar questions: (1) what should be the group's size; and (2) what
should be the level of the group's heterogeneity? These questions are important, and their answers cannot easily be summarized as single
sentence guidelines. Let us first consider the matter of group size.

Group size

Many studies have been conducted in response to the question,
"What should be the size of a decision group?" Two principal findings
have emerged. One is that leaderless groups of two, three, and four tend
to have difficulty solving problems and providing satisfaction for their
members. In two or four-person groups, stagnating confrontations tend
to develop with an equal number of members on either side of the issue.
This leads to low task accomplishment and low satisfaction. In three-
person groups, two members tend to dominate the third. This in turn
leads to the expected adverse effect on satisfaction. The other principal
finding is that the members of groups of six or more tend to derive lower
satisfaction than those of smaller groups. This is because of the lower
average level of participation that occurs in larger groups and because in
larger groups a few members tend to dominate the proceedings. As a
consequence of these findings, and some studies comparing the performance of five-member groups with other groups, decision scientists have
concluded that a decision group of five is the most effective.

Unfortunately, most studies leading to this conclusion were conducted with ad hoc groups, rather than groups whose members were
familiar to each other and who were operating in their usual roles, and

TABLE 9–1.   Guidelines for Planning, Organizing, and Staffing Decision
             Groups

A. Define the Assignment
   1. Define the issue to be dealt with.
   2. Define the responsibilities to be fulfilled.
   3. Define the requirements that must be met.
B. Plan the Overall Effort
   1. Divide the overall assignment into parts.
   2. Estimate the time and other resources needed for each part and the
      whole.
   3. Determine the time and other resources available, and take action to
      reduce differences between what is needed and what is available.
C. Assign People to Jobs
   1. Make sure that key information is available.
   2. Make sure that those who will be affected get to participate.
   3. Do not allow past practices to dictate group membership.
   4. Appoint a leader who is group oriented and yet willing and able to
      exert control.
   5. Consider having different members participate in different parts of the
      overall assignment.

with groups who either had no designated leader or whose designated
leaders had only minimal claim to the leadership position (e.g., had no
rewards with which to induce the other members to follow their directions). Consequently, because the settings of the studies were generally
unlike the settings in which many real decision groups operate, we should
be cautious in extrapolating the findings to our own decision situations
when they vary from the settings where the findings were obtained. For
example, if we appoint a group of four, but provide it with a "team
leader" who has a legitimate claim to the position, direct it to work in a
cooperative mode, and choose its members so that each has a unique
role, the tendency for the group to pair off into a two-against-two confrontation will be much less than it would be in the experimental settings
where this confrontation behavior has been observed.

     A similar example could be created that may cause us to be skep-
tical about the degree to which we should alter group size. In a three-per-
son group, two members may work together to dominate the third. Does
it seem reasonable to arbitrarily add two members, and use a five-person
team to take on an assignment that our earlier guidelines suggest could be
handled by a group of three? Very few managers, aware of the hours that
group efforts consume, would answer this question affirmatively.

Where, then, are we left with respect to the findings that groups of two and four had the tendency to become stalemated and the members of groups of two, three, and four reported high levels of conflict? The most that can be said is that we should keep these tendencies in mind and do what we can to overcome them, perhaps by appointing legitimate leaders, and instructing them in how to manage conflict.

Let us turn to the finding that members of larger groups derived less satisfaction and had a more difficult time organizing themselves to address their assignment. We can ask a question similar to the one posed earlier: Does it seem reasonable to appoint a task force of only five members when we honestly believe that concerns for breadth of expertise and constituency representation require a task force of nine members? Probably not, especially since the problems encountered by the experimental groups are not as prevalent in most organizational groups. For example, in groups larger than seven, members tend not to see other members as individuals. This loses much of its relevance, however, in situations where several of the members are previously known to each other, where the group interacts over an extended period of time, or where each member represents a different constituency or area of expertise. The finding that larger groups have difficulty getting organized to attack their assignments has less relevance when experienced chairpersons are appointed or elected.

Where does this leave us with respect to the findings that larger experimental groups tended not to perform much better than smaller groups and provided less satisfaction to their members? Again, the most that can be said is that we should keep these observations in mind and draw on them to the extent that they may be relevant. For example, these thoughts suggest that ad hoc groups of strangers should be kept smaller than ongoing groups of friends or coworkers, and that strong leadership will be even more important to the successful functioning of such groups. Let us consider the matter of group heterogeneity.

Group heterogeneity

Homogeneous groups are those whose members are similar, for example, in their attitudes and occupations. Heterogeneous groups are those whose members differ in such respects. Because the assignments given to decision groups generally require a variety of perspectives and information, we would expect that heterogeneous decision groups would be more effective. Research generally confirms this expectation. It supports the use of guidelines C–1 and C–2 of Table 9–1, suggesting that we staff so as to ensure availability of various informational items and points of view. In addition, research shows that heterogeneous groups are more likely to profit from the *assembly effect,* the condition where the group product is greater or better than could be obtained by aggregating the inputs from the individual members. For example, creative solutions are more likely to follow from a comparison of conflicting points of view than from a comparison of similar points of view.

An important exception to the general finding that heterogeneous groups are more effective occurs when the differences in attributes, such as status, attitude, or expertise, are so extreme that group members are unable to work together. This exception highlights the conclusions drawn by two eminent social-psychologists, Collins and Guetzkow, that although

> increasing the heterogeneity . . . within a group will . . . increase the problem solving potential of the group

it is also true that

> increasing heterogeneity . . . will [also] increase the difficulty of building interpersonal relations. (Collins and Guetzkow, 1964, p. 101)

To what sort of operational guidelines do these thoughts lead? They encourge us to make full use of the multiple expertise and perspectives that we obtain through the formation of a heterogeneous group, subject to the constraint that the differences in member attributes must not be so great that they interfere with the group's attempts to carry out its assignment. In organizing our group, we can help reduce the likelihood that heterogeneity will interfere with group functioning by appointing as group members people with either expertise in several areas or a broad general perspective. These people will be able to deal with a wider variety of information and perspectives and can be helpful in facilitating the exchange of information and the interpretation of views.

If our decision-aiding group is given a task where little creativity or judgment is required (as in the routine gathering of readily available data), then there is no need for heterogeneity, and we should appoint a homogeneous group. Such groups tend to work together more harmoniously and complete routine tasks more quickly than do heterogeneous groups.

SUMMARY AND OVERVIEW

This chapter provided guidelines, summarized in Table 9-1, for carrying out three important tasks: defining the group's assignment, planning the overall group effort, and organizing and staffing the group. The first two of these tasks are generally associated with the managerial function of planning. The third is associated with the functions of organizing and staffing.

Completion of these functions should precede, when possible, actual activation of the decision group. Although changes in plans, organization, and staff do take place, the functions of directing and controlling the group become predominant after activation.

Directing and controlling a decision group are seen as relatively difficult tasks by many people. The next chapter contains guidelines, tactics, and step-by-step procedures that make these tasks easier and lead to increased performance and satisfaction.

OPPORTUNITIES FOR FURTHER THOUGHT

1. Think of a decision situation where you would use a decision-aiding group, and write out the group's assignment in terms of issue, responsibilities, and requirements.
2. Recall a group situation that you observed where inadequate planning led to lowered group performance. Would careful adherence to the three planning steps described in the chapter have helped avoid the later difficulties? If not, what action would have been helpful?
3. Recall a group situation that you observed where inappropriate organizing or staffing led to lowered group performance. Would adherence to the five guidelines described in the chapter have helped avoid the later difficulties? If not, what action would have been helpful?

REFERENCES AND RELATED READINGS

Collins, B. E. and H. Guetzkow. *A Social Psychology of Group Processes for Decision Making.* New York, John Wiley and Sons, Inc., 1964.

Cummings, L. L., G. P. Huber, and E. Arendt. "Effects of Size and Spatial Arrangements on Group Decision Making. *Academy of Management Journal* 17 (Sept. 1974): 460–475.

Maier, N. F. *Problem Solving and Creativity in Individuals and Groups.* Belmont, Calif.: Brooks/Cole Publishing Company, 1970.

Shaw, M. E. *Group Dynamics.* New York: McGraw-Hill, Inc., 1971.

10

Group Decision Making and Committee Management: Directing and Controlling Individual Meetings

This chapter is concerned with managing the individual meetings of decision groups. In it we describe guidelines and tactics that have shown themselves to be useful in the direction and control of such meetings. When applied, they will enable the manager to be a more effective group leader or committee chairperson.

There are two reasons why it is important for managers to be skilled in directing and controlling group meetings. One is that both the performance and satisfaction of a decision group are determined to a great extent by the quality of its leadership. If the group leader or committee chairperson manages the meeting poorly, the group will tend to be ineffective in carrying out its tasks, and its members will tend to be frustrated, uncommitted, and reluctant to accept similar assignments in the future. If its leader manages it well, group performance and member satisfaction will both be favorable.

The second reason why it is important for managers to be skilled in the management of meetings is that the position of group leader or committee chairperson is highly visible. As a consequence, the group leader's strengths and weaknesses are readily observed and frequently discussed both inside and outside the group. This public review affects a manager's general image and his or her specific image as a group leader and consequently affects the scope of future assignments. Together these two reasons suggest the need for managers to seek out practical guidelines and tactics for directing and controlling the meetings of decision groups. The purpose of this chapter is to provide these guidelines and tactics.

The chapter is divided into two main sections. The first reviews the factors that interfere with the effectiveness of decision groups. The second describes guidelines and tactics that are useful in directing and controlling individual group meetings. Let us turn to a review of the factors that reduce decision group effectiveness.

SOCIAL AND PSYCHOLOGICAL FORCES THAT INTERFERE WITH EFFECTIVENESS OF DECISION GROUPS

In Chapter 3 we discussed a number of factors that interfere with effective decision making by an individual manager. In Chapter 8 we observed that the use of decision groups can help overcome or circumvent some of these factors. Decision groups themselves, however, have counterproductive tendencies that interfere with their effectiveness.

Perhaps we should define what we mean by effective group decision making. By this term we mean decision making that (1) meets the requirements of the decision situation (acceptable decision quality, acceptable use of member time, etc.), (2) results in the individual members being generally more satisfied than unsatisfied, and (3) does not impair the capacity of the group to continue to function. With this definition in mind, we can more meaningfully state what we will find to be a useful concept—that "the actual effectiveness of a decision group is equal to the potential effectiveness that follows from the combined inputs of the members minus the losses in effectiveness that follow from the group processes plus the gains in effectiveness that follow from the group processes." In a shorter form,

$$Actual\ Effectiveness = Potential\ Effectiveness - Process\ Losses + Process\ Gains.$$

The *process losses* include, for example, the loss in decision quality resulting from some member not having the opportunity to contribute his or her knowledge. The *process gains* include the gain in decision quality resulting from one member thinking of a new and useful idea as a result of listening to the discussion of other members.

As we noted in Chapter 9, in many respects the group's *potential effectiveness* is determined by how well the planning, organizing, and staffing functions are carried out. In contrast, as we will soon see, the *process losses* and *process gains* are largely determined by how well the directing and controlling functions are carried out. The question that naturally arises is "What are the causes of the *process losses?*" or, using some of our earlier terminology, "What are the social or psychological forces and counterproductive tendencies that interfere with the effectiveness of decision groups?"

The following is a summary listing drawn from both the management and decision science research literatures.

1. Group members with dominant personalities or intense interests in the decision situation tend to participate in the group discussion more than their contribution to the group's goal attainment merits. This in turn leads to lower quality decisions, by suppressing the contributions of other members and thereby restricting the availability of information. It also leads to lower satisfaction among the other group members whose participation is curtailed. Similarly, a willingness to persist stubbornly and thereby fatigue the opposition enables some individuals to affect the decision more than their information or knowledge justifies.

2. Low status members tend to defer to the opinions expressed by high status members, thus depriving the group of the potential contribution that justified the inclusion of these members to begin with.

3. Group pressures for conformity can suppress facts and opinions that are not in keeping with the direction that the group is headed, or not in keeping with the values held by other group members. As mentioned earlier, this behavior leads to lower quality decisions in that it restricts the availability of information.

4. As time passes, groups lose sight of their immediate task; they get into ruts and pursue peripheral issues, conversations, and trains of thought. This not only slows the process down (with the consequent negative effect on decision timeliness and member satisfaction), but also causes some information that would be useful in completing the task to be set aside and eventually forgotten.

5. In order to reduce the tension created by the presence of their overall assignment, decision groups involved in problem solving frequently give insufficient attention to the problem-exploration and alternative-generation steps. They move too quickly to the choice-making step, and thus increase the likelihood that they will choose an in-

appropriate or low-quality solution. For example, such groups tend to consider only readily available solutions and tend to push towards closure by stifling, circumventing, or bargaining away dissent or disagreement.

6. Group members tend to use some of their time establishing interpersonal relationships with other group members. Although this tendency towards socializing and status seeking appears unavoidable, it does absorb time that otherwise could be devoted to fulfilling the group's assignment.

7. The actual contributions of individual group members are adversely affected by their cognitive limitations and, in addition, by the miscommunications that occur as they attempt to share their information and reasoning with other group members. These difficulties directly interfere with the group's generation and interactive consideration of information. Because they often cause other group members to take time to help the individual having the difficulty, they indirectly interfere as well.

Thinking back to the discussion of Chapter 8, recall that to fully capitalize on the advantages to be gained from the use of decision groups, we must maximize the generation and the interactive analysis of the information possessed or acquired by the group members. Thus, as managers, we must direct the group so as to surface and collectively review as much of the relevant information and knowledge as we can. This is subject, of course, to the constraints on time and the availability of group members.

As our review of the above seven factors indicates, there are strong social and psychological forces that work against a complete sharing and review of information in groups. The prevalence and negative impact of these forces have led decision scientists and management practitioners to develop guidelines and tactics that help minimize the occurrence and impact of these forces. Consequently, they lead to the fuller generation and sharing of information necessary for improved decision making.

We turn now to a discussion of these devices. We begin with a guideline that focuses on the special situation of the first meeting.

Guideline 1. Help the group members get acquainted.

Psychological research and our everyday observations show that people have a strong urge to "get the facts" about new acquaintances, or old acquaintances and associates with whom they have not talked for some time. Apparently this urge and the questions that it prompts serve in part to minimize the chances that the people involved will relate to others in inappropriate ways. For example, people often ask questions such as "where are you from, who (what organization) are you with, and what have you been doing lately?" Such questions help the questioner to later speak positively about these locations, organizations, or activities. If the goal is to make a favorable impression, this helps him or her avoid making a blunder with respect to these matters. Similarly, the volunteering of information about ourselves is thought to be a device for ensuring that others do not inadvertently relate to us in an inappropriate way. Careful listening to the get-acquainted conversations of professionals will show that many of these early stage communications are attempts to clarify status or spheres of influence. Again, they are attempts to ensure appropriate behavior.

Knowing these tendencies will enable the manager of a newly formed group, or of an ongoing group whose members have not seen each other for some time, to more intelligently decide whether he or she should deliberately provide the opportunity for the group members to become acquainted with one another. Table 10-1 contains a wide-ranging "shopping list" of possible approaches for facilitating this familiarization. The fact that many are commonplace highlights the frequency with which managers recognize this universal urge of people to get to know one another before settling down to the business at hand.

Although we must regret the resultant loss of time, we must also accept the fact that if this opportunity is not provided, we will probably encounter the following consequences: (1) the group members may incorrectly relate to each other—for example, they may make unintentionally

---

TABLE 10-1.   Tactics for Helping Group Members Get Acquainted

a. Before the first meeting, send each member a brief biographical sketch of the other members, perhaps in conjunction with a description of the group's assignment, schedule of meetings, etc.
b. Before the first meeting, provide an opportunity for the members to socialize, such as a coffee or cocktail hour.
c. At the first meeting, introduce each member or have the members introduce themselves. (Generally the chairperson's introductions are more informative, as the members may be too modest to say much about themselves.)
d. During long meetings, provide breaks during which the members can engage in the social conversations that they have had to set aside while they focused on the group task.

offending statements or use terminology that is confusing to other members, and hence inadvertently interfere with the group's progress; (2) in order to avoid incorrectly relating to one another, individual members may not share all of their information or thinking, even though it may be relevant; and (3) the members may engage in side conversations during the meeting, in order to establish their relationship. Because these consequences could cause the group to be inefficient or unsuccessful in fulfilling its assignment, the manager should make an effort to ensure that the members quickly become acquainted.

Let us move on now to a guideline applicable to any meeting.

Guideline 2. Help the group follow the plan.

As we noted in Chapter 9, the effectiveness of decision making is determined, in part, by how well the decision-making process is planned. But any plan, including a good plan, is relatively useless unless it is implemented. Even when the plan must be changed, it is changed on the assumption that the new plan will be implemented. In the next several pages we describe four tactics that can be used to help ensure that the group implements the plan—that it focuses on carrying out its assignment by working through the individual tasks in the sequence of and according to the schedule established by its leader or its members.

As we will see, these tactics call for a simple systematic application of common sense. The importance of formalizing them on these pages follows from the fact that unsystematic application, or inadvertent nonapplication, causes the group leader to lose important opportunities for maximizing the group's performance. The first tactic is as follows:

a. At the beginning of each meeting, review the progress made to date and establish the task of the individual meeting • An example use of this tactic would be to say, "As you remember, at the end of the last meeting we had generated a list of eight approaches for cutting costs in the department and had laid out a strategy for evaluating them. Our schedule for today's meeting calls for a decision on how to get the information we need to make the evaluations." A more elaborate beginning, most useful with groups that meet more formally and less frequently might also include overviewing the items on an agenda distributed for the meeting.

Use of this tactic accomplishes several goals. First, by reviewing the progress to date, we highlight the group's past successes. This helps boost morale and esprit de corps and increases the motivation to continue progressing. Second, by reviewing the progress, we identify where the group is with respect to the plan. This, combined with identifying the task of the current meeting, helps ensure that each of the members has a common understanding of what needs to be done. Accomplishing these goals helps achieve the goal of minimizing confusion and misunderstanding and thus facilitates further progress.

Occasional reference to the particular task of the meeting can help keep the group properly focused, and occasional reference to the progress being made at the meeting, such as, "Well, we've successfully evaluated the first four alternatives, let's move on to number five," can help maintain interest and motivation.

The second tactic concerns the receiving of reports from group members who had preassigned tasks. Whether these reports should be elicited just before or just after the progress review and task establishment mentioned above depends on the nature of the report and the preference of the manager. The second tactic is as follows:

b. *At the beginning of each meeting, or as early as possible, get a report from each member with a preassigned task* • For example, we might say, "Before we move on, let's hear what Don found out about the company's plans for upgrading its computing equipment." Use of this tactic accomplishes three goals. One is that it helps establish an atmosphere of accountability. If members learn through observation or experience that they will be held responsible for completing their assignments, they will be more inclined to complete them in the future.

The second goal accomplished is the providing of public recognition for the reporting member. On those occasions when the progress of the meeting causes the group leader to forget to elicit a report, the resulting nonrecognition invariably leads to dampened enthusiasm on the part of the member. To some extent, postponement of a report to subsequent meetings has the same effect. Similarly, the group member whose report is held in abeyance generally does not participate as effectively during the intervening period. In some instances the member is concerned about whether or when he or she will receive credit for the completed assignment. In others he or she is concerned about the exact wording of the presentation.

There are, of course, some situations where reports may be premature and would require later repetition to be most useful. When this is the case, it is usually a better idea to simply but explicitly comment on the existence of the forthcoming report and the time when you will ask for it.

The third goal accomplished through this early elicitation of reports is the reduction, when it is present, of the tension that sometimes exists when some group members have information on a sensitive issue that others do not. Rather than being a primary consideration, the accomplishment of this goal is more of a favorable by-product of the use of the tactic to accomplish the two goals described above.

The last two tactics that help ensure that the group implements the plan are applied at the end of the meeting.

c. At the end of each meeting, summarize what was accomplished, where this puts the group on its schedule, and what will be the group task at the next meeting ● The goals accomplished through the use of this tactic are similar to those achieved by using the first tactic. By summarizing what was accomplished, we highlight the group's success and progress. This is especially helpful in those instances where not much measurable progress has been made—where all we can point to is the fact that we "exchanged views" or "examined alternatives." It is extremely important to highlight that something was accomplished, that information was shared, and that the communications will not have to be repeated.

By noting where the group is on its schedule and what the task of the next meeting will be, we minimize uncertainty and maximize the likelihood that the members will give some thought to forthcoming tasks.

The fourth tactic is as follows:

d. At the end of each meeting, make public and clear which members have which assignments to complete by the next meeting ● If the assignments are simple and the leader expects that they will be fulfilled, he may restate them himself, as "Bill, now as I understand it, you're going to get the information about the cost of leasing the computer terminals." It is usually a good idea, however, to seek some sort of response or acknowledgment, for example, by continuing the above summary statement with "Is that right?" or "Do you need any help from any of us to do that?" If the assignment is complex or the leader is intent on ensuring that a commitment to carry through has been made, he or she might have members with the assignments state the assignments. An example is "Now let's see what everyone's going to do between now and the next meeting. Mary, what will you be doing?"

Use of this tactic serves several purposes. One is that it helps reduce misunderstandings about assignments. Another is that, since the group hears who is to do what, use of the tactic tends to create a feeling of being responsible to the group as well as to the group leader. This tends to increase motivation. A third purpose that it serves is to highlight and recognize contributions that will be made by individual members.

This also tends to increase motivation. The overall effect of using this tactic is to ensure that the results and information needed at some subsequent time, usually the next meeting, will be available. Few things are as detrimental as a meeting where no progress is made because someone did not bring a key piece of information.

These four tactics are effective mechanisms for implementing the second guideline. Let us now turn to the third guideline. It draws heavily on ideas discussed in Chapters 3–7.

Guideline 3. Use information displays.

The use of information displays can help group members overcome their cognitive limitations and their communications difficulties. In Chapter 3 we noted that "each decision maker can mentally weigh and consider only a limited amount of information at one time" (Downs, 1966, p. 75). This problem is compounded in group meetings because the interaction that takes place is a distraction that actually increases the difficulty of individual information processing. What can we do to counteract the problem?

An answer to the question follows from Chapters 4–7, where we saw that models and explicit information-processing strategies could be used to overcome cognitive limitations. In group settings we should carry this strategy a step further and make extensive use of chalkboards, flip charts, and handouts to display cognitive and communication aids, such as listings (of, say, constraints), information displays (e.g., utility models or decision trees), and process guides (e.g., agenda items or step-by-step computational procedures).

If the group is generating alternatives, we should list them on a large flip chart. This stimulates the thinking of others, minimizes unwanted redundancy, and reduces the tendency of members to worry about others forgetting their particular idea or contribution. If the group is thinking through contingencies, we should use a chalkboard to lay them out in the form of a decision tree. This way there is no ambiguity or unrecognized disagreement about what the contingency implies or where it fits in the overall analysis.

In addition to helping individual members overcome their cognitive limitations, experience shows that these public displays are extremely useful in facilitating communication and understanding among the group members.[1] This means, in effect, that the models and techniques of Chapters 4–7 are often more useful to groups than they are to individuals. A final benefit to the manager from the use of information displays is that physical control of information—a critical group resource—is helpful in controlling the group.

The usefulness of displaying information highlights the need to generate the information to begin with. This task is facilitated with the fourth guideline:

Guideline 4. Help the group achieve equitable participation by managing the discussion.

Equitable participation is the level of participation that is in keeping with the individual's information, knowledge, or other contribution to the group's efforts. Inequitable participation is participation to a degree that is either greater or less than that which is in keeping with the person's contribution. In the meetings of most decision groups, unmanaged or "natural" rates of participation are inequitable, with some people participating more than their contribution justifies and some participating less. Several of the causes of this commonplace occurrence are contained in our earlier enumeration of the forces that interfere with group effectiveness. Whatever the cause, it is a common observation that some people, whether due to habit, special interest, or innate verbosity, participate in meetings to a degree unwarranted by their actual contribution to the group's assignment and progress.

Exactly equal or absolutely uniform participation is also generally inequitable. It is unlikely that on any given matter every group member has equal information, or ability to direct the discussion, or whatever contribution is required at the time.

In either case, whether the variation in participation among members is too great or too little, the effectiveness of the group will suffer. Performance will suffer for two reasons. One is that the time used by the member with inequitably high participation levels will be unavailable to those who could have used it to make more valuable contributions. The second is that some members, who presumably are present because

[1]Because of its appropriateness, we recall from Chapter 7 a statement from an executive describing a meeting of his company's planning board that ". . . it wasn't until we put a decision tree on the board that people began to realize that we had all been talking about different problems!" (Hayes, 1969, p. 109)

they have the potential to make a contribution, feel inhibited and do not contribute even when time is available. Research shows that satisfaction will also suffer as those who feel that their participation was curtailed will react adversely to the overall process. This is especially unfortunate when we realize that one of the potential payoffs from the use of decision groups is the increased enthusiasm and acceptance that accompanies the act of participating. The key question is, of course, what tactics can a manager use to direct the group toward more equitable participation? The following two tactics have shown themselves to be especially helpful.

a. Establish "fairness" as a standard • This is accomplished through the use of guiding comments. For example, after an unnecessarily long or repetitious comment by one group member, we might say "Okay John, I think we understand your point of view. In all fairness, we should now give someone else the opportunity to be heard on the matter." Guiding comments can also be used to ensure equitable distribution between points of view, for example by saying "Well, we've just heard an argument for the proposal. Now I think it's only fair that we hear an argument against it."

In each of the above instances we were indicating to the speaker that it is only fair that he or she *not* participate for a while. We can be more aggressive but still tactful, such as "Ruth, we've heard your argument in favor of the proposal. Maybe we ought to let someone else contribute the remaining arguments that favor it." Also, in each of these instances we were not only closing the door, but with the second statement, we were opening the door to another speaker and thus not shutting off discussion. This can be stated explicitly as, "I don't mean to shorten the discussion—I just think that it's important that we share the opportunities to speak."

Guiding comments can be used to increase the participation of certain members, as when saying "Mr. Smith, we haven't heard from you on this proposal. What ideas do you have on the matter?" However, forcing people to speak can cause them to withdraw even further. In general, the better strategy is simply to provide openings in the discussion, as indicated above, and make general appeals to broaden participation. One could say, "I hope that before we close this discussion we get to hear from some of you who haven't yet made your contribution."

The above paragraphs focused on the use of guiding comments to establish as standard behavior the maintenance of fairness with respect to opportunities to participate in the group discussion. There is a second tactic for helping the group achieve equitable participation.

*b. Use the **round-robin** technique* • This is a very useful technique for attaining equitable participation when the group's immediate task is to identify and share key items. Examples of such items include possible constraints on choice making, possible candidates for a job opening, questions that the members feel should be addressed, or items for a meeting agenda. The procedure is to go around the table or other seating arrangement and ask for one item from one member at a time. As each item is put forth, the group leader writes it onto the chalkboard or flip chart and then proceeds to ask for one item from the next group member. This elicitation and listing process continues around the table until the first person is reached. A second round then begins.

When group members whose turn it is have nothing to contribute, they simply say "pass." When their turn occurs again, on a subsequent round or cycle, they may have thought of another idea and are allowed to reenter the process, or they could pass again. The cycling is continued until all ideas are listed (i.e., until everyone passes on the same round). In general, some members will have fewer ideas and will therefore contribute in fewer rounds. At the same time, the structure of the process has provided the opportunity for equitable participation.

The round-robin technique is an excellent device for allowing everyone an equal opportunity to participate without forcing everyone to participate equally. Thus, it is an important aid in achieving equitable participation. In addition, it is quite useful for separating the generation of ideas from the evaluation of these ideas. In the application of the technique, the leader usually asks that the idea simply be stated and not argued for or elaborated upon until all ideas have been elicited from all of the members. Finally, the insistence that only one item be put forth during each member's turn is useful in preventing the boredom and frustration that sets in among the members of a group when one member insists on enumerating all of his or her thoughts on a matter.

The fifth and last guideline deals with the issue of consensus—the condition that exists when a choice is made that is not unacceptable to any group member. Research shows that decision groups work hard to achieve consensus, and they they will often (and generally unintentionally) sacrifice decision quality in an effort to obtain the necessary agreement.

For example, one member may hold out adamantly for an alternative that others feel to be inferior. It is then likely that he or she would be able to "fatigue" the others into yielding to what no one else really believes to be the best of the alternatives available. Thus quality is lost, but consensus, as it is typically thought of, is achieved. As another example, in order to ensure that everyone is satisfied, the group members may engage in compromises or trade-offs that facilitate consensus but create an alternative that is inferior in quality. The possible occurrence of this consensus-achieving, but quality-sacrificing behavior often causes managers to retain final decision-making authority.

Because we wish to avoid sacrificing decision quality when possible, it is appropriate to consider approaches that will avoid or minimize this trade-off of quality for consensus. We will consider three. The first two are familiar and will be considered briefly. One of these is for the manager to retain final decision-making authority. Of course, this approach does not apply to autonomous groups who are bound to make their own decisions, or to decision-aiding groups with tasks such as estimating resources or making recommendations.

The second approach to circumventing the loss in decision quality associated with consensus seeking is to vote on the issues about which the members disagree. Its principal disadvantages are the clear identification of "losers" and the lower satisfaction or commitment that goes along with this approach to resolving disagreements. As a consequence, the use of voting as a choice-making mechanism is in violation of the aspirations and customs of many groups.

These two approaches cover only a limited number of cases encountered in actual managing practice. Many other cases will be encountered where groups must make decisions, and yet wish to avoid the use of voting. This fact prompts the question, "Is there an approach to consensus seeking that reduces the likelihood of a loss in decision quality, and yet still results in outputs that are acceptable to all members?"

The answer to this question is "yes." Specifically, this third approach is to implement the following:

Guideline 5. Focus on agreement about the reasonableness of the reasoning rather than on agreement about the choice itself.

There are three tactics for implementing this guideline. The first, used at a very early point in the choice-making step, is as follows:

a. Early in the choice-making step, have the group agree on how it will ultimately make its choice • This tactic is most easily applied when the problem is highly structured, as were the problems discussed in

Chapters 4–7. As we will see, it is also applicable when the problem is less structured. It is most effective when applied well before the group reaches the choice point.

An example of a moderately structured problem where this tactic might be useful would be the screening or selection of key personnel. Rather than leaping right to an interactive discussion of the candidates, the manager should first have the group discuss components of the decision situation such as criteria, constraints, and decision rules. Perhaps the manager should even develop a multiattribute utility model using the step-by-step procedure described in Chapter 5. In many cases, a higher quality decision will be reached if the group first agrees on the elements of a decision model and on a decision rule than if it moves directly to ranking the alternatives.

Even when the problem is less structured or perhaps more political, abbreviated forms or certain components of decision models and rules may be useful. Simple listings of the alternatives, criteria, and future conditions are often helpful. For example, as part of a consulting assignment, the author was once asked for advice by the chairperson of a committee of department managers that had been directed to design a new organizational structure. As each alternative design had been offered, it had been vigorously attacked by whichever department managers felt it was adverse to their interests. After approximately sixteen hours of meetings, the group was no further along than when it had started.

At the next two-hour meeting, the author had the group focus its attention on developing and ranking the criteria and constraints that it would use to evaluate organizational designs offered in the future. The tenor of the discussions at this meeting was quite analytic, as is often the case when the task is of this nature. It was in sharp contrast with the heated and political discussions of previous meetings. Using the very rudimentary multiattribute utility model, the committee in its subsequent meetings was able to proceed rapidly to agreement on an organizational design.

An important benefit of having the group decide how it will make its choice early in its deliberations is that the discussion tends to identify the information that must be sought before the final choice can be made. The second tactic for minimizing the inclination to sacrifice quality for consensus is as follows:

b. Have the group agree to be satisfied with the situation where all members understand the reasoning that leads to the group choice • Careful reading of this tactic shows that it is similar to but more general than the first tactic. Both call for a review of the reasoning leading to a choice. The first tactic requires public agreement on the decision model and decision rule. This second tactic calls for understanding of (though not necessarily agreement on) the reasoning that supports the apparent choice of the majority.

The aspiration of many decision groups is to convince each member that the group choice is the best of the alternatives. This is a high aspiration but, as we noted earlier, it does not improve decision quality. In fact, it tends to reduce it.

On the other hand, the tactic just stated reflects a lower aspiration. The group leader might introduce the idea with, "I'm sure we hope that all of us are in full agreement with whichever is the committee's choice for the site of this new facility. On the other hand, I'm sure we also recognize the difficulty of choosing from among the widely varying list of sites that we have in front of us. In view of this, let me suggest that we work hard to make sure that everyone understands the reasoning that leads us to whichever site we choose. It may be too much to ask for 100 percent agreement on sites, but I think we should attempt to get agreement that a reasonable person could choose whichever seems to be favored."

Examination of this tactic shows that, although it reflects a lower aspiration concerning consensus, it will lead to higher quality decisions. This observation follows from the fact that its use questions and brings into full view the reasoning leading to the choice. This process of specification and critique will often tease out errors in reasoning that, in some cases, helped lead the group toward favoring a lower quality alternative.

c. Obtain an explicit indication that the prevailing reasoning is understood by each group member • Depending on the situation, the leader might seek outright verbal agreement, or be satisfied with nods of the head. Or, the leader could ask, "Is there anyone who wonders about the defensibility of the reasoning that seems to have led us to this choice?" Use of this tactic tends to increase the feeling of shared control. It also surfaces disagreement that can be useful in identifying weak reasoning and promotes a sense of commitment among the group members.

The above considerations are summarized in Table 10–2 as a checklist of guidelines and tactics for directing and controlling individual meetings.

TABLE 10-2.   Guidelines and Tactics for Managing Decision-Group
Meetings

1. Help the group members get acquainted.*
2. Help the group follow the plan.
   a. At the beginning of each meeting, review the progress made to date and
      establish the task of the individual meeting.
   b. At the beginning of each meeting, or as early as possible, get a report
      from each member with a preassigned task.
   c. At the end of each meeting, summarize what was accomplished, where
      this puts the group on its schedule, and what will be the group task at
      the next meeting.
   d. At the end of each meeting, make public and clear which members have
      which assignments to complete by the next meeting.
3. Use information displays.
4. Help the group achieve equitable participation by managing the discussion.
   a. Establish "fairness" as a standard.
   b. Use the *round-robin* technique.
5. Focus on agreement about the reasonableness of the reasoning rather than
   on agreement about the choice itself.
   a. Early in the choice-making step, have the group agree on how it will
      make its choice.
   b. Have the group agree to be satisfied with the situation where all
      members understand the reasoning that leads to the group choice.
   c. Obtain an explicit indication that the prevailing reasoning is understood
      by each group member.

Example tactics for implementing this guideline are shown in Table 10-1.

SUMMARY AND OVERVIEW

In the first section of the chapter we reviewed the social and
psychological factors or forces that interfere with the effectiveness of
decision groups. In the second part we examined five guidelines and a
number of tactics that group leaders can use to help overcome or circumvent some of these factors.

The focus of the chapter was on the use of guidelines for managing the meetings of the face-to-face, interacting groups that are familiar
to all of us. The focus of the next chapter is on the use of special techniques that, when the group's task is to provide information, are
sometimes even more effective in overcoming the counterproductive
tendencies that reduce group effectiveness.

OPPORTUNITIES FOR FURTHER THOUGHT

1. Table 10–1 lists four tactics for helping group members get acquainted. Have you encountered, or can you think of, any others that would be helpful?
2. Review the tactics that can be used to help the group adhere to its plans. List two adverse consequences of not implementing each tactic.
3. Recall a group situation that you observed where inequitable participation seemed to reduce either the performance or satisfaction of the group members. Would the two tactics described in the chapter have been helpful in achieving more equitable participation? If not, what tactics would have been helpful?

REFERENCES AND RELATED READINGS

Delbecq, A. L., A. H. Van de Ven, and D. H. Gustafson. *Group Techniques for Program Planning*. Glenview, Ill.: Scott, Foresman and Company, 1975.

Downs, A. *Inside Bureaucracy*. Boston: Little, Brown and Company, 1966.

Hackman, J. R. and C. G. Morris. "Group Tasks, Group Interaction Process, and Group Performance Effectiveness: A Review and Proposed Integration." *Advances in Experimental Social Psychology*. vol. 8. pp. 45–99. New York: Academic Press, 1975.

Hall, J. and H. W. Watson. "The Effects of a Normative Intervention on Group Decision Making Performance." *Human Relations* 23 (1970): 229–317.

Hayes, R. H. "Qualitative Insights From Quantitative Methods." *Harvard Business Review* 47 (July–August 1969): 108–117.

Steiner, I. D. *Group Process and Productivity*. New York: Academic Press, Inc., 1972.

11
Special Group Techniques: Procedures and Examples

This chapter describes three techniques that are useful to managers who are attempting to use groups to generate information. The techniques focus on overcoming or circumventing the social and psychological forces that often adversely affect the potential performance of face-to-face interacting groups.

Each of these techniques—individual brainstorming, the nominal group technique, and the Delphi technique—has been studied, tested, and found to be useful by both managers and decision scientists. Several relevant studies, applications, and step-by-step procedures are described in the chapter. We begin by discussing the brainstorming technique, then move on to discussions of the nominal group technique and the Delphi technique.

BRAINSTORMING: A TECHNIQUE FOR USING GROUPS TO IDENTIFY ALTERNATIVES

In trivial or routine decision situations it is often reasonable to accept the problem description as it is presented and, further, to quickly adopt some easily identified alternative, rather than expend the time and energy necessary for exploring the problem and identifying a more creative alternative. An example situation is where we need an answer to a question and, with little thought, "choose" to ask a person who has answered similar questions in the past.

There are, however, other situations where there are no easily thought of alternatives, perhaps because the problem is an unusual one. There are still other situations where the readily identified alternatives are lacking in quality. Perhaps they seem inferior to those that we believe could be identified if we put our minds or the minds of a group to the matter. Consider, for example, a problem that was widely discussed in the late 1950s and early 1960s:

> *Education problem.* Because of the rapidly increasing birthrate beginning in the 1940s, it is now clear that by 1970 public school enrollment will be much greater than it is today. In fact, it has been estimated that if the student-teacher ratio were to be maintained at what it is today, 50 percent of all individuals graduating from college would have to be induced to enter teaching. What different steps might be taken to insure that schools will continue to provide instruction at least equal in effectiveness to that now provided?

Clearly, this was a problem where creative thinking was justified and necessary. As another example, consider the following:

> *Tourist problem.* Each year many American tourists visit Europe. But suppose that our country wished to get many more European tourists to visit America during their vacations. What steps can you suggest that would get more European tourists to come to this country?

In both these problems, new ideas seem called for. In particular, problems similar to the second problem (e.g., marketing or fund-raising problems) very often seem to justify a conscious and formal effort to identify creative approaches to their solutions. The question to be addressed in this section is "How can a manager use subordinates or coworkers to help identify creative solutions to a particular problem?"

One technique that has been developed in response to this question is called *group brainstorming*. This technique involves the use of a group whose members have had the problem defined for them and who have been asked to identify alternative approaches for solving it. The procedure for managing the group's interaction involves the application of four basic rules:

1. *Criticism is ruled out.* Judgment or evaluation of ideas must be withheld until the idea-generation process has been completed. (This includes adverse judgments of your own ideas as well as adverse judgment of the ideas of other participants.)

2. *"Freewheeling" is welcomed.* The wilder or more radical the idea, the better. (It is easier to tame ideas down than to think them up.)

3. *Quantity is wanted.* The greater the number of ideas, the greater the likelihood of a superior idea.

4. *Combination and improvement are sought.* In addition to contributing ideas of their own, participants should suggest how ideas of others can be turned into better ideas, or how two or more ideas can be joined into still another idea.

The purposes of brainstorming are to push people to think harder and to free them from inhibition, self-criticism, and criticism by others. In this way, they will produce as many different ideas as possible in response to a specific problem. The assumption is that the larger the number of ideas produced, the greater the probability of achieving an effective solution.

Group brainstorming gained considerable popularity as a management technique during the 1950s. It was used in many major companies, units of the army, navy, and air force, and various federal, state, and local agencies. Its use resulted in the identification of more ideas than a manager alone could identify. It was also an exciting and stimulating experience for the participants.

Beginning in the late 1950s and continuing through the early 1970s, a series of studies by decision scientists found that another technique, called *individual brainstorming,* was even more effective for identifying creative solutions to problems than was group brainstorming. The purposes of individual brainstorming are the same as those of group brainstorming. The approach differs in that the procedure used to free the participants from the inhibiting influence of possible criticism from others is to have them work independently, often by physically separating them from one another. The basic rules for individual brainstorming are the following:

1. *Self-criticism is ruled out.* Adverse judgment of your ideas must be withheld until later.

2. *"Freewheeling" is welcomed.* The wilder the idea, the better. (It is easier to tame ideas down than think them up.)

3. *Quantity is wanted.* The greater the number of ideas, the greater the likelihood of a superior idea.

In order to show the effectiveness of individual brainstorming, let us quickly review the results of some field studies. We will then move on to a detailed description and evaluation of this powerful technique.

The first rigorous comparison of individual and group brainstorming was done at Yale University.[1] Two problems for which creative solutions were sought in these studies were the "education" and "tourist" problems described previously. For the participants who worked alone, the average number of different solutions to the education problem was eighteen. For the interacting groups of four persons each, the average number of different solutions was thirty-three. The corresponding numbers for the tourist problem were twenty-one and thirty-eight. Clearly, group brainstorming resulted in more ideas than the average individual was able to generate.

This was not a surprising finding. What was surprising was that when the solutions from the forty-eight participants who had worked as individuals were pooled into twelve synthetic groups of four persons each, the average number of different, nonoverlapping ideas for the synthetic groups was sixty-four for the education problem and sixty-nine for the tourist problem. These results indicated that when people brainstormed as individuals they generated more ideas than when they brainstormed in an interacting group.

Results such as these have been replicated in a number of industrial settings. Table 11–1 shows the results of a study where the participants were employees of the Minnesota Mining and Manufacturing Company (3M). Forty-eight of the participants were research personnel and forty-eight were employed in the central staff advertising department. Entries in the table are the total number of ideas or solutions for both the education and the tourist problems together. They are for synthetic groups of four noninteracting individuals and for four-person interacting groups. As can be seen, the synthetic groups were more effective in terms of the quantity of ideas or solutions.

[1]D. W. Taylor, P. C. Berry, and C. H. Block, *"Does Group Participation When Using Brainstorming Facilitate or Inhibit Creative Thinking?"* Administrative Science Quarterly 3 *(June 1958): 23–47.*

TABLE 11–1.   Mean Total Number of Different Ideas Under Conditions
                of Group and Individual Brainstorming*

	Interacting Groups of Four Members	Synthetic Groups of Four Individuals
Research Personnel	49.3	62.2
Advertising Personnel	37.3	58.5

*From M. D. Dunnette et al., "The Effect of Group Participation on Brain-Storming Effectiveness for Two Industrial Samples," from *Journal of Applied Psychology, Vol. 47,* 1, pp. 30–37. Copyright 1963 by the American Psychological Association. Reprinted by Permission.

Procedure and discussion: Individual brainstorming

The step-by-step procedure for using the individual or *synthetic group* brainstorming technique is as follows.

Step 1. Describe the problem, and then describe the task as identifying as many solutions to the problem as is possible • Experience shows that good results are obtained when the problem is posed as a question (e.g., "How can we get people interested?") and when the question is made available in written form.

Step 2. Describe how privacy is to be attained • Privacy can be attained either by physical separation of the participants or by firm instructions that there is to be no discussion while the participants write out their list of ideas or solutions.

Step 3. State the three basic rules of individual brainstorming (described above) and state that the participants will have ten minutes to write down their solutions • Experience shows that ten to twelve minutes is long enough to elicit the ideas that the individuals have without being so long that the participants become aggravated.

Step 4. Have the participants write down their ideas as per the instructions given in Step 3.

As can be seen, the thrust of both group and individual brainstorming is toward quantity of ideas.

But what about quality? Isn't the average quality less for the technique that generates the greater quantity? In order to answer this question, the researchers evaluated the ideas or solutions on a scale of 0–4, where 0 meant "no conceivable contribution to solution of problem" and 4 meant "clearly a major contribution to solution of problem." The evaluation was done without the researchers knowing which technique had produced which ideas or solutions. The average quality ratings are shown in Table 11–2. If anything, the quality of the ideas and solutions

TABLE 11-2.   Mean Total Quality Scores Under Conditions of Group and
                Individual Brainstorming†

	Interacting Groups of Four Members	Synthetic Groups of Four Individuals
Research Personnel	94	128
Advertising Personnel	65	116

†From M. D. Dunnette et al., "The Effect of Group Participation on Brain-Storming Effectiveness for Two Industrial Samples," from *Journal of Applied Psychology, Vol. 47,* 1, pp. 30–37. Copyright 1963 by the American Psychological Association. Reprinted by Permission.

generated by these research and advertising personnel was greater when they worked as individuals rather than when they worked in a group.

The fact that these studies both used the same problems and the same size groups should not lead us to believe that the results do not generalize. Other studies using different problems and groups of up to nine members have resulted in the same findings.

The key components of the individual brainstorming technique include the following instructions:

1. The ideas are to be as creative and original as possible.
2. The participants are not to critique their ideas.
3. The participants are to generate as long a list as possible.

The additional component of group brainstorming is the instruction that the participants should attempt to develop ideas of their own as a result of hearing the ideas of other group members. Whether or not this *piggybacking* takes place to any significant degree is not known. What is known is that if it does take place it is more than offset by the inhibiting influence of the other participants in the group. Even when the participants know that their ideas will not be publicly criticized, they unconsciously or consciously suppress some of the ideas that they would identify if they were working alone.

As can be seen, individual brainstorming seems to be a powerful technique for generating creative solutions to problems. There are two conditions where it seems to be especially appropriate. One is where it appears that there is a need for creative ideas or solutions, as contrasted with the ideas or solutions that might be readily available to anyone familiar with the problem. The second is where the descriptions of the alternatives sought are not so complex that they cannot be briefly written down (i.e., the task is not one of designing a solution to the problem).

Brainstorming focuses on only one part of the decision-making process, the alternative-generation step. It seems to facilitate the accomplishment of this step very well; the number of alternatives generated is surprisingly large. How can we use a group to sort out the alternatives into those few that should be considered further and those that, due to lack of resources or some other reason, should not? In other words, how can we use a group to generate ideas and make an initial evaluation of them? One approach is to use the *nominal group technique.*

THE NOMINAL GROUP TECHNIQUE: A TECH-NIQUE FOR USING GROUPS TO GENERATE AND EVALUATE INFORMATION

In many situations, managers know that they should obtain the ideas of a number of individuals and should attempt to obtain some degree of public agreement on the value of these ideas. One example is the situation where a manager is looking for ways to increase sales and wants to be sure to obtain the ideas of the sales representatives on how this could best be accomplished. Another example is the situation where the president of the school board wants to obtain ideas on new programs or initiatives that the local schools should undertake. Clearly such situations require that the ideas of those who will be affected should be obtained and, in some cases, publicly considered.

These are not easy situations to deal with. How can they best be managed? How should a manager obtain the opinion or knowledge of people who might have different goals, different beliefs about the best way to achieve their common goals, or different information about the decision situation?

A group management procedure that has been developed in response to these questions is called the *nominal group technique.* It is explicitly designed to obtain and review sensitive information in a group setting. It is conceivable that the managers described could obtain the ideas or information from their salespeople or the other managers with personal interviews or a survey questionnaire. But there are instances when (perhaps in order to protect themselves from charges of favoritism or to make sure that everyone understands the situation) managers may want to obtain the information in a public group setting. It is for these situations that the nominal group technique was developed.[2]

---

[2]*See A. L. Delbecq, A. H. Van de Ven, and D. H. Gustafson.* Group Techniques for Program Planning. *(Glenview, Ill.: Scott, Foresman and Company, 1975.)*

We should note here that the information desired could be of several types. Recall that in individual brainstorming, the information sought is the identity of alternative solutions to a problem. For example, the nominal group technique is frequently used to identify concerns or worries that the group members have about a problem solution that might be adopted. In other words, it is used to identify the criteria and constraints that the members would use to evaluate a solution. As another example, the technique is also used to identify the problems that the members see in their present situation. In other words, it is used in the problem-exploration phase of the overall decision-making effort.

Procedure and discussion: Nominal Group Technique

The nominal group technique was developed in the late 1960s by Andre Delbecq and Andrew Van de Ven from social-psychological studies of decision conferences, management-science studies of aggregating group judgments, and social-work studies of problems surrounding citizen participation in program planning. Since that time, the technique has gained extensive recognition and has been widely applied in health, social service, education, industry, and government organizations.

The technique involves a structured group meeting which proceeds along the following format. Imagine a meeting room in which seven to ten individuals are sitting around a table in full view of each other. At the beginning of the meeting they are not speaking to one another. Instead, each individual is writing ideas on their pads of paper. At the end of five to ten minutes, a structured sharing of ideas takes place. Each individual, in round-robin fashion, presents one idea from his or her private list. A recorder or leader writes that idea on a flip chart in full view of other members. There is still no discussion at this point of the meeting—only the recording. Round-robin listing continues until all members indicate they have no further ideas to share.

The output of this nominal phase of the meeting is a list of ideas, such as alternatives or criteria. As can be seen, this phase includes aspects of individual brainstorming, discussed previously, and of the round-robin technique discussed in Chapter 10. Discussion of a very structured nature occurs during the next, interactive phase of the meeting. The approach is to sequentially ask for questions or comments about each item listed on the flip chart. When this process is complete, independent evaluation of the ideas takes place. Each member, privately, indicates preferences by rank-ordering the subset of alternatives that he or she most favors. The initial group output is the mathematically pooled outcome of these two phases.

Turning now from this summary overview of the first two phases, let us examine the step-by-step procedure for using the technique in its entirety.

Step 1. Have the participants generate their ideas or information in a nominal group setting.[3]

This step is very similar to individual brainstorming. There are only two differences. One is that we always have the participants work in the presence of each other. The other is that we prevent them from criticizing each other's ideas by giving firm instructions not to communicate with each other, rather than by using physical separation. For example, we might say, "During this ten minutes of independent thinking, I ask that you not talk to other members, interrupt their thinking, or look at their worksheets." Our purpose in deliberately causing the participants to work in the presence of each other is to create some degree of task-oriented tension. By putting each participant in a social environment where the objective of creating an extensive list is so specific and clearly being striven for by others, the individual members will be highly motivated to seek the same objective.

The second difference is that, contrary to the procedure in individual brainstorming, we do not assure the participants that their ideas will not be shown to the other participants. The next step in applying the technique involving the structured exchange of ideas and information is in fact just the opposite. It involves the sharing of the ideas from all the participants. The reasoning behind this procedure follows from research telling us that when the group members know in advance that they will be stating their ideas or information to the other members, they will be motivated to work harder at the task (i.e., develop better ideas). On the other hand, we also know that they will feel more inhibited because of possible criticism of their ideas. A procedure for dealing with these conflicting arguments is described under Step 2.

Experience shows that if the manager is using the nominal group technique to get at sensitive, political, or personal problems in the problem-exploration phase, he or she will be more effective if this step is

---

[3]*A nominal group is a group that does not verbally interact and, in this sense, is a group "in name only."*

conducted twice. The first time, technical or operational (i.e., imper-
sonal) problems are elicited. The second time, political (i.e., emotional)
problems are elicited. If this two-step process is not used, these sensitive
and uncomfortable items tend not to surface.

Step 2. Have the participants share their ideas using a round-robin recording procedure.

In this step, the information the members have written down is
recorded on a flip chart or chalkboard that is visible to the entire group.
Round-robin recording means going around the table where the participants are seated and asking for one idea from one member at a time.
The leader writes the idea of a group member on the flip chart and then
proceeds to ask for one idea from the next group member in turn. The
benefits of round-robin recording are:

1. Equal participation in the presentation of ideas.
2. Increase in problem-mindedness.
3. Depersonalization—the separation of ideas from specific
personalities.
4. Increase in the ability to deal with a larger number of ideas.
5. Tolerance of conflicting ideas.
6. Encouragement of hitchhiking.[4]
7. Provision of a written record and guide.

The fact that a list is written is of particular importance. A written
idea is more objective and less personal than a verbal statement. If the
idea is in writing, individuals are better able to separate it from the per-
sonality or position of the individual contributing it. Also, from our
earlier discussions of cognitive limitations, we know that the group
members will be able to deal with a larger number of ideas if these ideas
are written down and displayed.

Delbecq, Van de Ven, and Gustafson (1975) offer the following as
important hints for effective recording:

[4] *"Hitchhiking" as used here refers to the fact that ideas listed on the flip chart by
one member may stimulate another member to think of an idea not written on
the worksheet during the silent period. In this case, the member is free to add the
new idea to the worksheet and report it for listing on the flip chart when his or
her turn arrives.*

1. Record ideas as rapidly as possible.
2. Record ideas in the words used by the group member.[5]
3. Provide assistance in abbreviating only in special situations.
4. Make the entire list visible to the group by tearing off completed sheets from the flip chart and taping them to the wall.

There is a concern that the participants may be inhibited in generating ideas if they know that these ideas will be made public to the other group members. If the manager feels that this inhibition might be critical, he or she can have the written lists passed in anonymously. He or she then writes down an item from the first list, then writes an item from the next list, and so forth, in round-robin fashion. Applying the round-robin technique to the written lists maintains the participant's interest more effectively than would listing all the items from one person's list before moving on to the next person's.

Step 3. Have the participants discuss each recorded idea in a predetermined sequence.

This discussion gives the originators of the ideas, as well as other group members, an opportunity to clarify their meaning and intent. The members can share their thoughts concerning the importance, feasibility, and merits of the idea. In other words, the discussion provides for the sharing of information.

In the early development and applications of the nominal group technique, this step was carried out in a highly controlled manner—only explanations (rather than evaluations) were allowed. Recent research and experience with applications indicate that a more open discussion leads to greater member satisfaction, and because it facilitates information exchange, it also leads to improved decision quality. The continued requirement that some predetermined sequence be used to order the discussion helps ensure that the discussion of one idea is not curtailed by references to ideas still to be discussed. It also ensures that all ideas do

[5]*The advantages of using the words of the group member are: (1) an increased feeling of equality and member importance, (2) a greater identification with the task, and (3) a lack of feeling that the leader-recorder is manipulating the group. Substituting our words for the group member's words is in poor taste and tends to cause resentment.*

get discussed. Occasionally, in order to be certain that all ideas are discussed, the group leader will want to limit the discussion time devoted to any one idea.

Step 4. Have the participants use **rank-voting** to indicate their feelings concerning the importance of the ideas. Then determine the group output by summing the ranked votes.

The typical approach for implementing this step is for the leader to ask each participant to (1) select the five ideas that he or she thinks are most important, (2) rank them in order of their importance, and (3) assign a score of five points to the first-ranked idea, four to the second, and so forth.[6] The *group's preference* is determined by summing the point scores for each idea. Thus, the preferred idea is typically the one that received several five-point or four-point votes.

If the leader or group feels that some members will not vote their true feelings if the individual votes are made public, the voting can be done with a secret ballot. In many cases, however, it is convenient for the group leader to point to one of the recorded ideas and ask for those who assigned five points to the idea to raise their hands. He or she then writes down next to the idea the number of fives that are indicated. The process is repeated for all rankings. This vote-elicitation cycle is repeated for each of the listed ideas.

The use of rank-voting allows all participants to influence the relative evaluation of several ideas. It appears to be more satisfying than allowing each participant to have only one vote to allocate to just one idea.

Step 5. Discuss the results of the voting and decide if an additional rank-voting cycle is necessary.

Once voting and tabulating are completed, the nominal group meeting often proceeds to a discussion of the voting results. This helps achieve a sense of closure and accomplishment.

[6]*Use of rankings rather than ratings ensures that the evaluations from each member have the same average and variation about that averge. This, in turn, reduces the possibility that one member can manipulate the group output by rating one alternative very high and the others all the same and very low.*

If the meeting includes this step, it is often useful to emphasize discussion of those ideas that were ranked quite differently by different members of the group. For example, we should encourage the group to talk about ideas that receive individual point scores of five, as well as one (or zero, if some members do not even include the idea in their list of the best five ideas). If this discussion indicates that some members would like to change their votes, it is appropriate to repeat Step 4 (i.e., to rank-vote again).

As can be seen, the nominal group technique can be used in each phase of the decision-making process, in *problem exploration,* in *alternative generation,* and in *choice making.* Thus it can be used in place of the typical interactive group meeting with which we are all familiar. Its advantage is that it helps the group leader overcome or circumvent several of the social and psychological factors that diminish decision group effectiveness. Its disadvantages are that, even though its nominal phase is effective in surfacing information, the high level of control during the discussion phase may inhibit the full evaluation of this information. It has been especially effective in dealing with groups where wide differences in status or opinion were likely to lead to little generation or sharing of information or opinions. It is also useful when the manager wants a preliminary and public evaluation of ideas or alternatives that he or she intends to draw upon more thoroughly at a later time.

The brainstorming and nominal group techniques are useful for eliciting information in a group setting. They allow us to capitalize on the fact that groups have more information than do individuals. Sometimes, however, it is not possible to bring the people together from whom we want information. The next part of the section describes a technique that has shown itself to be useful to managers faced with this situation.

THE DELPHI TECHNIQUE: A TECHNIQUE FOR OBTAINING JUDGMENTS FROM A LARGE PANEL OF EXPERTS

In many planning situations, historical data are not very good indicators of future events. For example, the demand for home appliances in 1990 will be so affected by the shortages of resources and the advances in technology that statistical projections of historical trends will be meaningless. When an organization's future environment or performance cannot be reasonably forecasted from historical events, the organization's managers will tend to rely on expert judgments.

A well-known technique for systematically obtaining the judgments of a large number of experts is the Delphi technique. This technique was originally developed by the RAND Corporation and is now widely used to develop forecasts of future events as a part of the overall organizational-planning process. In the next few pages we will describe the Delphi technique as it is usually implemented and will discuss two applications in some detail. We will then describe some variations of the technique and review where it seems to be an especially effective procedure for gathering information from knowledgeable people.

The Delphi technique can be viewed as an advanced form of an opinion survey or communications procedure. As originally conceived and generally used, the technique has three features: (1) anonymity, (2) opportunity for opinion revision, and (3) summary feedback.[7] Anonymity is maintained by avoiding face-to-face communications and instead using mailed questionnaires or some other formal procedure (such as on-line computer communications). Opportunity for opinion revision is obtained by conducting the overall survey in a series of "rounds," where in each round the participants are allowed to provide revised opinions. Statistical feedback is obtained by providing participants with a summary of the responses from the previous round before asking for revised opinions.

These three features allow the technique to take advantage of the information from a large panel of experts and still avoid some of the problems encountered in face-to-face meetings. We have discussed some of these problems in Chapter 8, but note here that the technique minimizes the problems associated with the following types of panel members:

1. The status-conscious expert who feels called upon to defend his publicly stated opinion.

2. The senior executive with whom subordinates are reluctant to disagree.

3. The silver-tongued salesman who can convince anyone to his point of view.

Let us turn now to a discussion of two published applications of the Delphi technique.

The first was concerned with forecasting developments in

[7]For an application that incorporated all three features, see S. Basu and R. G. Schroeder, "Incorporating Judgments in Sales Forecasts: Application of the Delphi Method at American Hoist and Derrick." Interfaces 7 (May 1977): 18–27.

medicine.[8] This study was conducted to aid the planning of a large pharmaceutical company. The panel members were researchers or practitioners in biomedicine and related areas. None were company employees. One hundred and eleven experts were originally contacted, of which 78 agreed to participate. Forty-two participated in the first phase of the study and 35 in the second phase.

The first round involved sending the participants a brief definition of the five fields that the company was interested in (biomedical research, diagnosis, medical therapy, health care, and medical education). They were asked to list important discoveries, breakthroughs, changes in methods, and other events that might occur in each field in the next fifty years. The managers of the study then combined the 867 events, many of which were very similar, into 209 events.

The second round involved sending the participants the list of 209 events and asking them to estimate the date by which they were 50 percent certain that the event would occur and the date by which they were at least 90 percent certain that the event would occur. Experts who felt that the event would not occur within the next fifty years were asked to mark the "never" column. The managers of the study then took these responses and summarized them.

The summary of the results of this Delphi study was prepared in two forms. The first was a diagram for each event showing the proportion of participants who had chosen various dates as the date by which the event was 50 percent (or 90 percent) certain to have occurred. Only those events for which there was some consensus were included in this summary. Consensus was defined as agreement by at least 60 percent of the experts that the event had a 50 percent (or 90 percent) probability of occurring within a particular ten-year period.

The second form of the summary consisted of *scenarios,* or descriptions of the various events that would be taking place in a given field at a particular time. This form was derived from the first by choosing any given date and observing from the several diagrams which events would most likely be taking place at that time.

Other information obtained during the second round included the medical need and social-ethical desirability of the described event. Although it is not reported whether this information was summarized, it may have been useful in identifying for the company planners which events might have professional, social, or economic resources behind them.

[8]*A. D. Bender, A. E. Strack, G. W. Ebright, and G. Von Halter, "Delphic Study Examines Developments in Medicine."* Futures *1 (June 1969): 289–303.*

Another published application of the technique was concerned with forecasting developments in technology. This study took place in a large aerospace corporation.[9] The participants were 135 scientists and engineers selected by middle management from the more than 6000 who worked for the organization. The purpose of the study was to aid Research and Development managers in modifying their long-range plans. These plans were later subjected to the usual executive evaluation to determine how well they meshed with corporate plans and objectives.

In the first round, each panel member was assigned to one of fourteen technological categories and asked to list probable technical events in that category that could have significant impact on the company. In addition, the participant was asked to weigh each event on the basis of the following factors:

1. *Desirability from the customer's viewpoint* (i.e., reflecting potential market demand). A three point response scale was used—"needed desperately," "desirable," and "undesirable but possible."

2. *Feasibility from the producer's viewpoint* (i.e., reflecting feasibility and the difficulty of achieving prerequisite developments). Again a three-point scale was used—"highly feasible," "likely," and "unlikely but possible."

3. *Timing.* The date by which there was a 10 percent chance of occurrence, the date by which there was a 50 percent chance of occurrence, and the date by which there was a 90 percent chance of occurrence.

The first round produced 2100 predicted events. Four editings, conducted primarily by middle-level technical managers, eliminated duplicate and trivial or irrelevant events and reduced the list to 1186 items.

In the second round, each participant was sent a list of those items related to his or her technological category or a closely related category. Again they were asked to assess the desirability and feasibility of each event as well as the probability that it would ever occur. Then they were asked to assume that the event would in fact occur and to indicate the three dates by which the event would have occurred with a 10 percent, 50 percent, and 90 percent probability. Finally they were asked to indicate the extensiveness of their familiarity with the technology necessary to make the judgments required.

[9] D. L. Pyke, "A Practical Approach to Delphi." Futures 2 (June 1970): 143–152.

The third and final round involved only those participants who rated their familiarity as "excellent" rather than "fair" or "good" and who, because their response on one or more parameters was outside arbitrarily established limits, were thought to have information not generally available to the other panelists. These panel members received the summarized results from the second round, plus a "challenge" note. The note highlighted the questions on which their estimate was far from the norm and asked for information that might have caused their estimate to be what it was. If, after seeing the summary estimates from the second round, they wanted to review their estimates, they could, but they were not pressured to do so. In addition, they could explain their second-round estimates but were not pressured to do so. Throughout this process they had complete anonymity. When this round was completed, its results were incorporated into the information obtained in the second round.

The summary of the study was numerical in nature. The three possible responses on desirability and feasibility were scored $+1$, 0 and -1. The average of these values was reported for each event, as was the average probability of occurrence. The median of the .1, .5, and .9 probability dates was also shown, and an asterisk was included if one or more minority opinions from one of the challenged experts was available in a separate appendix. A special report volume was prepared containing the results from each of the fourteen technological panels. In addition, the data were all maintained as a management information system that allowed management to receive answers to such questions as, "What are the events in the field of composite materials that have desirability index greater than .2 and a .5 probability-of-occurrence date of 1985 or earlier?"

Variations of the technique, general procedure, and discussion

Although neither of the two example applications demonstrated the fact, the originally conceived and frequently implemented version of the Delphi technique provides feedback to all participants of the results from the previous round. In light of the information they then have about the opinions of others on the question at hand, it also asks them to provide either a new judgment or retain their original judgment. This feedback and request for another judgment step can be repeated several times over, but in actual practice, it is seldom repeated more than once.

There are two purposes for these iterative rounds involving feedback and the opportunity to revise judgments. One is to increase the degree of agreement or consensus among the experts. The other is to increase the accuracy or quality of the overall group response.

Research and experience have shown that the first purpose is almost invariably achieved. The variation among the responses of the participants is reduced, with more responses being close to the group average in the later rounds. It appears that the second purpose is achieved only if there is some variability among the participants about how knowledgeable they believe they are about the question. Participants who regard themselves as less knowledgeable tend to revise their judgments further toward the group average than do those who see themselves as quite knowledgeable. Thus, the tendency is for the group average to shift in the correct direction.

In some applications, the feedback in these iterations is more than just a numerical summary of what the overall panel estimates were for the previous round. Sometimes it is diagnostic (i.e., it contains the explanations from various panel members about why they made the judgments they did). Such a procedure tends to cause panel members to revise their opinion in the direction of those members with more convincing arguments. This generally increases the quality of the final group judgment.

The fact that this iterative procedure was not followed in the two applications described shows that variations of the Delphi technique are possible and sometimes desirable. As an example, some Delphi applications are being made with telephones hooked into a computer-controlled recording system so that participants can receive instructions and feedback from the monitor and ask and answer questions of other participants at their leisure. In some applications, the iterative rounds are eliminated, such as in the first study discussed. Although there were two rounds, there was no attempt to use feedback to achieve consensus or improve accuracy. Some authorities argue that unless a study has all the features of the original Delphi technique—including the opportunity for all panel members to revise their judgments in light of feedback about how other members answered the same question—then it ought not to be regarded as an application of "the" Delphi technique. Others argue that it is better to be liberal in using the term than to create a whole list of terms to cover all possible variations of the typical features. We will follow the latter point of view here.

With these comments in mind, let us summarize the general procedure in the following five steps.

Step 1. Define the problem to which the Delphi study is a solution, and design a questionnaire • Explicitly defining the problem aids in questionnaire design by providing a criterion for evaluating which questions will be included. Designing the questionnaire is a crucial activity because the participants may be either unable to ask clarifying questions or not inclined to ask such questions. Also, a well-designed questionnaire ensures that all of the necessary information is gathered. If time permits, the questionnaire should be pretested.

Step 2. Determine who should participate in the Delphi process, and request that they participate • Who participates in a Delphi process is an important determinant of the usefulness of the information obtained. How many experts participate will be a function of the criteria used for identifying "experts," the inducements used to involve the experts, and the resources (e.g., staff support for processing questionnaires) available for conducting the study.

Step 3. Mail all of the appropriate background materials and the first round questionnaire to the participants.

Step 4. Tabulate and summarize the results from the first round questionnaire, and design the second round questionnaire.

Step 5. Mail all of the appropriate summaries, feedback messages, and the second round questionnaire to the participants.

Step 6. Analyze the results of the second round questionnaire.

If additional rounds of questionnaires seem necessary, Steps 4 and 5 can be repeated.

Proponents of the Delphi technique suggest that there are at least five situations where it has an advantage over other alternatives for systematically obtaining the judgments of experts:

1. Where the individuals needed to contribute knowledge to the examination of a complex problem have no history of adequate communication, and the communication process must be structured to insure understanding.

2. Where the problem is so broad that more individuals are needed than can meaningfully interact in a face-to-face exchange.

3. Where disagreements among individuals are so severe that the communication process must be refereed.

4. Where time is scarce for the individuals involved and/or geographical distances are large, thereby inhibiting frequent group meetings.

5. Where a supplemental group communication process would be conducive to increasing the efficiency of a subsequent face-to-face meeting.

SUMMARY AND OVERVIEW

This chapter described three techniques that are useful in overcoming or circumventing the forces and counterproductive tendencies that often interfere with the effectiveness of decision groups. The techniques are useful when the special circumstances of the decision situation suggest that application of the guidelines of Chapter 10 would not fully respond to difficulties that the manager might face.

OPPORTUNITIES FOR FURTHER THOUGHT

1. Use the individual brainstorming technique on yourself. Provide a written problem, and work on generating your ideas for ten minutes. Assess the merits of the technique in your particular "application."
2. Recall a group situation that you observed where lack of control led to poor group performance or low member satisfaction. Would any of the three techniques, or modifications of them, have been helpful? If not, describe aspects of the situation that would have interfered with their being helpful.
3. Think of a decision situation where the Delphi technique would be useful, and complete Step 1 of the technique.

REFERENCES AND RELATED READINGS

Basu, S. and R. G. Schroeder. "Incorporating Judgments in Sales Forecasts: Application of the Delphi Method at American Hoist and Derrick." *Interfaces* 7 (May 1977): 18–27.

Bender, A. D., A. E. Strack, G. W. Ebright, and G. von Halter. "Delphic Study Examines Developments in Medicine." *Futures* 1 (June 1969): 289–303.

Delbecq, A. L., A. H. Van de Ven, and D. H. Gustafson. *Group Techniques for Program Planning.* Glenview, Ill.: Scott, Foresman and Company, 1975.

Dunnette, M. D., J. Campbell, and K. Jaastad. "The Effect of Group Participation on Brainstorming Effectiveness for Two Industrial Samples." *Journal of Applied Psychology* 47 (February 1963): 30–37.

Osborn, A. F. *Applied Imagination.* New York: Charles Scribner's Sons, 1957.

Pyke, D. L. "A Practical Approach to Delphi." *Futures* 2 (June 1970): 143–152.

Souder, W. E. "Effectiveness of Nominal and Interacting Group Decision Processes for Integrating R & D and Marketing." *Management Science* 23 (February 1977): 595–605.

Taylor, D. W., P. C. Berry, and C. H. Block. "Does Group Participation When Using Brainstorming Facilitate or Inhibit Creative Thinking?" *Administrative Science Quarterly* 3 (June 1958): 23–47.

12
Predicting and Influencing Organizational Decisions[1]

In Chapter 1 we stated that the purpose of this book was "to help managers improve their decisions and the decisions of their subordinates and associates as well." As subsequent chapters showed, our approach to achieving this purpose was to introduce techniques that can help individuals and groups overcome the intellectual limitations and counterproductive behaviors that tend to reduce the quality of their decisions. We repeatedly noted that both scientific studies and managerial experience have shown that the use of these techniques, or even of scaled-down versions of the techniques, can increase decision quality.

Chapters 4–11 focused on improving decisions through the use of formal decision-aiding techniques. There are other factors (besides the use of formal techniques) that both influence decisions in organizations and are predictors of such decisions. The next section of this chapter is concerned with these factors—the buttons and knobs that control the

[1]*An organizational decision is a decision made on behalf of an organization by a member or members of the organization. The criteria used in making such a decision usually reflect both the stated goals of the organization and the personal goals of the decision maker(s). The relative importance given the various goals and criteria vary considerably with the situation.*

outcomes of organizational decisions. The subsequent and last section is an integrative overview of the book.

THE BUTTONS AND KNOBS

All of us have observed organizational decisions that did not seem to make sense. "I'll never understand how they chose that blankety-blank" is a frequently heard exclamation of exasperation. In many instances the speaker has just found that his or her prediction of what the choice would be was wrong, and consequently so was his or her planning. In other instances, the alternative that he or she thought was best was not the one selected by the organization. In either case, the outcomes include disappointment and a loss of resources and momentum.

The purpose of this chapter is to review some of the factors that determine organizational decisions and to provide some practical advice on how to use these factors in *predicting* and *influencing* such decisions. If we increase our ability to do either, we can both be more useful to our associates and more successful in furthering our own career goals.

There are, of course, many determinants of organizational decisions. We will discuss five of the most important ones. Each of the five satisfies two criteria. One is that scientific studies have documented that it affects organizational decisions, and the other is that it leads to operational strategies. Let us begin.

1. Availability of conspicuous alternatives

There is probably nothing more closely associated with the likelihood that a particular alternative will be selected than is the conspicuousness of that alternative in the mind of the decision maker. Research demonstrates that conspicuous alternatives are much more frequently chosen than their nature would generally merit. This finding follows from the fact that most people and organizations tend to undersearch for alternatives and instead oversearch for information to bolster their early (and often relatively uninformed) choices. We and our organizations tend to be lazy searchers and do not, as we should, view the cost of search as an investment toward obtaining what could be a superior outcome.

Fifty years ago a piece of advice frequently given to young men beginning their careers in business was "Son, get a desk near the president's office." In those days people drew on experience and observation to come up with this insight, an example of what research has since shown us to be a generalizable phenomenon: decison makers tend to select the conspicuous alternative.

Given this fact, how can we use it to further the objectives of our organizational unit or ourselves? One strategy is to make sure our favored alternative (e.g., our product or ourselves) is conspicuous. The tactics with which this can best be done cannot be identified in the abstract; the particular approach for making something conspicuous must be specific to the decision situation. But one point should be made. In many situations, by the time we or our unit get around to forcefully putting forth our alternative, it will be too late—the decision will have been made.

We cannot afford to be only reactive to evolving decision processes. In many settings we must also be proactive. For example, we cannot always wait for a request for a bid or a proposal before making a customer aware of our products or talents. In many cases, the buyer's choice will have been made before the bid elicitation or request for proposal is written. We must cause our favored alternatives to be conspicuous in the minds of people who might be making decisions in the future. That, of course, is what mass media advertising is all about—future purchases. We should note that, especially in less formal decision situations, a "decision" in many respects is simply the near-random intersection of a problem looking for a solution and a solution looking for a problem. We need to make sure that our favored alternative is one of the more active and conspicuous of the solutions that are out there looking for problems.

We must sound a note of caution here. There are undoubtedly circumstances where conspicuousness becomes abrasive or pushy, and while we may gain our end in the short run, we will damage our relations with the decision makers in the long run. Again, the exact tactics to be used depend on the situation. One approach is to make people generally aware of our alternative and then to make them particularly aware of it near the time that the choice is to be made (assuming that the process signals that the choice point is near). It is safe to say that inconspicuous alternatives seldom get chosen, and so we should do what we can to make sure our favored solutions are not inconspicuous.

All right, you say, I've got the message and I'm smart enough to figure out how to implement it, but what if we know that the decision maker has already begun to focus in on some other alternative, one that is not the one we think should be chosen? How can we compete? How can we overcome the effects of this "natural law" when it is working against us? These are important questions that can be answered. We will be better able to answer them, however, after we have reviewed some of the other determinants of decisions. Let us set these questions aside for now and agree to pick them up again when we are more familiar with a wider set of factors affecting organizational decisions.

2. Time available for making the decision

In general, decision makers try to solve their problems with old "tried and true" solutions. "Off the shelf components" that have served well in the past are the ones rationalized as fitting today's new problem. This approach is frequently used because it minimizes the time required for dealing with the problem.

As you can see, we have again highlighted the importance of conspicuousness, but we have also highlighted the fact that the time available for making the decision is a powerful determinant of how much information will be sought and thus brought to bear in the choice-making process. This is especially true with respect to information concerning the availability of alternatives. If there is little time available, whether due to deadlines or workloads, there will tend to be little search for alternatives. Thus we can predict that in a situation where time is short, readily identifiable or available alternatives will have even a greater tendency to be chosen. Assuming that we know which possible solutions are conspicuous, and our experience and confidants will usually let us know this, we can be good predictors of organizational choices when the time for decision making is limited.

While in general we do not want decision makers to be rushed, a need for haste does increase our ability to predict outcomes. It also can cause our favored solutions to be adopted if they are in the more conspicuous set. Thus, if we know that the alternative that we think best is also the one in the lead, then we should not do anything that would lengthen the time used to make the decision. Instead we should attempt to do (within the bounds of ethics, good taste, and our future relations with the people involved) what we can to cause the decision process to come to a close.

218 MANAGERIAL DECISION MAKING

3. Relative ambiguity associated with various data

When decision makers use information, they do not use it uniformly. Some information has a greater impact than does other information. Research shows that hard data has a greater effect than soft data, and that unambiguous data has a greater impact than ambiguous or less interpretable data. Consequently, we can assume that, all else being equal, the solutions that score high on criteria where there is hard data will tend to be selected over solutions that score high on soft data. It is true that other factors affect the relative importance of data besides their relative ambiguity. Nevertheless, the ambiguity associated with potentially key data can be an indicator in forecasting organizational choices.

How can we use the knowledge that ambiguity is a determinant of decisions? A number of strategies can be used. One is to make sure that our favored alternative looks as good as it possibly can on the quantitatively assessed criteria. Another that should not be overlooked when reasonable is to challenge the relevance or usefulness of data sets in which our product or proposal does not score well. Finally, if time and additional search for information will reduce the ambiguity associated with criteria that favor what we see as the best alternative, then we should encourage the expenditure of that time and search effort. Again, of course, this must all be done within the bounds of professional ethics and good taste.

This issue—that criteria are weighted in part by the ambiguity associated with the relevant data—has implications for the role of organizational politics in decision making. It seems timely to turn now to this important subject.

4. The influence and interest of powerful persons

We all know of situations where what seemed to be the best solution on technical or economic grounds was not chosen because of political reasons. And we all know of cases where the technical and economic arguments either overcame political arguments or seemed to be the only arguments considered. Here we are interested in being able to predict when nonpolitical criteria will dominate the decision and when political criteria will dominate.[2] Armed with this knowledge, we will be

[2]*For two years preceding this writing, the author was employed part-time as a lobbyist at the Wisconsin legislature. The present subsection in particular reflects not only the organizational literature but his own observations and experiences concerning the role of this factor in collective decisions.*

better able to predict the outcomes of the decision pro(
able to choose our strategy for affecting it.

A mistake that is frequently made in attempti..
fect organizational choices by analyzing or manipulating the a..
powerful persons is to assume that these people are interested in solutions to the problem, and willing to use their influence. Do not make it.
Powerful people are usually involved in many issues, and the problem
that is of paramount interest to us may not be of paramount interest to
them. In addition, organizational power is a scarce resource, and while
use of it sometimes creates more power, overuse sometimes merely
dissipates the reserve. There are very few people who are willing to use
their power in every instance that comes along. If we are counting on
someone's influence to help our cause, we must make certain they are interested enough to use this influence. Many who assumed that such
assistance was forthcoming have been disappointed. We have heard
them. "Boy, did he ever let us down," or "They let me climb out on the
limb and then sat back and watched while those other idiots sawed it
off." That is not the way everyone saw it, of course. The powerful person who was counted on saw either that other problems were more
demanding of attention or that the influence would be best saved for use
in another battle. There are always other battles.

Now that we have a better understanding of when organizational
power might be used, we should consider when it will be effective. The
answer to the question of when political criteria will dominate economic
and technical criteria hinges to some extent on the concept of ambiguity.
If the "scores" for the various alternatives are such that it is unclear
which should be chosen (i.e., if there is ambiguity on the nonpolitical
criteria), then the setting is ripe for power to dictate choice. If, on the
other hand, the balance or role of power is ambiguous, then nonpolitical
criteria tend to dominate. The balance or role of power will be ambiguous when (a) equally powerful coalitions support different solutions;
(b) the powerful persons appear uninterested or unwilling to exert influence; or (c) the situation is such that the use of or capitulation to
power would be highly visible and would violate organizational norms.

Some of the strategies that follow from the above remarks are obvious. For example, if our favorite alternative appears to score well on
economic or technical criteria, then we might try to both minimize
whatever ambiguity there might be in the scores and get closure before
political criteria can be brought to bear. Or, if our cause has a powerful
enemy, we might try to counteract this person with powerful friends.
Some of the strategies, though, are a bit more subtle. For example, we
might take steps to reduce the interest of the powerful enemy by dragging
out the decision process until he or she is occupied elsewhere. We could

also satisfy his or her principal concern with a minor alteration to our solution package. We could also take steps to make the use of power be a violation of organizational norms by appealing to codified procedures, past practices, professional ethics, or whatever else seems reasonable.

Before leaving this important set of strategies, let us mention two strategies that can be very effective when attempting to diminish the power of someone opposing what we feel is the best solution. One of these is to restrict the use of power by making the decision process more public. Publicity is not the friend of politics, especially where organizational norms lean toward the use of economic and technical criteria. Thus we might agree to publish the minutes of decision-making meetings, review committee progress with superiors, bring in neutral but decision-relevant observers, or hold open meetings. The second strategy is to dilute the power by enlarging the decision-making group with neutral parties and push for essentially a one-man, one-vote decision or advisory rule. These two strategies have the added advantage of reducing the level of conflict—a goal often striven for by those involved in on-going organizations.

5. Availability of resources

Anyone knows that limitations on the resources available for solving a problem allow some alternatives to continue as contenders and cause other alternatives to be eliminated. It makes good sense to try to fit our alternative to the resource constraints. If the situation demands it, however, we should try to design or redesign the constraints to fit our alternative.

Although these are useful strategies, we need not dwell on them since they are part of our general knowledge. Instead, we should spend time examining some of the more subtle implications of resource limitations.

One of these is that when there is an adverse change in the equilibrium between resources and problems (i.e., when there are fewer resources and the same problems or the same resources and more problems), then the competition for resources to solve problems increases. This leads to increases in organizational conflict and tends to drive the decision makers away from the use of problem-solving strategies and toward the use of competitive ones like bargaining and politicking. These strategies increase the propensity for the use of power. Thus, for predictive purposes, we can say that with an adverse change in the resource-to-problem equilibrium, we would expect to see power play a more important role in decision making.

Another subtle implication of resource limitations is that if our favorite solution to the problem exceeds the resources available for solving the problem, our solution may be large enough to solve other problems. Their solutions together with that of the first problem would justify exceeding the original resource limitation. Thus, a common tactic of vendors is to propose an expensive piece of equipment and then point out that it solves problems we did not know we had. Perhaps it has "reserve capabilities" or "capacity to fit our growing needs." To generalize this vendor behavior, we can say that a useful strategy highlights the fact that our favorite alternative is actually more like a portfolio of solutions that solve multiple problems, all of them important, and that in aggregate these problems justify the expenditure of the added resources.

Several paragraphs ago, in our discussion of the availability of conspicuous alternatives, we agreed to address the question of what to do when an alternative that we do not feel is the best choice is the front-runner (i.e., the most conspicuous alternative). We now have some answers. One is to extend the time available for decision making so that other alternatives are likely to receive more extensive scrutiny and so become more conspicuous. A second is to identify ambiguities in the data or logic supporting the front-running alternative. A third is to try to alter the distribution of power being brought to bear on the decision process. The fourth is to cause the fit between the resources available and the alternatives under consideration to be altered in favor of the alternative we believe best. This can be done by pointing out either that it can fulfill more needs than the conspicuous alternative or that it is sufficient but not as demanding on the organization's resources.

Assuming that we are competent and well-intentioned professionals, it is in the best interest of our own unit and of our parent organization for us to be adept in predicting and influencing organizational decisions. There are a number of factors that are useful in carrying out these two processes. Among them are: (1) the availability of conspicuous alternatives, (2) the time available for making the decision, (3) the relative ambiguity associated with various data, (4) the influence and interest of powerful persons, and (5) the availability of resources. The thrust of this section was to describe strategies that might be useful in employing these factors as mechanisms for predicting and influencing (within the bounds of professional ethics, good taste, and continuing relationships) organizational decisions. Let us turn now to a brief and integrative overview of the book.

AN INTEGRATIVE OVERVIEW

In this book we examined a variety of decision-aiding techniques. Each of these techniques has shown itself to be useful in improving the decisions of individuals, groups, or organizations. In these last few paragraphs we will briefly review the content of the individual book chapters and highlight some of the integrative relationships that exist among techniques that were presented in different chapters.

Chapters 1 and 2 were introductory in nature, and Chapter 3 examined some of the difficulties faced by decision-making managers. In Chapters 4 and 5 we first encountered a formal decision-aiding technique. It was in these two chapters in particular that we discussed the use of multiattribute utility models as mechanisms for overcoming some of the intellectual limitations of an individual decision maker faced with a multicriterion problem. Our purpose here is to note that the concepts and procedures associated with this technique, even though presented in the context of individual decisions, are also useful in aiding the decision making of groups and organizations. The visual displays associated with this technique (e.g., the utility curves and payoff tables) are also valuable in group and organizational decision settings, where they can be used as aids in both the communication and identification of sources of confusion or the causes of disagreement. When employed in this latter, diagnostic role, the models and displays can be useful in identifying either the information needed to reconcile differences of opinion or in identifying the nature of alternatives that would satisfy all of the parties concerned.

In Chapters 6 and 7 we discussed the use of decision matrices and decision trees as devices for dealing, in a systematic way, with uncertainty and risk. As was true in the case of MAU models, the displays associated with these techniques are also useful as communication and diagnostic aids in group and organizational decision settings. In addition, we should note that the "value of information" concept of Chapter 7 can be helpful when groups or organizations are attempting to decide when to close off their search for information and move on to making a choice. For example, if we feel the decision process should be slowed, we might suggest that some analysis should be directed toward determining if additional information would be cost-effective. If we feel that time is being taken to obtain unnecessary information, we could use a decision tree analysis to examine and challenge the cost-effectiveness of the proposed or ongoing information search.

In Chapters 8–11 we examined techniques for managing decision-aiding groups. In particular we noted that one approach to gaining acceptance for decisions is to involve people in the analyses that lead to these decisions. The strategy that this suggests is the use of groups as advisors in the employment of the decision aids that were introduced here as being useful to individual decision makers. For example, the techniques of Chapters 8–11 can be advantageously used to manage groups that are employing the analytic techniques of Chapters 4–7 such as in designing payoff tables, determining utility curves, or developing the shape and content of decision trees. Thus, group techniques can be useful in employing the analytic techniques and analytic techniques can be useful in managing groups.

Lastly, in this chapter we discussed strategies and tactics for predicting and influencing organizational decisions. A review of these shows that organizational choices are determined by both the information available and the decision process used. Since the techniques of the previous chapters are themselves decision processes and since they greatly influence the information that is brought to bear on the problems, their use tends to have a strong impact on organizational decisions. In particular, the techniques of the previous chapters affect organizational decisions in the following ways.

1. They tend to lead to the identification of more alternatives and thus reduce the propensity to choose the most conspicuous alternative.

2. They tend to increase the time used to make a decision because they identify the need for information that otherwise might not be sought. On the other hand, when decisions are being delayed because of conflict or confusion, the use of these techniques can often reduce the conflict or confusion. This leads to a quicker decision.

3. They tend to reduce the ambiguity associated with certain data (e.g., the subjective probabilities generated in Chapter 7 are less ambiguous than is the phrase "reasonably likely"). They also tend to reduce the ambiguity felt toward any data in that they clearly specify the role of this data in the decision process.

4. They tend to redistribute power among the interested parties by giving more power to those who provide the information used in the models and by giving less power to those whose goals are not reflected by the criteria used in the models or processes.

5. They tend to increase the relationships between organizational decisions and organizational resources. For example, utility curves quantify the benefits to be received for each additional increment of resources, and decision trees identify the organizational value of information. The explicit scheduling of the meetings and activities decision groups links the time to be expended to the time that is available.

In essence, these last few paragraphs tell us that the use of the decision-aiding techniques presented in this book tends to rationalize and improve organizational decisions both directly and indirectly.

SUMMARY AND OVERVIEW

At this point there seem to be a few thoughts that bear repeating. One is that our careers and our personal satisfactions can be greatly enhanced if we improve our decision making. Good decisions lead to successful outcomes on which we can build. Poor decisions lead to hours and days of remedial undertakings and foregone opportunities. There is a great gap between what the average quality of our decisions is and what it could be.

The second thought is that the techniques described in this book can be valuable aids in helping managers improve their decisions and the decisions of their subordinates, associates, and organizations as well. Each of the techniques has been tested and found to be useful by both decision scientists and practicing managers.

The third thought is that I enjoyed writing this book. I hope that the reader has enjoyed using it.

OPPORTUNITIES FOR FURTHER THOUGHT

1. Describe a situation where you attempted to influence an organizational decision. Which of the factors described in this chapter played a part in your efforts? How successful were you?

2. Identify another factor or two, besides those discussed in this chapter, that might be useful in predicting or influencing organizational decisions. Describe the strategies or tactics that might be used in employing the factor(s) to influence a decision.

REFERENCES AND RELATED READINGS

Allison, G. T. "Conceptual Models and the Cuban Missile Crisis." *The American Political Science Review* LXIII (September 1969): 689–718.

Beach, L. R. and T. R. Mitchell. "A Contingency Model for the Selection of Decision Strategies." *Academy of Management Review* 3 (July 1978): 439–449.

Bryan, S. E. "TFX: A Case in Policy Level Decision Making." *Academy of Management Journal* 7 (March 1964): 54–70.

Cecil, A. A. and E. G. Lundgren. "An Analysis of Individual Decision Making Behavior Using a Laboratory Setting." *Academy of Management Journal* 18 (September 1975): 600–604.

Cohen, M. D., J. G. March, and J. P. Olson. "A Garbage Can Model of Organizational Choice." *Administrative Science Quarterly* 17 (March 1972): 1–25.

Cyert, R. and J. March. *A Behavioral Theory of the Firm.* Englewood Cliffs, N.J.: Prentice–Hall, Inc., 1965.

Gerwin, D. "Towards a Theory of Public Budgetary Decision Making." *Administrative Science Quarterly* 14 (March 1969): 33–46.

Lindblom, C. G. "The Science of 'Muddling Through.'" *Public Administrative Review* 19 (Spring 1959): 155–169.

Logsdon, J. *The Decision to Go to the Moon.* Chicago: The University of Chicago Press, 1976.

Pfeffer, J. "Power and Resource Allocation in Organizations." In *New Directions in Organizational Behavior,* B. M. Staw and G. R. Salancik, eds., pp. 235–266. Chicago: St. Clair Press, 1977.

Index